Choral Connections

Level 1 Mixed Voices

Teacher's Wraparound Edition

Teacher's Manual

GLENCOE

McGraw-Hill

New York, New York   Columbus, Ohio   Mission Hills, California   Peoria, Illinois

Meet the Authors

SENIOR AUTHOR

Mollie G. Tower - As Coordinator of Choral and General Music of the Austin Independent School District, Mollie Tower was recently nominated "Administrator of the Year." She is very active in international, national, regional, and state music educators' organizations. Ms. Tower was contributing author, consultant, and reviewer for the elementary programs *Share the Music*, and *Music and You*. Senior author of *Música para todos*, *Primary and Intermediate Dual Language Handbooks for Music Teachers*, she has also written and consulted for many other publications. A longtime advocate of music education, Mollie is a popular clinician who conducts workshops across the country.

Marc Erck
Choir Director

Marc Erck has more than ten years of choral directing experience. He received his Bachelor of Music Education from Southwestern University. Marc is currently the director of choirs at Hill Country Middle School in the Eanes Independent School District and Choir Director at University United Methodist Church in Austin, Texas.

Ruth Phillips
Choir Director

Ruth Phillips has taught choral music in junior high and middle school for 17 years in both the Dallas/Fort Worth area and in San Marcos, Texas. She is currently in her eighth year at Goodnight Junior High. Ms. Phillips received a Bachelor of Science degree in All Level Music Education from McMurry University in Abilene, Texas.

Linda S. Wyatt
Choir Director

With 27 years of choir directing experience, Linda S. Wyatt is presently Director of Choirs at Murchison Middle School in Austin, Texas. After receiving her Bachelor of Music Education degree from Southwest Texas State University, she taught at John Marshall High School and Sul Ross Middle School in San Antonio.

Contributing Writers

Dr. Susan Snyder has taught all levels of vocal music over the last 25 years. She holds a B.S. in music education from the University of Connecticut and an M.A. from Montclair State College. She holds a Ph.D. in curriculum and instruction from the University of Connecticut and advanced professional certificates from Memphis State University and the University of Minnesota. Teaching at Hunter College and City University of New York, Dr. Snyder was coordinating author of the elementary music program, *Share the Music*, and a consultant on *Music and You*. She has published many articles on music education and integrated curriculum and is an active clinician, master teacher, and guest conductor.

Vocal Development, Music Literacy
Katherine Saltzer Hickey, D.M.A.
University of California at Los Angeles
Los Angeles, California
Choir Director
Pacific Chorale Children's Choruses
Irvine, California

The National Standards for Music Education are reprinted from *National Standards for Arts Education* with permission from Music Educators National Conference (MENC). Copyright ©1994 by MENC. The complete National Standards and additional materials relating to the Standards are available from Music Educators National Conference, 1806 Robert Fulton Drive, Reston, Virginia 22091. (Telephone 800-336-3768.) A portion of the sales of this material goes to support music education programs through programs of the Music Educators National Conference.

Glencoe/McGraw-Hill
A Division of The McGraw-Hill Companies

Send all inquiries to:
Glencoe/McGraw-Hill
15319 Chatsworth Street
Mission Hills, California 91345

ISBN 0-02-655527-1 (Student's Edition)
ISBN 0-02-655536-0 (Teacher's Wraparound Edition)

Printed in the United States of America.

2 3 4 5 6 7 8 9   MAL   02 01 00 99 98 97 96

Table of Contents

SECTION Selection	Concepts and Skills	1	2	3	4	5	6	7	8	9	Teacher's Resources	
TEACHING LESSONS												
Bound for Jubilee	Melodic movement stepwise and in thirds. Singing in four parts.	a				a				a	📁	
A Red, Red Rose	Rhythmic reading; part independence.	d				a	a				📁	
Over There	Finding movable *do*; reading syncopation.	c, d		a				a			📁	
Dare to Dream!	Stepwise movement; staggered entrances.	d				c					📁	
The Tiger	Rhythms in 6/8 meter; repetitive entrances.					a		a				
Shalom, My Friends	*La* tonal center (minor mode); relationship between parts.	c					c					
Whisper! Whisper!	Tonic triad in broken and block style; call and response.	d			c	c	c	b				
Mansions in the Sky	Three-part singing; unison and chords; stepwise and skipwise melodies.	d				e	c	a	b		📁	
Down by the Riverside	Syncopated rhythms; part independence.	c, d				c					📁	
Something Told the Wild Geese	Phrasing; tuning.	a, c				a, c						
Praise Ye the Lord, All Nations	Part independence; read rhythms in 3/4 meter including half, quarter, and eighth notes.	a, c, d				a	b	a, b				
Wiegenlied	Phrase building; I, IV, and V chords; German language.	c				a	c	a, b		b	📁	
Nightfall	Breathing technique; legato singing.	a, d					c	a	b	a	📁	
Riu, Riu, Chiu	*La* tonal center; meter changes; Spanish language.	b, c				c	c	a, b		a	📁	

SECTION		National Standards									Teacher's Resources	
Selection	Concepts and Skills	1	2	3	4	5	6	7	8	9		
HISTORICAL LESSONS												
Renaissance Period	Understanding the development of choral music during the Renaissance.						c		a, b	a, b, c	transparency, headset, folder	
Kyrie Eleison	Polyphonic singing; part independence; Greek pronunciation.					a, c	b, c	b		a, b	folder	
Baroque Period	Understanding the development of choral music during the Baroque period.			b			c		a, b	a, b, c	transparency, headset, folder	
Alleluia from *For Us a Child Is Born*	Breathing techniques: dynamics	a, c, d, e				a, b, c				a	folder	
Classical Period	Understanding the development of choral music during the Classical period.						a	a, b	a, b	a, b, c	transparency, headset, folder	
Dies Irae from *Requiem*	Singing in Latin; blended choral sound.	d, e				e		a	b	a	folder	
Romantic Period	Understanding the development of choral music during the Romantic period.				b, c		a		a, b	a, b, c	transparency, headset, folder	
In Stiller Nacht	Detached and connected articulation; singing in German; sustained crescendo/decrescendo.	c, d, e				b, e		a, b	a, b	a, b, c	folder	
Contemporary Period	Understanding the development of choral music during the Contemporary period.		c		b, c		a, c		a, b	a, b	transparency, headset, folder	
River, Sing Your Song	Phrasing, dynamics.	a, c, e		c		a, b, c, d		a		b		

ADDITIONAL PERFORMANCE SELECTIONS
I Hear Liberty Singing
It's Time to Fly Away
Shenandoah
Three Yoruba Native Songs of Nigeria
The Tree of Peace

The folder icon indicates that Teacher Resources (such as listening maps, blackline masters, etc.) are available to support the learning process.

The transparency projector icon indicates that there are overhead transparencies available to enhance learning.

The headset icon indicates that there are listening selections specifically chosen to aurally illustrate the music of the period.

National Standards Middle School Grades 5-8

The National Standards for Music Education were developed by the Music Educators National Conference. Reprinted by permission.

MUSIC

The period represented by grades 5-8 is especially critical in students' musical development. The music they perform or study often becomes an integral part of their personal musical repertoire. Composing and improvising provide students with unique insight into the form and structure of music and at the same time help them to develop their creativity. Broad experience with a variety of music is necessary if students are to make informed musical judgments. Similarly, this breadth of background enables them to begin to understand the connections and relationships between music and other disciplines. By understanding the cultural and historical forces that shape social attitudes and behaviors, students are better prepared to live and work in communities that are increasingly multicultural. The role that music will play in students' lives depends in large measure on the level of skills they achieve in creating, performing, and listening to music.

Every course in music, including performance courses, should provide instruction in creating, performing, listening to, and analyzing music, in addition to focusing on its specific subject matter.

1. **Content Standard:** Singing, alone and with others, a varied repertoire of music

   Achievement Standard:
   Students
   a. sing accurately and with good breath control throughout their singing ranges, alone and in small and large ensembles
   b. sing with *expression and *technical accuracy a repertoire of vocal literature with a *level of difficulty of 2, on a scale of 1 to 6, including some songs performed from memory
   c. sing music representing diverse *genres and cultures, with expression appropriate for the work being performed
   d. sing music written in two and three parts

   Students who participate in a choral ensemble
   e. sing with expression and technical accuracy a varied repertoire of vocal literature with a level of difficulty of 3, on a scale of 1 to 6, including some songs performed from memory

2. **Content Standard:** Performing on instruments, alone and with others, a varied repertoire of music

   Achievement Standard:
   Students
   a. perform on at least one instrument[2] accurately and independently, alone and in small and large ensembles, with good posture, good playing position, and good breath, bow, or stick control
   b. perform with expression and technical accuracy on at least one string, wind, percussion, or *classroom instrument a repertoire of instrumental literature with a level of difficulty of 2, on a scale of 1 to 6
   c. perform music representing diverse genres and cultures, with expression appropriate for the work being performed
   d. play by ear simple melodies on a melodic instrument and simple accompaniments on a harmonic instrument

   Students who participate in an instrumental ensemble or class
   e. perform with expression and technical accuracy a varied repertoire of instrumental literature with a level of difficulty of 3, on a scale of 1 to 6, including some solos performed from memory

3. **Content Standard:** Improvising melodies, variations, and accompaniments

   Achievement Standard:
   Students
   a. improvise simple harmonic accompaniments
   b. improvise melodic embellishments and simple rhythmic and melodic variations on given pentatonic melodies and melodies in major keys
   c. improvise short melodies, unaccompanied and over given rhythmic accompaniments, each in a consistent *style, *meter, and *tonality

4. **Content Standard:** Composing and arranging music within specified guidelines

   Achievement Standard:
   Students
   a. compose short pieces within specified guidelines,[3] demonstrating how the elements of

music are used to achieve unity and variety, tension and release, and balance

b. arrange simple pieces for voices or instruments other than those for which the pieces were written

c. use a variety of traditional and nontraditional sound sources and electronic media when composing and arranging

5. **Content Standard:** Reading and notating music

Achievement Standard:
Students

a. read whole, half, quarter, eighth, sixteenth, and dotted notes and rests in 2/4, 3/4, 4/4, 6/8, 3/8, and *alla breve meter signatures

b. read at sight simple melodies in both the treble and bass clefs

c. identify and define standard notation symbols for pitch, rhythm, *dynamics, tempo, *articulation, and expression

d. use standard notation to record their musical ideas and the musical ideas of others

Students who participate in a choral or instrumental ensemble or class

e. sightread, accurately and expressively, music with a level of difficulty of 2, on a scale of 1 to 6

6. **Content Standard:** Listening to, analyzing, and describing music

Achievement Standard:
Students

a. describe specific music events[4] in a given aural example, using appropriate terminology

b. analyze the uses of *elements of music in aural examples representing diverse genres and cultures

c. demonstrate knowledge of the basic principles of meter, rhythm, tonality, intervals, chords, and harmonic progressions in their analyses of music

7. **Content Standard:** Evaluating music and music performances

Achievement Standard:
Students

a. develop criteria for evaluating the quality and effectiveness of music performances and compositions and apply the criteria in their personal listening and performing

b. evaluate the quality and effectiveness of their own and others' performances, compositions, arrangements, and improvisations by applying specific criteria appropriate for the style of the music and offer constructive suggestions for improvement

8. **Content Standard:** Understanding relationships between music, the other arts, and disciplines outside the arts

Achievement Standard:
Students

a. compare in two or more arts how the characteristic materials of each art (that is, sound in music, visual stimuli in visual arts, movement in dance, human interrelationships in theatre) can be used to transform similar events, scenes, emotions, or ideas into works of art

b. describe ways in which the principles and subject matter of other disciplines taught in the school are interrelated with those of music[5]

9. **Content Standard:** Understanding music in relation to history and culture

Achievement Standard:
Students

a. describe distinguishing characteristics of representative music genres and styles from a variety of cultures

b. classify by genre and style (and, if applicable, by historical period, composer, and title) a varied body of exemplary (that is, high-quality and characteristic) musical works and explain the characteristics that cause each work to be considered exemplary

c. compare, in several cultures of the world, functions music serves, roles of musicians,[6] and conditions under which music is typically performed

Terms identified by an asterisk (*) are explained further in the glossary of *National Standards for Arts Education*, published by Music Educators National Conference, © 1994.

2. E.g., band or orchestra instrument, *fretted instrument, electronic instrument

3. E.g., a particular style, form, instrumentation, compositional technique

4. E.g., entry of oboe, change of meter, return of refrain

5. E.g., language arts: issues to be considered in setting texts to music; mathematics: frequency ratios of intervals; sciences: the human hearing process and hazards to hearing; social studies: historical and social events and movements chronicled in or influenced by musical works

6. E.g., lead guitarist in a rock band, composer of jingles for commercials, singer in Peking opera

INTRODUCTION

Choral Connections is a four-level series designed to build music literacy and promote vocal development for all students and voice categories in grades 6–12. The series is a multi-textbook program supported with print materials and audio listening components. This enables students to develop music skills and conceptual understanding, and provides teachers with a flexible, integrated program.

Choral Connections presents beginning, intermediate, and advanced-level literature for various voice groupings: mixed, treble, and tenor-bass. This comprehensive choral music program includes student texts, teacher's wrap-around editions, teacher's resource binders, and optional audio recordings designed to enhance student learning while reducing teacher preparation time.

Choral Connections is a curriculum that provides your students with a meaningful, motivating choral music experience, and will help you and your students make many connections. This choral music program . . .

Connects to . . . the National Standards

The National Standards are correlated to each lesson for quick-and-easy identification and reference. The performance standards related to singing and reading notations are explicit in each lesson, and by using the extension activities, teachers can connect the musical elements through improvisation and composition. Analysis and evaluation are an active and consistent component of lessons throughout the series. Additional student activities connect the lessons to the other arts, as well as provide a consistent historical and cultural context.

Connects to . . . Skill Development

Through vocal warm-ups and sight-singing exercises, students build vocal skills and master the vocal and sight-reading skills necessary to perform each piece. Rhythmic melodic and articulation skills are developed as needed for expressive interpretation. Students are encouraged to develop listening skills and use their perceptions to improve individual and group performance.

Connects to . . . Performance

Fundamental to a quality choral music program is the student performance of the literature. Student performance provides opportunities for young musicians to demonstrate musical growth, to gain personal satisfaction from achievement, and to experience the joy of music making. To help develop skills, *Choral Connections* provides exercises in warming-up and sight-singing which help prepare students to successfully sing each piece.

Conceptual understanding is built throughout the teaching/learning sequence, as the performance is prepared.

Connects to . . . the Arts and Other Curriculum Areas

Choral music provides a rich opportunity to connect the musical experience to other art disciplines (dance, visual arts, theatre), and to enhance the learning in other subject areas. It also provides a vehicle to help students gain knowledge and understanding of historical and cultural contexts across the curriculum.

PROGRAM PHILOSOPHY

Responding to Trends in Choral Music Education

Choral Connections is consistent with current educational philosophy that suggests:

- Performance is a product which should be the end result of a sound educational process, building conceptual understanding and skills as the performance is prepared.

- Students are motivated through materials and concepts that are connected to their own lives and interests, and they should be exposed to high-quality, challenging musical literature.

- Students learn best when they are active participants in their learning, and when they clearly understand and help set the goals of the learning process.

- Students understand concepts better when they have background information and skills which allow them to place their learning into a larger context.

- Students need to actively manipulate musical concepts and skills through improvisation and/or composition in order to fully assimilate and understand them.

- Students improve when they receive fair, honest, and meaningful feedback on their successes and failures.

- Students should be encouraged to assess themselves individually and as a group, learning to receive and process constructive criticism, which leads to independent self-correction and decision making.

Scope and Depth of Music Literature

Most students are capable of performing more difficult material than they can sight-sing. Therefore, the literature in *Choral Connections* is drawn from many periods and styles of music. The wide range of composers and publishers ensures variety, and allows for various skills and concepts to be developed as each new piece is encountered. The high standards set in *Choral Connections* provides selections that are inherently powerful and exciting for students. Rather than working with contrived songs to teach skills or concepts, students learn through discovery and interaction with quality literature.

Addressing the National Standards

The National Standards for Arts Education, published in 1994 and reprinted with permission on pages T6–T7, launched a national effort to bring a new vision to arts education for all students. The National Standards provides a framework for achievement in music, with outcomes suggested for grades 4, 8, and 12. *Choral Connections* addresses the National Standards in several ways.

The most obvious and predominant National Standards addressed in choral ensemble are: (1) singing and (5) reading notation. However, good performance requires musical understanding which only occurs when all aspects of musical experience are incorporated. The preparation of vocal performance is enriched and deepened by involvement in all nine of the National Standards.

As you teach with *Choral Connections*, there will be frequent opportunities to deepen or extend student learning through: (2) playing through and creating accompaniments, (3) improvisation, (4) composition and arranging, (6) analyzing, (7) assessing, (8) linking with other arts and other academic disciplines, and (9) understanding historical and cultural contexts. The National Standards identified for each lesson and the Teacher's Wraparound extension activities help you become aware of the National Standards, and the depth of learning that will occur as you implement this choral music program.

Promoting Music Literacy

Choral Connections promotes music literacy. Literacy includes oral and aural aspects of music communication—reading, writing, singing, and listening. Each lesson begins with a *vocal warm-up* during which the student builds vocal skills through singing and listening. The lesson then proceeds to *sight-singing exercise(s)*, emphasizing reading development. These exercises may be rhythmic, melodic, harmonic, or a combination thereof; and emphasize the musical elements which are the objectives of the lesson. The sight-singing exercises lead directly into the *musical selection*. Students are encouraged to sight-sing in every lesson, and are assessed in an increasingly rigorous way as the text progresses from lesson to lesson. Sight-singing is approached as a challenge, and a means to the student's musical independence.

Literacy goes beyond reading pitch and rhythm and extends to the expressive elements of music and appropriate interpretation. Students are frequently asked to explore interpretive aspects of music making, and encouraged to suggest their own ideas for phrasing, dynamics, and so on. Through careful listening and constructive critique of their own work, they will gradually become more discriminating about the quality of performance, and the impact of that performance on the audience.

Including Authentic Student Assessment

The assessment in *Choral Connections* is systematic, objective, and authentic. There is ongoing *informal assessment* by teacher observation throughout the lessons. The text is written as a series of action steps for the student, so there are many opportunities for the director to hear and see the level of accomplishment.

Students will find objectives at the beginning of each lesson, and two types of assessment questions at the end. First, factual questions that check for understanding of concepts and skills are presented. Next, there are questions which require higher-level thinking through analysis, synthesis, and/or evaluation. The questions are always related directly to the lesson objectives, and allow students to demonstrate their understanding. By answering the questions, and demonstrating as suggested, students are involved in *self-assessment*. Many times students are involved in their own assessment, constructing rubrics or critiquing their performance, and identifying their next challenge.

The Teacher's Wraparound Edition includes lesson objectives and each lesson is taught so the concepts and skills are experienced, labeled, practiced, and reinforced, then measured through *formal assessment*. These assessment tasks match the lesson objectives, allowing students to demonstrate understanding of concepts and skills through performance, composition, or writing. Students are frequently required to produce audio or video tapes. This authentic assessment technique keeps testing of rote learning to a minimum, and allows measurement of higher-level application of knowledge and skills. A portfolio can be constructed for individual students, groups, or the whole ensemble; demonstrating growth over time.

Connecting the Arts and Other Curriculum Areas

Lessons in *Choral Connections* integrate many appropriate aspects of musical endeavor into the preparation of a piece. Students compose, improvise, conduct, read, write, sing, play, listen/analyze, and assess on an ongoing basis that builds understanding, as well as high standards. In this way, the many aspects of music are integrated for deeper learning.

As one of the arts, music can be linked to other arts through similarities and differences. Throughout the text, and particularly in the historical section, music is compared and contrasted with other arts to determine aspects of confluence, and the unique features of each art.

As one way of knowing about the world, music can be compared with concepts and skills from other disciplines as seemingly different as science or mathematics. The integrations between music and other disciplines are kept at the conceptual level, to maintain the integrity of both music and the other subjects. For example, mathematical sets of 2, 3, 4, 5, and 6 might be explored as a link to pieces with changing meter; or the text of a piece might become a starting point for exploration of tone painting. In Making Historical Connections, a time line connects music to social studies, and a list of authors for each period provides a link to language and literature.

Providing a Variety of Student Activities

Choral Connections begins with the choral experience, and builds understanding through active participation in a range of activities including singing, playing, improvising, composing, arranging, moving, writing, listening, analyzing, assessing, and connecting to cultures, periods, or disciplines. Lessons are written with the heading "Have students . . .", so there is always an emphasis on learning by doing.

Fitting Your Classroom Needs

Effective classrooms are characterized by many features, including student participation, a positive environment, clear sense of purpose, challenging content, high motivation, and a sense of sharing between teacher and student. These probably describe your choral ensemble classroom, and *Choral Connections* will allow you to make the most of these characteristics.

With *Choral Connections*, your students will be clear about purpose and direction, have multiple routes to success, and be involved in their own learning. The lessons will guide you and your students to share in the excitement of music making, and help you to grow together. The lessons are written the way you teach, and allow you to maintain and strengthen your routines, while adding flexibility, variety, and depth.

ORGANIZATION AND FLEXIBILITY

Each *Choral Connections* text is divided into the following sections:
- Preparatory Materials

- Lessons
- Making Historical Connections
- Additional Performance Selections

Preparatory Materials

Preparatory Materials introduce such basic concepts as notes and their values, rests and their values, rhythm patterns, breathing mechanics, solfège and hand signs, frequently found intervals, and pitch. Activities provided in the Teacher's Wraparound Edition suggest ways to use these materials as beginning exercises if your students have little or no music background. If your students are familiar with choral music, these Preparatory Materials can be both a quick review and a convenient reference.

Lessons

The Lessons are designed to be taught over a period of time. Each lesson is developed around a piece of quality authentic music literature. The lesson includes warm-ups, sight-singing, and rhythmic or melodic drills, all of which are directly related to preparation of the piece. Objectives are clearly stated, and a motivational opening activity or discussion is provided. The Teacher's Wraparound Edition outlines a carefully sequenced approach to the piece, with multiple entry points, and clear assessment opportunities to document achievement and growth.

Making Historical Connections

Making Historical Connections provides narrative, listening, and choral experiences for each of the five main historical periods. A *narrative lesson* provides a brief and interesting exposition of the main characteristics of the period, leading from the previous period, and outlining the achievements and new styles that emerged. A time line guides the student to place the musical characteristics into a larger historical and cultural context. The *listening lesson* includes both vocal and instrumental listening selections from the period, with listening maps and teacher wraparound lessons to guide student listening. The third component, a *literature lesson*, rounds out the student experience through a preparation of a piece to be sung from the period.

Additional Performance Selections

Additional Performance Selections provide a range of additional literature featuring popular pieces and multicultural selections that can be used to enhance the repertoire of your choral music performance. Warm-up exercises and suggestions to help you guide your students through the score are given, as well as program tips.

Lesson Objectives

Each lesson has objectives that emphasize and build conceptual understanding and skills across the lessons. The objectives in this book are:

LESSON OBJECTIVES	
LESSON 1 Bound for Jubilee	• Identify notes moving stepwise and in thirds. • Sing in four parts.
LESSON 2 A Red, Red Rose	• Read and clap rhythms from three staves, maintaining part independence. • Sing in three parts using solfège, numbers, or text.
LESSON 3 Over There	• Sight-sing in different keys using solfège. • Sight-read syncopated rhythms.
LESSON 4 Dare to Dream!	• Read stepwise passages with solfège and hand signs. • Recognize and sing staggered entrances.
LESSON 5 The Tiger	• Read rhythms in 6/8 meters. • Locate repetitive entrances.
LESSON 6 Shalom, My Friends	• Sight-sing pitches in D minor. • Identify different relationships between vocal parts. • Sight-sing a piece in three parts, using solfège or text.
LESSON 7 Whisper! Whisper!	• Distinguish between broken and block versions of the tonic chord. • Perform call-and-response segments of a choral piece.
LESSON 8 Mansions in the Sky	• Read and sing in three parts. • Distinguish between and sing unison and chords. • Distinguish between and sing stepwise and skipwise melodic motion.
LESSON 9 Down by the Riverside	• Read and clap syncopated rhythms. • Sing in two parts with independent melody and rhythm lines.
LESSON 10 Something Told the Wild Geese	• Perform correctly shaped musical phrases. • Demonstrate good intonation while singing with two other parts.
LESSON 11 Praise Ye the Lord, All Nations	• Sing your part independently with the other voice parts. • Read notation in 3/4 meter including half, quarter, and eighth notes.
LESSON 12 Wiegenlied	• Sing, demonstrating an understanding of phrase. • Use correct German pronunciation for the song text. • Build a I, IV, and V chord in the key of E♭.
LESSON 13 Nightfall	• Describe and demonstrate correct breathing mechanics. • Describe and demonstrate legato singing style.
LESSON 14 Riu, Riu, Chiu	• Read in F minor, using solfège syllables and hand signs or numbers. • Perform correct meter changes from 2/2 to 3/2 and back. • Use correct Spanish pronunciation.

LESSON OBJECTIVES (continued)

RENAISSANCE PERIOD	• Describe the developments that took place in music during the Renaissance Period. • Compare the differences in sacred music from the Middle Ages and the Renaissance. • Define *madrigal*, *Renaissance*, and *polyphony*.
Kyrie Eleison	• Sing voice parts independently. • Identify polyphonic textures. • Demonstrate knowledge of correct Greek pronunciation.
BAROQUE PERIOD	• Describe some developments that took place during the Baroque period. • Identify some forms and characteristics of Baroque instrumental and vocal music. • Compare characteristics of Baroque art/architecture and music. • Define *oratorio*, *cantata*, and *opera*.
Alleluia from *For Us a Child Is Born*	• Sing with proper breathing techniques. • Define and perform dynamic markings.
CLASSICAL PERIOD	• Compare qualities of music written in the Classical and Baroque styles. • Identify two major composers from the Classical period. • Define *sonata-allegro form*.
Dies Irae from *Requiem*	• Singing in Latin with correct pronunciation. • Sing with a blended choral sound.
ROMANTIC PERIOD	• Compare qualities of music written in the Romantic and Classical styles. • Identify major composers and forms from the Romantic period. • Define *nationalism*, *art songs*, and *symphony*.
In Stiller Nacht	• Sing with detached and connected articulation. • Sing in German with correct pronunciation. • Identify sustained crescendo and decrescendo.
CONTEMPORARY PERIOD	• Compare qualities of music written in the Contemporary and Romantic styles. • Identify several characteristics and styles of twentieth-century music. • Define *dissonance*, *twelve tone music*, and *aleatoric* or *chance music*. • Define *fusion*.
River, Sing Your Song	• Demonstrate correct dynamics. • Determine and perform correct phrasing.

Student Text

Lessons

The lessons, through which students systematically build musical skills and conceptual understanding, comprise the majority of the text. These lessons are structured as follows:

- **FOCUS** . . . tells the student the main concepts and skills addressed in the lesson. By having only a few main goals, students and teacher will keep focused on these objectives as work progresses.

- **SIGHT-SINGING EXERCISES** . . . build rhythmic, melodic, and expressive sight-singing skills through exercises that are directly related to some aspect of the upcoming musical selection. Through sight-singing practice every day, students gain confidence and skills to become independent readers.

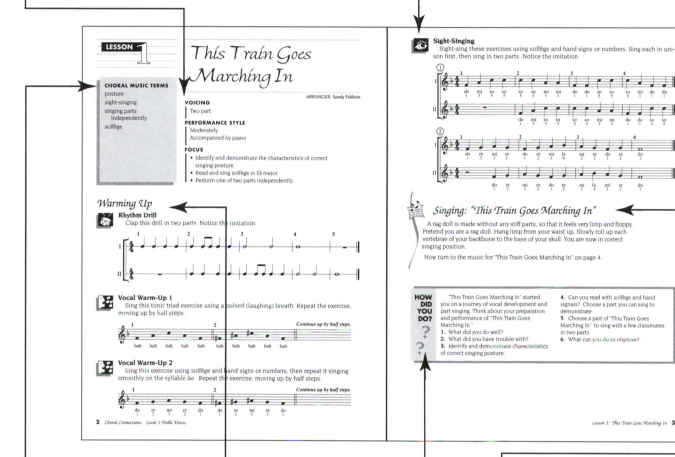

- **CHORAL MUSIC TERMS** . . . give the students an opportunity to build a musical vocabulary essential for clarity of thought in communicating about music to others.

- **WARM-UP EXERCISES** . . . allow the students to warm-up their bodies, voices, and minds at the beginning of every class, while immediately exploring the main rhythmic, melodic, and skill issues that will arise in preparing the piece. These exercises are designed to sequentially build skills.

- **SINGING** . . . provides a motivating introduction to the piece of music, related to the student's perspective, which begins with a familiar idea and asks the student to think about or explore some concept or skill. Through interest and active participation, the student is then led logically into the piece.

- **STUDENT SELF-ASSESSMENT—HOW DID YOU DO?** . . . gives the student ways to assess accomplishment, growth, and needs, for both self and group. Beginning with recall, comprehension and application questions, the final questions ask for analysis, synthesis, and evaluation, guiding the student to higher-level thinking and the ability to self-assess.

Making Historical Connections

The Historical section of the text provides a survey of Western music history through exploration of the culture and music of the five overarching periods: Renaissance, Baroque, Classical, Romantic, and Contemporary. Each period is addressed in the following ways:

- **Historical Narrative Lesson** . . . provides a brief, student-oriented historical context of the period through visual art, architecture, historical events, musical developments, artistic characteristics, musical personalities, and listening selections. Students are encouraged to imagine this time period as if they were living in it, and experience the music from the perspective of the period.

- **Historical Listening Lesson** . . . provides one choral and one instrumental listening selection, to give students an aural experience with the styles, sounds and forms of the period. Listening maps are provided in the Teacher's Resource Binder so the student can follow along as a visual guide to listening.

- **Historical Literature Lesson** . . . is paired with the narrative lesson for each period, and provides the opportunity to perform a piece with appropriate characteristics and performance style. The selected materials reflect the period, and provide a concrete example of those characteristics introduced in the previous narrative.

Additional Performance Selections

Each book provides additional performance selections which meet the various needs of the ensemble and director. Each selection is accompanied by a specifically designed warm-up to build appropriate vocal skills.

- **Patriotic Selections** . . . provide excellent openers and closers for concerts, and are particularly useful when performing at patriotic celebrations.

- **Holiday Selections** . . . acknowledge the need for performance literature appropriate for winter holidays and during the spring season.

- **Multicultural selections** . . . provide an opportunity for performance of music that has different criteria than Western art music, allowing exploration of different languages, vocal tone color, styles, movement, and cultural characteristics.

- **Proven Audience-Pleaser Selections** . . . allow you to round out your programs with appropriate rousing or sentimental pieces that provide a change of pace or variety.

Glossary

The glossary provides brief, accurate definitions of musical terms used in the text.

TEACHER'S WRAPAROUND EDITION

National Standards Connections

Choral Connections affords multiple opportunities to address the National Standards. Correlations between lesson content, extension activities, and bottom-page activities are listed to show the relationship between lesson activities and the standards.

Teaching Sequence

Each lesson is organized to follow a logical progression from warm-ups through assessment, while providing maximum flexibility of use for your individual situation. Each lesson is linked to one musical selection, and provides learning opportunities based on the inherent concepts and skills required to understand and perform the piece. The lessons of the Teacher Wraparound Edition are structured as follows:

- **Focus** . . . gives the teacher a brief overview of concepts and skills which form the content of the objectives and assessments in the lesson.

- **Objectives** . . . provides concrete, measurable objectives allowing an interconnected approach to lesson segments. Each objective will be assessed in three ways during the lesson.

- **Choral Music Terms** . . . identifies the terms used during the lesson to build understanding and skills.

- **Warming Up** . . . includes rhythm and vocal warm-up exercises, as well as sight-singing exercises. The vocal warm-ups are designed to sequentially develop vocal skills, and start each class immediately with singing. The sight-singing exercises are designed to systematically build sight-singing skills, and lead directly into the upcoming piece. The purpose of each exercise is stated clearly for the teacher and student at the beginning of the lesson. These exercises may all be done before the piece is introduced, or they may be presented cumulatively, one each day, and concurrent with developing understanding of the piece.

- **Singing** . . . provides motivation and an entree to the piece of literature. Many different approaches are utilized, but they all draw the student into the piece through active learning and thinking.

- **Suggested Teaching Sequence** . . . returns to each warm-up activity and reviews, then guides you directly from the warm-up into the piece of literature. In this way, you have multiple entry points, so your approach is new and different each day the ensemble works on the piece. Specific rehearsal techniques, based on sight-singing, sectional work, and analysis of difficulties build skills and conceptual understanding as the performance is refined day after day. Each lesson includes recommended steps for organizing students into small groups by voice part to sight-sing the song separately before coming together in full ensemble to perform the selection.
- **Assessment** . . . provides Informal Assessment, Student Self-Assessment, and Individual Performance Assessment. There is appropriate assessment for each lesson objective.

Assessment

Informal Assessment is accomplished through teacher observation during the lesson. Each objective is observable, and the text indicates the checkpoint for teacher assessment.

Student Self-Assessment is accomplished through oral or written response to questions in the Student Text.

Individual Performance Assessment requires the student to demonstrate a skill or understanding through individual assessment. This is frequently done through audio or video taping, creation of rubrics to assess the quality of the performance, or a written exercise to demonstrate understanding. Individual Performance Assessment can be done by the teacher, student, peers, or a combination thereof. The tapes may be compiled into a portfolio which shows growth and development of understanding.

Extensions and Bottom-Page Activities

Extensions and bottom-page activities in each lesson afford a plethora of background information, teaching strategies, and enrichment opportunities.

- **Enrichment activities** in the side columns provide opportunities for movement, improvisation, composition, and analysis based on lesson and selection content.
- **Vocal development strategies** give detailed information about specific techniques that facilitate vocal production, style, and negotiation of difficult passages within the piece.
- **Music literacy strategies** help students expand their ability to read and analyze music.
- **Teaching strategies** are available to reinforce concepts or skills that may be difficult for students,

or elaborate on classroom management techniques suggested within the lesson.
- **More about** boxes provide background historical, cultural, and/or biographical information to give deeper understanding of the piece.
- **Curriculum connections** provide strategies to help students build bridges between music and other disciplines.

Performance Tips

In the Additional Performance Selection section, you are provided with performance suggestions that identify specific strategies that have worked successfully for choral music teachers, and potential "hot spots" you may need to address. Each selection is accompanied by a suggested program, including selections from the book. These recommendations should be extremely helpful for the beginning choral director, and provide many interesting alternatives for the experienced conductor.

TEACHER'S RESOURCE BINDER

The Teacher's Resource Binder contains teaching materials designed to reduce teacher preparation time and maximize students' learning. The following categories are provided to assist with meeting the individual needs and interests of your students.

Skill Masters. The *Skill Masters* provide sequential musical concepts that can be used to review and reinforce musical concepts in the areas of rhythm and pitch, music literacy, vocal development, and pronunciation guides.

Blackline Masters. The *Blackline Masters* are designed to enhance the concepts presented in the student text lessons.

Assessment. Assessment activities provide performance assessment criteria, rubrics, and other activity pages to help teachers with individual and group assessment.

Fine Art Transparencies. Full color overhead transparencies of the visual art pieces that introduce each of the historical sections are provided.

Listening Maps. Blackline masters of listening maps are provided and feature choral and instrumental selections. These help reinforce learning about the five major historical periods. Teachers may wish to make a transparency of the blackline master and have students follow along as the teacher points to the overhead transparency.

FEATURED LISTENING SELECTIONS

The Listening Program provides rich resources of sound to reinforce learning about the five major Western historical periods. Two selections for each period, one choral and the other instrumental, are accompanied by listening maps. At first, students listen as observers, watching the teacher guide their listening with a transparency of the map on the overhead projector. In the next listening, they then follow their own copies of the map, showing their ability to hear specific musical features. The Teacher's Wraparound Edition provides the CD number and track at point of use for each selection. Many more historical period examples are included on the CD sets than are referenced in the text. You're invited to use them to supplement and extend your lessons, or to have students create their own maps to creatively demonstrate understanding of musical and/or historical elements.

Choral Connections

Teacher's Wraparound Edition

LEVEL 1
MIXED VOICES

GLENCOE

McGraw-Hill

New York, New York
Columbus, Ohio
Mission Hills, California
Peoria, Illinois

Cover Photos: Paul Chen/Masterfile and Eureka Collection/SuperStock, Inc.

Glencoe/McGraw-Hill

A Division of The McGraw·Hill Companies

Send all inquiries to:
Glencoe/McGraw-Hill
15319 Chatsworth Street
Mission Hills, California 91345

ISBN 0-02-655527-1 (Student's Edition)
ISBN 0-02-655536-0 (Teacher's Wraparound Edition)

Printed in the United States of America.

2 3 4 5 6 7 8 9   MAL   02 01 00 99 98 97 96

Meet the Authors

Senior Author

Mollie G. Tower—As Coordinator of Choral and General Music of the Austin Independent School District, Mollie Tower was recently nominated as "Administrator of the Year." She is very active in international, national, regional, and state music educators' organizations. Ms. Tower was contributing author, consultant, and reviewer for the elementary programs *Share the Music* and *Music and You*. Senior author of *Música para todos, Primary and Intermediate Dual Language Handbooks for Music Teachers*, she has also written and consulted for many other publications. A longtime advocate of music education, Mollie is a popular clinician who conducts workshops across the country.

Marc Erck
Choir Director

Marc Erck has more than ten years of choral directing experience. He received his Bachelor of Music Education from Southwestern University. Marc is currently the director of choirs at Hill Country Middle School in the Eanes Independent School District and Choir Director at University United Methodist Church, both in Austin, Texas.

Ruth Phillips
Choir Director

Ruth Phillips has taught choral music in junior high and middle school for 17 years in both the Dallas/Fort Worth area and in San Marcos, Texas. She is currently in her eighth year at Goodnight Junior High. Ms. Phillips received a Bachelor of Science degree in All Level Music Education from McMurry University in Abilene, Texas.

Linda S. Wyatt
Choir Director

With 27 years of choir directing experience, Linda S. Wyatt is presently Director of Choirs at Murchison Middle School in Austin, Texas. After receiving her Bachelor of Music Education degree from Southwest Texas State University, she taught at John Marshall High School and Sul Ross Middle School in San Antonio.

Consulting Author

Dr. Susan Snyder has taught all levels of vocal music over the last 25 years. She holds a B.S. in music education from the University of Connecticut and an M.A. from Montclair State College. She holds a PhD. in curriculum and instruction from the University of Connecticut and advanced professional certificates from Memphis State University and the University of Minnesota. Teaching at Hunter College and City University of New York, Dr. Snyder was coordinating author of the elementary music program, *Share the Music*, and a consultant on *Music and You*. She has published many articles on music education and integrated curriculum and is an active clinician and master teacher.

Consultants

Choral Music
Stephan P. Barnicle
Choir Director
Simsbury High School
Simsbury, Connecticut

Vocal Development, Music Literacy
Katherine Saltzer Hickey, D.M.A.
University of California at Los Angeles
Los Angeles, California
Choir Director
Pacific Chorale Children's Choruses
Irvine, California

Music History
Dr. Kermit Peters
University of Nebraska at Omaha
College of Fine Arts
Department of Music
Omaha, Nebraska

Contributors/Teacher Reviewers

Dr. Anton Armstrong
Music Director and Conductor, St. Olaf Choir
St. Olaf College
Northfield, Minnesota

Jeanne Julseth-Heinrich
Choir Director
James Madison Middle School
Appleton, Wisconsin

Caroline Lyon
Ethnomusicologist
University of Texas at Austin
Austin, Texas

Caroline Minear
Supervisor
Orange County School District
Orlando, Florida

Judy Roberts
Choir Director
Central Junior High School
Moore, Oklahoma

Dr. A. Byron Smith
Choir Director
Lincoln High School
Tallahassee, Florida

Table of Contents

ADDITIONAL PERFORMANCE SELECTIONS

CHORAL MUSIC TERMS

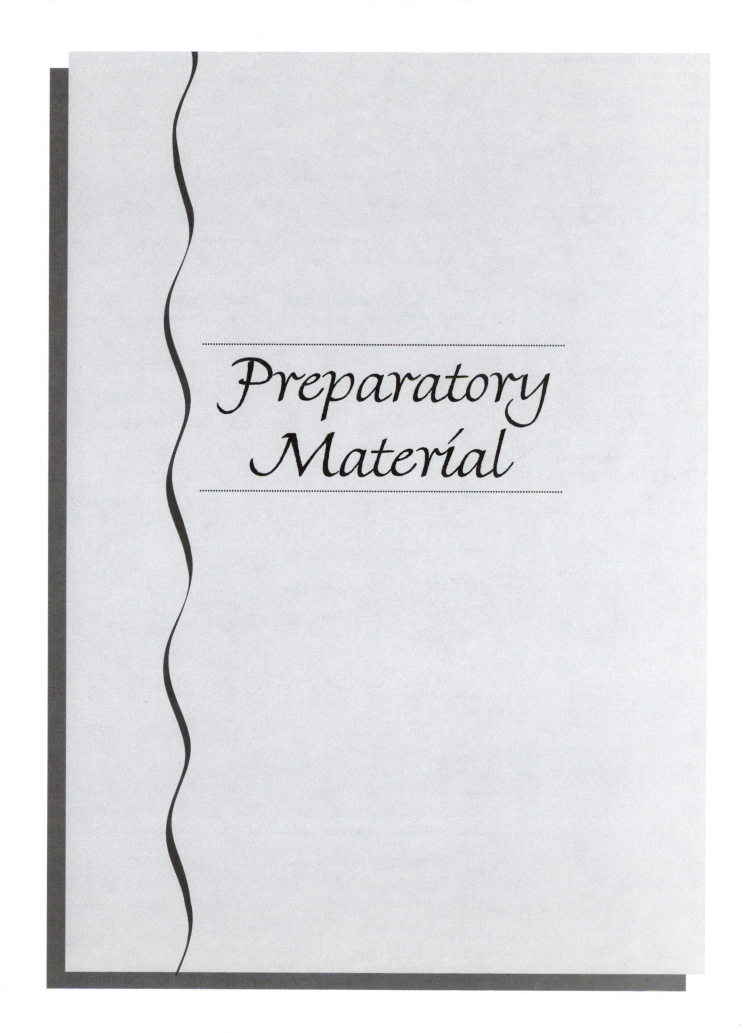

Preparatory Material

Using the Preparatory Material

The preparatory material found on these pages is designed to build a basic rhythmic, melodic, and sight-singing vocabulary. By working through the challenges, students will build the skills required for successful work in the upcoming lessons.

- If your students have little or no music background, take a day or two to introduce this musical vocabulary. Have them sing a few rounds to get them familiar with basic conducting, breathing, and working together.

- If your students have a rich music background, and have participated in a solid elementary music program, review these challenges quickly, stopping to answer questions and clarify any misunderstandings. Then proceed to Lesson 1. Refer back to these pages during lessons when necessary.

Notes and Rests

The alignment of notes and rests on this page show the relationship between notes or rests of different value. Encourage students to learn these concepts early.

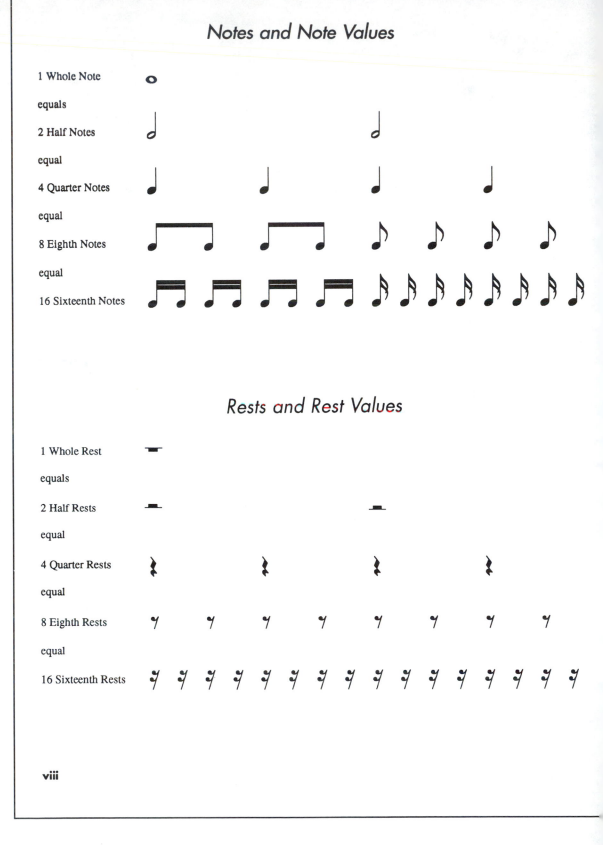

Notes and Note Values

1 Whole Note

equals

2 Half Notes

equal

4 Quarter Notes

equal

8 Eighth Notes

equal

16 Sixteenth Notes

Rests and Rest Values

1 Whole Rest

equals

2 Half Rests

equal

4 Quarter Rests

equal

8 Eighth Rests

equal

16 Sixteenth Rests

viii

Rhythm Challenge in 4/4 Meter

Directions: Accurately count and/or perform the following rhythms without stopping!

When presenting a rhythm challenge, allow students the chance to read through the whole challenge first, answering any questions, and helping them resolve any concerns. Then offer students the opportunity to perform the challenge without pressure.

At the beginning of the year, too much pressure for those with no previous experience might discourage them for the rest of their lives! Some techniques to consider are:

- Have students design a chart in the form of a graph with approximately 15 columns that represent the same number of trials. One or more trials can be attempted at the beginning of each class. After each trial, each student should record the number of the measure where the first mistake was made. After fifteen trials, most students should show, by a line graph, considerable improvement.
- Encourage students to design their own method of tracking their improvement. Students with access to computer programs might take it upon themselves to create a personalized chart for individuals or one for the entire class.

ix

More Rhythm Challenges

To increase students' skill at reading rhythms, have them:

- Speak or clap each rhythm challenge as a group or in small ensembles, isolating and practicing measures and phrases that pose difficulty.
- Practice in small groups for a predetermined amount of time, such as 5 minutes. At the end of that time, assess rhythmic reading in one of the following ways: each student speaks and claps the pattern; each group speaks and claps the pattern; the whole class speaks and claps the pattern.
- Students should keep a record of their progress by recording the first measure where an error is made on each successive attempt.

Directions: Accurately count and/or perform the following rhythms without stopping!

x

Breathing Mechanics

Singing well requires good breath control. Support for singing comes from correct use of the breathing mechanism. Deep, controlled breathing is needed to sustain long phrases in one breath. Also, correct breathing will support higher, more difficult passages.

Posture
Posture is very important in breath support.
- Keep your body relaxed, but your backbone straight.
- To stretch your back: Bend over and slowly roll your back upward until you are standing straight again. Do this several times.
- Hold your rib cage high, but keep your shoulders low and relaxed.
- Facing front, keep your head level. Imagine you are suspended by a string attached to the very top of your head.
- When you stand, keep your knees relaxed and do not "lock" them by pushing them all the way back. Keep your feet slightly apart.
- When you sit, keep both feet flat on the floor and sit forward in your chair.

Inhaling
- Expand the lungs out and down, pushing the diaphragm muscle down.
- Inhale silently without gasping or making any other noise.
- Imagine taking a cool sip of air through a straw.
- Expand your entire waistline, keeping the shoulders low and relaxed.

Breath Control
To help you develop breath control do the following:
- Hold one finger about six inches from your mouth imagining that your finger is a birthday candle. Now blow out a steady stream of air to blow out the flame of the candle.

Summary

STANDING
Feet slightly apart
Knees relaxed
Backbone straight
Rib cage high
Shoulders low
Head level

SITTING
Feet on the floor
Sit on edge of chair
Backbone straight
Rib cage high
Shoulders low
Head level

Breathing Mechanics
Remind students that vocal tone, resonance, and intonation are affected by posture and breathing. Basic singing posture is a relaxed, but firm, body stance. Have students read through the text on this page and practice correct posture and breathing.

Diaphragmatic Breathing
Have students:
- Feel the sensation of muscle expansion by placing thumbs above the small of the back with fingers pressing the top of the hips. Sip a long, deep breath and feel the action of the muscles.
- Feel the action of the diaphragm muscle by pressing the fingertips of both hands into the midsection of the torso just below the rib cage. Take a startled, quick surprise breath and feel the action of the muscle. Ask: How did the diaphragm react?
- Feel the diaphragm muscle expand outward as they sip a long, cool breath.
- Pant like a dog or bark like a dog (use *arf* and *woof*). Feel the action of the diaphragm.
- Use unvoiced consonants, such as *sh, f, p, t,* and *k* in different rhythms and tempos to create the diaphragmatic action.

What is Signing?

Signing in music describes the use of hand signals to represent relative sounds of pitches. The signs were used by Reverend John Curwen from a method developed by Sarah Glover of Norwich in the nineteenth century. The *do* is movable and was intended to teach beginners to sing accurate pitches. The system has been adopted by the Kodaly approach and Tonika-Do system in Germany.

Intervals

Help students remember intervals by relating them to the first two pitches of the following familiar songs:

Major 2nd —"Frère Jacques"

Major 3rd—"Taps"

Perfect 4th—"Here Comes the Bride"

Perfect 5th—"Twinkle, Twinkle Little Star"

Major 6th—"My Bonny Lies Over the Ocean"

Octave—"Somewhere, Over the Rainbow"

Have students:

• Challenge one another in pairs, one singing an interval, the other telling what interval was heard.

• Check any disagreements with another pair.

• Take turns singing intervals.

Composing with Frequently Found Intervals

Have students:

• Compose an exercise of eight measures, using at least three different intervals shown on this page.

• Notate their melodies.

• Describe their piece and perform it to a classmate.

Solfège and Hand Signs

Solfège is a system designed to match notes on the staff with specific interval relationships. Hand signs provide additional reinforcement of the pitch relationships.

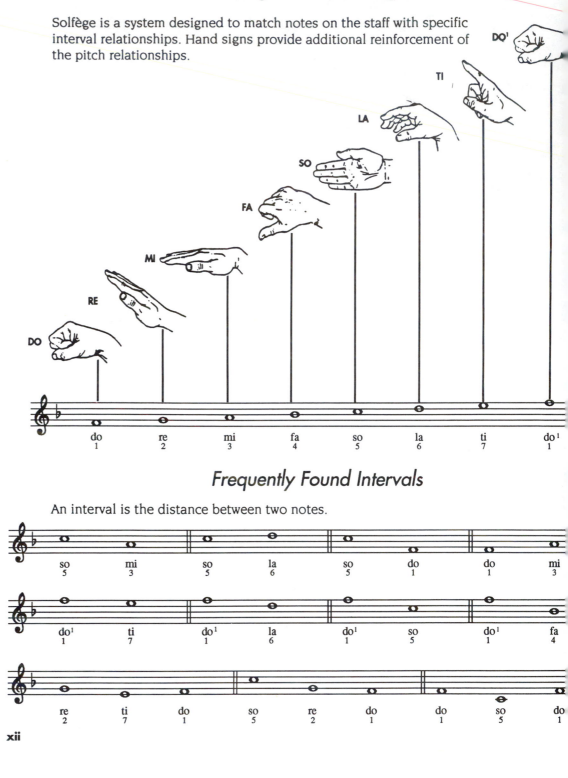

Frequently Found Intervals

An interval is the distance between two notes.

Pitch Challenge

Directions: Accurately sing each measure on solfège using hand signs and without stopping! During the measure of rest, look ahead to the next challenge.

The best way to get better at pitch accuracy is to get feedback about which pitches are sung flat or sharp. The following activity is excellent for both the singer and listener. However, use confident volunteers only, as students will be critiqued openly in front of peers.

Have students:

- Listen to volunteers who are willing to have their pitch accuracy assessed as they perform the Pitch Challenge on this page with a partner.
- If the pitch is accurate, listeners should point thumbs to the side; if sharp, point thumbs up; and if flat, point thumbs down.
- Repeat this activity with as many volunteers as time permits.

Lessons

Bound for Jubilee

COMPOSER: Joyce Elaine Eilers
TEXT: Joyce Elaine Eilers

Focus

OVERVIEW
Melodic movement stepwise and in thirds; singing in four parts.

OBJECTIVES
After completing this lesson, students will be able to:
- Distinguish between melodic movement stepwise and in thirds.
- Sing in four parts.

CHORAL MUSIC TERMS
Define the Choral Music Terms for students, giving pronunciation, and answering any questions that may arise.

Warming Up

Vocal Warm-Up
This Vocal Warm-Up is designed to prepare students to:
- Establish a pattern of doing warm-ups at the beginning of each class.
- Sing using solfège and hand signs or numbers.
- Warm up their voices by repeating the pattern one step higher each time.
- Distinguish between melodic segments in which the notes move stepwise or in thirds.

Have students:
- Study Blackline Master 1, *Stepwise Movement and Thirds.* (Answer any questions that may arise.)
- Read through the Vocal Warm-Up directions.
- Sing, following your demonstration.

Bound for Jubilee

COMPOSER: *Joyce Elaine Eilers*
TEXT: *Joyce Elaine Eilers*

CHORAL MUSIC TERMS
chord
four-part singing
melodic movement in thirds
melodic stepwise movement
unison

VOICING
SATB

PERFORMANCE STYLE
Spirited
A cappella

FOCUS
- Identify notes moving stepwise and in thirds.
- Sing in four parts.

Warming Up

 Vocal Warm-Up
Sing this warm-up exercise using solfège syllables *do, re, mi, fa,* and *so* or numbers. Repeat the warm-up pattern, beginning one step higher each time. Decide which notes move up or down stepwise, and which move in thirds.

TEACHER'S RESOURCE BINDER
Blackline Master 1, *Stepwise Movement and Thirds,* page 75
Blackline Master 2, *C Major Scale as a Round,* page 76

National Standards
Through involvement with this lesson, students will develop the following skills and concepts:
1. Singing, alone and with others, a varied repertoire of music. **(a)**
5. Reading and notating music. **(a)**
9. Understanding music in relation to history and culture. **(a)**

Sight-Singing

Sight-sing these parts using solfège syllables or numbers. Look at and listen to the beginning and end of this exercise. How is the ending different? Use the terms *unison* and *chord* in your comparison.

Singing: "Bound for Jubilee"

What do you think the word *jubilee* means?

Jubilee comes from the Hebrew language. In Biblical times, it was a year of celebration that came about every 50 years. During that time there was no farming, and all slaves were freed and their lands restored. During the slavery period in the United States, the term was associated with liberation from bondage, and often had the same meaning as heaven.

Now turn to the music for "Bound for Jubilee" on page 4.

HOW DID YOU DO?

Think about your performance of the Vocal Warm-Up, Sight-Singing, and "Bound for Jubilee."
1. What did you do well?
2. Where do you need more work?

3. How might you demonstrate what you have learned to your classmates or teacher?
4. Explain what you enjoyed most about this lesson.

TEACHING STRATEGY

Sight-singing: Making Mistakes

The goal of sight-singing is to perform a piece of music at first sight, without studying it beforehand. At the beginning, students are likely to make a lot of mistakes. Help them understand that mistakes are how people learn, and that with practice they will get much better. Discuss how laughing at mistakes of others can be hurtful, but that if everyone laughs together during these first few attempts, it will reduce the pressure until everyone's sight-singing improves.

Sight-Singing

This Sight-Singing exercise is designed to prepare students to:
- Sight-sing using solfège and hand signs or numbers.
- Compare beginning and ending sounds.
- Distinguish between unison and chord.
- Distinguish between melodies moving in thirds and stepwise.

Have students:
- Read through the Sight-Singing exercise directions. Answer the question.
- Read each voice part rhythmically, using rhythm syllables.
- Sight-sing through each part separately.
- Sing all parts together.

Singing: "Bound for Jubilee"

Define *jubilee*. Have students:
- Read the question in the student text, page 3, "What do you think the word *jubilee* means?"
- Discuss possible answers.
- Read the text to learn the definition.
- Predict what the title "Bound for Jubilee" might mean.

Hand out Blackline Master 2, *C Major Scale as a Round*, and have students:
- Sing the C major scale up and down in unison without pausing.
- In each voice part begin two beats after the previous voice—beginning with the sopranos.
- Discuss what chords were formed in the round.

3

Suggested Teaching Sequence

1. Review Vocal Warm-Up.

With students, go over the Vocal Warm-Up on page 2 and Blackline Master 1, *Stepwise Movement and Thirds.*

Have students:

- Review the Vocal Warm-Up exercise.
- Read the text and determine which parts of the exercise are stepwise (last five pitches) and in thirds (*do-mi-so* segments).
- Try writing some examples of melodies moving stepwise and in thirds on the board.

2. Review Sight-Singing.

Use solfège. Identify *unison* and *chord.*

Have students:

- Review the Sight-Singing exercise on page 2, reading through each part with solfège and hand signs or numbers.
- Sight-sing all parts together.
- Read the text, and then listen and identify the first sound as unison (all singing the same pitch), and the final sound as a chord (each part singing a different pitch).
- Identify where their melody line moves in steps and thirds.

Bound for Jubilee

Words and Music by
JOYCE ELAINE EILERS

3. Sight-sing "Bound for Jubilee" using solfège and hand signs or numbers.

Have students:

- Divide into voice sections (SATB) and read each part rhythmically, using rhythm syllables.
- Still in sections, sing their parts, using solfège and hand signs or numbers, identifying and working on problem areas.
- Sing the piece with solfège and hand signs or numbers with full ensemble.
- Divide into sections and recite the text rhythmically for each part.
- Sing the piece through with text as a full ensemble.

4. Add choreography.

Have students:

- Put hands on their knees on the phrase "or the Devil might come and take me away."
- Raise hands above their head and shake them on the last syllable of the last word in the song (*Jubi-lee*).

Bound for Jubilee **5**

The Term "Jubilee"

During the Middle Ages, the term *jubilee* was carried over from the Biblical definition into music, and applied to several notes that formed a *melisma* (a group of several notes sung to one syllable of text) on the last syllable of the word *alleluia*.

THE EVALUATION PROCESS

You will find three different evaluation procedures in each lesson.

- The first is informal, and done by teacher observation at specific checkpoints during the lesson, where the students are demonstrating the skill or understanding in an observable way.
- The second, student self-evaluation, helps students reflect upon what learning has taken place, and self-assess where more work is necessary. Sometimes there will be an open-ended question that allows students to offer opinions and preferences.
- Finally, the formal assessment requires each student to make a response or perform in a way that is individually measurable. By mixing these assessment techniques, you should be able to construct an objective grading system for students which has many components. Share your assessment plans with students, so they will know the benchmarks of success.

MUSIC LITERACY
Alla Breve

Introduce or review *alla breve* ¢ meter. Explain that spirited, fast music demands precise conducting. All note values are cut in half—two beats per measure with a half note equaling one beat, a quarter note equaling a half-beat, and so forth.

To help students expand their music literacy, have them:

- Listen and follow their music as you tap the beat and speak the text in rhythm.
- Repeat the exercise, but this time they will speak the text in rhythm while you tap the beat.
- Repeat the exercise again, while you conduct in 2.
- Take turns conducting the group.

Informal Assessment

In this lesson, students showed the ability to:

- Sing in four parts during the Sight-Singing exercise and in "Bound for Jubilee."
- Distinguish visually between melodic movement in steps and thirds.

Student Self-Assessment

Have students:

- Return to page 3 and read the questions in the How Did You Do? section.
- Answer the questions individually. Discuss their answers in pairs or small groups, and/or write their responses on a sheet of paper.

Individual Performance Assessment

To further demonstrate accomplishment, have the student:

- Point to examples of melodic movement in steps and thirds in "Bound for Jubilee."
- Sing the Sight-Singing exercise in a double quartet.

Bound for Jubilee **7**

TEACHING STRATEGY

Reinforcing the Bass Line

It is possible that the bass section will need a little help.

- Double the voices on piano, electronic keyboard, or bass guitar, if needed. (You may have students in your group who can easily play this part.)

VOCAL DEVELOPMENT

Tessitura

The tessitura of "Bound for Jubilee" is low for females. To help students cultivate a light, but articulated head voice, have them:

- Explore vocal range with easy natural sounds, high to low. For example: sighs, glissandi, or *whoos.*
- Determine the use of head register by singing octave leaps (D D' D) on *la-hoo-la* while holding their hand on their chest. Work for full tone with minimum of chest vibration.
- Vocalize from head tone down, using all vowels, beginning on C^2.

Next, have them:

- Using a spirited style that is fast, light, accented, and relaxed:
  1. Accent each beat and syncopation.
  2. Use head tone.
  3. Exaggerate the pronunciation of each syllable for articulation.
- Resonate or ring on the *oo* sound of "*hallelu*" or "*jubilee.*"

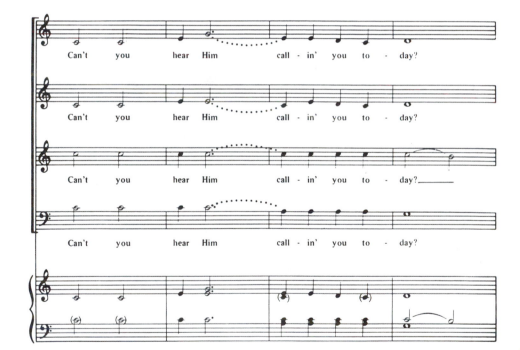

TEACHING STRATEGY

Register

Because of the style and range of this piece, it is a good time to introduce heavier and lighter registration, and their stylistic appropriateness. Explore the difference between the heavier, chestier feeling, and a lighter head tone quality. Listen for examples of each on the radio. Discuss the necessity to maintain in-tune singing and diction regardless of registration. This piece can be sung in heavier registration, or with a blended sound, giving a very different feeling from the pure, lighter registration sound.

Extension

Reinforcing Understanding of Stepwise and Skipwise Melodic Movement through Composition

Providing opportunities for improvising, composing, and/or arranging will build understanding of new concepts encountered, while encouraging sight-singing skills. Have the students compose short melodies in a familiar key, using only melodic motion that is stepwise and in thirds. Arranging can then be done by devising an introduction and/or ending. Arranging can also be done by making choices in "Bound for Jubilee" about tempo or another expressive contrast. Students can try the piece several ways (fast, medium, slow), then decide which they like best—or create an arrangement that has the piece performed several times at different tempos.

National Standards

The following National Standards are addressed through the Extension and bottom-page activities:

4. Composing and arranging music within specified guidelines. **(a)**
7. Evaluating music and music performances. **(b)**
9. Understanding music in relation to history and culture. **(a)**

DEVELOPING LEADERSHIP SKILLS

During the year, you will want to encourage leadership in many ways. Some possible suggestions are:

- Encourage students to make suggestions and/or decisions about performance style, tempo, etc.
- Invite responsible and interested students to conduct pieces.

10 *Choral Connections   Level 1 Mixed Voices*

CULTURAL CONNECTIONS
Festival in Any Language

The idea of festival, whether the term is *fiesta, Mardi Gras, pow wow,* or *jubilee,* connotes a release from the burdens of the work day with celebration, laughter, music, games, speeches, food, dance, and many other activities. Most folk songs of the world come from the daily experiences of people as they live, love, work, and play.

A Red, Red Rose

COMPOSER: *Daniel Burton*
TEXT: *Robert Burns (1759–1796)*

CHORAL MUSIC TERMS
part independence
solfège syllables
soprano, alto, bass
steady beat
text

VOICING
SAB

PERFORMANCE STYLE
Tenderly and expressively
A cappella

FOCUS
- Read and clap rhythms from three staves, maintaining part independence.
- Sing in three parts using solfège syllables, numbers, or text.

Warming Up

 Rhythm Drill
Clap the following exercise in 2/4 meter as someone keeps a steady beat. Try each part separately. Then in three groups, clap all three lines at the same time. Listen carefully to your beat keeper. Find three different sounding claps for the three lines.

Vocal Warm-up
Sing the chord drill using solfège.

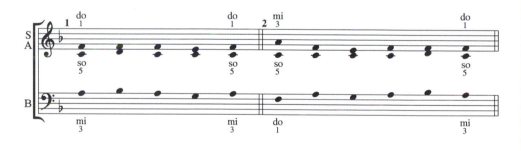

Lesson 2: A Red, Red Rose **11**

TEACHER'S RESOURCE BINDER
Blackline Master 3, *Vocal Development Rubric,* page 77

National Standards
Through involvement with this lesson, students will develop the following skills and concepts:
1. Singing, alone and with others, a varied repertoire of music. **(d)**
5. Reading and notating music. **(a)**
6. Listening to, analyzing, and describing music. **(a)**

LESSON 2

A Red, Red Rose

COMPOSER: Daniel Burton
TEXT: Robert Burns (1759-1796)

Focus

OVERVIEW
Rhythmic reading; part independence.

OBJECTIVES
After completing this lesson, students will be able to:
- Read and clap rhythms from three staves, maintaining part independence.
- Sing in three parts using solfège and hand signs, numbers, or text.

CHORAL MUSIC TERMS
Define the Choral Music Terms for students, giving pronunciation, and answering any questions that may arise.

Warming Up

Rhythm Drill
This Rhythm Drill is designed to prepare students to:
- Read and clap rhythms in 2/4 meter over an audible steady beat.
- Read different voice lines: soprano, alto, and bass.
- Perform imitative rhythms within "A Red, Red Rose."
- Clap rhythms in ensemble to learn their parts in the ensemble.
Have students:
- Read through the Rhythm Drill directions.
- Perform the drill.

Sight-Singing

This Sight-Singing exercise is designed to prepare students to:

- Sight-sing using solfège and hand signs or numbers.
- Use their ability to read quarter notes, eighth notes, and half notes.
- Sing three-part harmony.
- Sight-sing segments of "A Red, Red Rose" (measures 53-57).

Have students:

- Read through the Sight-Singing exercise directions. Answer the questions.
- Read each part rhythmically, using rhythm syllables.
- Sight sing each part separately.
- Sing all parts together.

Singing: "A Red, Red Rose"

Identify and sing a round. Introduce "A Red, Red Rose." Have students:

- Read the text on student page 12.
- Sing a round of their choice or yours, and answer any questions that may arise.
- Listen to "A Red, Red Rose" as they follow their music, then tell where it sounds like a round. (The bass line imitates the soprano line nearly all the way through the piece.)

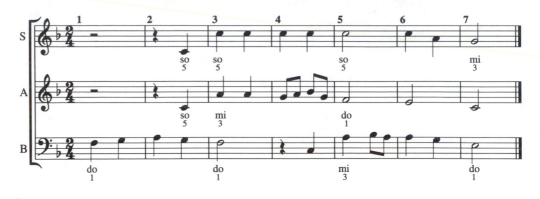

Sight-Reading

Sight-read these parts using solfège syllables or numbers. Find the measures in "A Red, Red Rose" that are similar. Are they the same? If not, what's different?

Singing: "A Red, Red Rose"

Do you know what a *round* is?

A *round* is one melody with two or more parts beginning the melody at different times. The result is harmony created by the layering of pitches.

Sing a round of your choice. How many different melodies are being sung? How is each part different? How do you keep singing with your section? Listen to "A Red, Red Rose." What parts sound like a round?

Now turn to the music for "A Red, Red Rose" on page 13.

HOW DID YOU DO?

Think about your performance of the Rhythm Drill, Sight-Singing, and "A Red, Red Rose."

1. What did you do well?

2. Where do you need more work?

3. Could you perform the rhythm or sight-singing exercise with only six performers—two on each part?

4. What did you enjoy most about this lesson?

Composer Daniel Burton

Perhaps best known for his choral compositions, Daniel Burton's published works include music for harp, organ, vocal solo, and string orchestra. Characteristics of his choral style are a rich harmonic freshness, great vocal sensitivity, and a marked preference for beautiful and unusual texts.

Organist and composer in residence at First United Methodist Church of San Diego since 1973, Mr. Burton concertizes on both the organ and the concert harp. Before moving to San Diego, he held positions as a university instructor in chorus, music theory and literature, and keyboard.

A Red, Red Rose

Robert Burns (1759–1796)
Daniel Burton

SAB, A cappella

A Red, Red Rose **13**

Suggested Teaching Sequence

1. Review Rhythm Drill.
Have students:
- Review the Rhythm Drill on page 11.
- Read and clap these rhythms in 2/4 meter over an audible steady beat.
- Perform different voice lines: soprano, alto, and baritone.
- Perform imitative rhythms within "A Red, Red Rose" by clapping to learn their parts in the ensemble.

TEACHING STRATEGY
Hand Clapping - Soprano, Alto, and Baritone

Have students experiment with hand clapping to find ways of clapping that are equally loud, but higher, middle, and lower in pitch. For example: clapping fingertips on the palm creates a high pitched clap; using more of the hand to clap creates a middle pitched clap; cupping hands creates a lower pitched clap. Remind the students that high and low pitch are different from loud and soft, and all clapping should be at a medium dynamic level.

Reading Rhythms

If students are not familiar with rhythmic notation, refer to the Rhythm Challenges on pages ix and x, to help build confidence and skill at reading rhythmic notation.

2. Sight-sing "A Red, Red Rose" using solfège and hand signs or numbers.

Have students:

- Divide into voice sections (SAB) and read each part rhythmically, using rhythm syllables.
- Still in sections, sing their parts, using solfège and hand signs or numbers, identifying and working on problem areas.
- Sing the piece through using solfège and hand signs or numbers with the full ensemble.
- Divide into sections and recite the text rhythmically for each part.
- Sing the piece through with text as a full ensemble.

3. Review Sight-Singing.

Have students:

- Review the Sight-Singing exercise on page 11.
- Sight-sing using solfège and hand signs or numbers, demonstrating their ability to read quarter notes, eighth notes, and half notes.
- Sing three-part harmony.
- Sing a segment of "A Red, Red Rose" (measures 53-57).

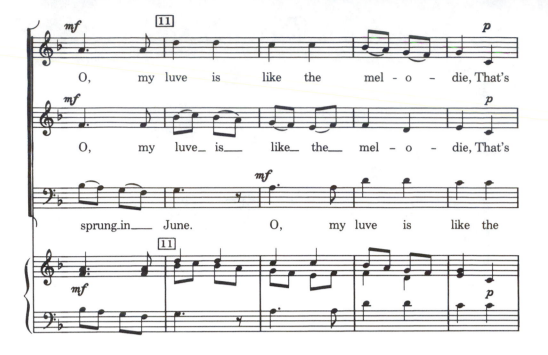

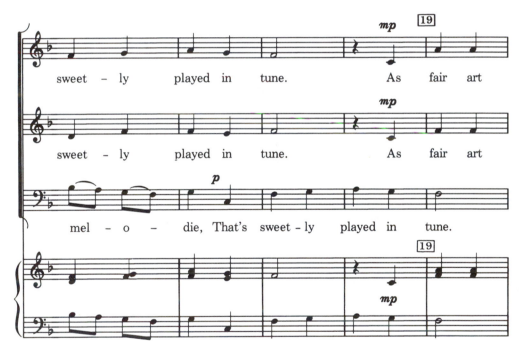

TEACHING STRATEGY
Watching for Directions

Write the chords that appear on the bottom of student page 11 on a chart or the board, and have the students sing the chords using solfège or numbers. Decide together how they will know when it is time to move to the next pitch (a signal from you or one of the students). In this way they will begin to understand about watching for directions and staying together. Encourage careful listening both to others within the section and to the other two sections, so the chords are well tuned.

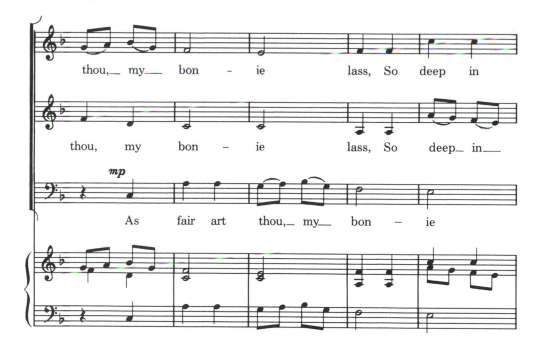

thou,_ my_ bon - ie   lass, So deep in

thou, my bon - ie   lass, So deep_ in_

As   fair art thou,_ my_ bon - ie

luve_ am_ I,   And   I will luve thee

luve am I,   And   I_ will_ luve_ thee_

lass, So   deep in   luve_ am_ I,   And

Informal Assessment

In this lesson, students showed the ability to:
- Read rhythms in three parts during the Rhythm Drill.
- Sight-sing using solfège and hand signs or numbers during the Sight-Singing exercise.
- Sight-sing using solfège and hand signs or numbers during "A Red, Red Rose."

Student Self-Assessment

Have students:
- Return to page 12 and read the questions in the How Did You Do? section.
- Answer the questions individually. Discuss them in pairs or small groups, and write their responses on a sheet of paper.

Individual Performance Assessment

To further demonstrate accomplishment, have student:
- Perform either of the exercises on page 11 within a small, randomly selected group of two sopranos, two altos, and two basses.

A Red, Red Rose **15**

**VOCAL
DEVELOPMENT**

Reminder Check-Off List

Using Blackline Master 2, *Vocal Development Rubric,* have students rate their own techniques.

1. Diction.
2. Use of identical vowel sounds on *luve, newly, June,* and *tune* throughout.
3. Flip the *r* for Scottish burr.
4. Drop the consonant *r* that follows a vowel.
5. Use the diphthong.
6. Modify the final vowel on the words *melodie* and *bonnie* with an *oo* sound.
7. Clearly articulate the slurred eighth notes each time they occur.

CURRICULUM CONNECTIONS

Creative Writing

Robert Burns lived from 1759-1796. His text has ideas that we can understand, but in Scotland during the historical period in which he lived, language was used differently than it is today.

Write the text of the song on the board, eliminating any repetitions, and discuss the meaning of the poem. Have students write a similar message using contemporary language, but keeping the feeling of Burns' poem. They may share their work or keep it in a journal, and share it only with you. Encourage students to use both nontraditional and modern electronic instruments to compose a simple melody to accompany their messages.

Phrase Length

The phrases in this piece are unusual. Some phrases are four measures long, but some are five. The five-measure phrase precedes the four-measure one, providing a little extra tension and a quicker release. Students might enjoy speculating as to why the composer chose this phrase arrangement for this specific text.

National Standards

The following National Standard is addressed through the Extension and bottom-page activities:

4. Composing and arranging music within specified guidelines. **(b, c)**

Composed in the Style of
a Spiritual
MUSIC and TEXT: Jerry Ray

Focus

OVERVIEW
Finding movable *do*; reading syncopation.

OBJECTIVES
After completing this lesson, students will be able to:
- Sight-sing with solfège and hand signs or numbers in different keys.
- Read syncopated rhythms found in "Over There."

CHORAL MUSIC TERMS
Define the Choral Music Terms for students, providing correct pronunciation, and answering any questions that may arise.

Warming Up

Vocal Warm-Up
This Vocal Warm-Up is designed to prepare students to:
- Sing scalewise patterns in unison using solfège and hand signs or numbers.
- Sing in different keys.
- Perform rhythm patterns including syncopation.

Have students:
- Read through the Vocal Warm-Up exercise directions.
- Sing, following your demonstration.

Over There

COMPOSER: Jerry Ray
TEXT: Jerry Ray

CHORAL MUSIC TERMS
cambiata voice
key signature
phrase
scale
syncopation

VOICING
SAB

PERFORMANCE STYLE
Syncopated
Accompanied by piano

FOCUS
- Sight-sing in different keys using solfège.
- Sight-sing syncopated rhythms.

Warming Up

 Vocal Warm-Up
Sing the following scales in unison with solfège or numbers. Sing the scale in C major using rhythm pattern 1. Sing the whole rhythm pattern on each pitch before moving to the next one. Repeat this with the scale in D♭ major, using rhythm pattern 2.

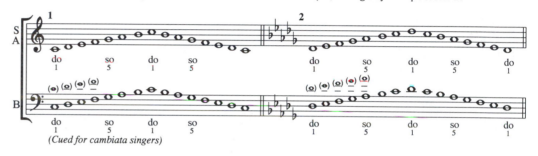

(Cued for cambiata singers)

Clap the following exercise in 4/4 meter as someone keeps a steady beat. Clap each line separately. Then in two groups clap the two lines at one time paying close attention to the syncopated rhythms in line 2.

TEACHER'S RESOURCE BINDER
Blackline Master 4, *Circle of Fifths,*
    page 78
Blackline Master 5, *Syncopated Rhythms,*
    page 79

National Standards

This lesson addresses the following National Standards:
1. Singing, alone and with others, a varied repertoire of music. **(c, d)**
3. Improvising melodies, variations, and accompaniments. **(a)**
8. Understanding relationships between music, the other arts, and disciplines outside the arts. **(a)**

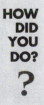

Sight-Singing

Sing each phrase using solfège and hand signs. Notice the key changes. Do you recognize either one of the rhythm patterns from the warm-up activity in this exercise?

Singing: "Over There"

You can improve your sight-singing skills if you learn to watch for clues. The key signature (the number of sharps or flats at the beginning of each staff) tells you what key to sing in. *Do* is on a different pitch in each key.

Now turn to the music for "Over There" on page 22.

HOW DID YOU DO? **?**

The more you read, the more rhythm and melody patterns will seem familiar. Think about your experiences with "Over There."
1. What did you learn that was new?
2. What do you need to know more about?
3. Can you point to two examples of syncopation and the different key signatures in "Over There"? Can you name the keys that each key signature indicates?
4. What are some of the qualities of this piece that reflect a spiritual style?
5. Tell one thing you enjoyed about this lesson.

Sight-Singing

This Sight-Singing exercise is designed to prepare students to:
- Sing in three parts written on two staves.
- Sight-sing in three different keys using solfège and hand signs or numbers.
- Read notation containing syncopated rhythm.
- Sing complete phrases.
- Read and sing a fermata.
Have students
- Read through the Sight-Singing exercise directions.
- Sight-sing each part separately.
- Sing all parts together.

Singing: "Over There"

Warm-up with the scale.
Help students build sight-singing skills by:
- Reading the text in the Singing section on page 21.
- Singing the scale starting on three different pitches chosen by three students. Have them discuss differences in vocal ranges, and why some keys are better for sopranos, altos, and basses.

MORE ABOUT...

Composer Jerry Ray

Although his music education specialized in choral, voice and piano, Jerry Ray's skills as a composer, arranger, and keyboardist have touched many phases of today's popular music. Currently he is an associate music director at one of the largest nondenominational churches in Los Angeles, California.

Also, he has written television and radio jingles for commercial products. As a composer, most of Ray's original works are for the piano. He also has formed his own company, and worked as an accompanist, producer, arranger, or composer for many of Hollywood's musical talents.

Suggested Teaching Sequence

1. Review Vocal Warm-Up.

Identify key signatures and syncopated rhythm patterns. Have students:

- Review the directions of the Warm-Up exercise on page 20. Then sing the two scales with solfège and hand signals or numbers.
- Discuss how to find *do* with different key signatures. You may wish to use Blackline Master 4, *Circle of Fifths*, to help explain where *do* is found for each key signature.
- Clap the two rhythm patterns.
- Sing the scales using one rhythm pattern for each, repeating the whole pattern on each successive scale tone.

2. Review Sight-Singing.

Have students:

- Review the directions for the Sight-Singing exercise on page 21.
- Sing through each part with solfège and hand signs or numbers, isolating parts as necessary.
- Find the syncopated rhythm in the second measure, and identify syncopation as a type of rhythm in which stressed sounds occur on weak beats or in between beats.

Over There

Words and Music by
JERRY RAY

SAB with Piano

I'm a-gon-na lay down my bur-dens o-ver there, o-ver there. Let me take my bur-dens o-ver

7515

MUSIC LITERACY

You may want to call students' attention to the following points regarding "Over There."

- **Alla breve meter.**
- **Syncopation** (augmented and hidden)—practice eighth-dotted quarter rhythm.
- **Key changes**—sing different scales with solfège or numbers.
- **Coda at measure 94**—based on triad inversions.
- **Structural form**—analyze phrases to determine form. Discover similarities and differences.

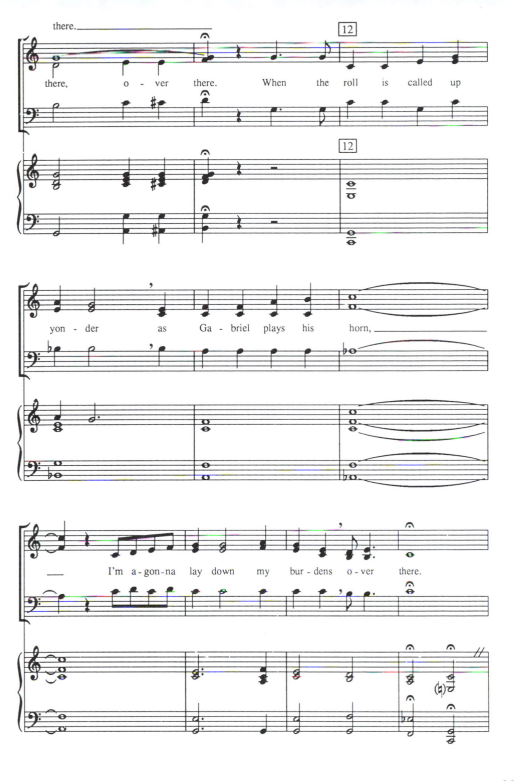

3. Sight-sing "Over There" using solfège and hand signs or numbers.

Have students:

- Divide into voice sections (SAB) and read each part of "Over There" rhythmically, using rhythm syllables.
- Discuss where the scalewise patterns and syncopated rhythms are found.
- Identify the key changes, and point to the key signatures, naming the keys (measure 1, key of C; measure 41, key of D♭; measure 58, key of D; measure 75, key of E♭), and noticing that although these are different keys, they are close to one another on the staff.
- Still in sections, sing with solfège and hand signs or numbers, identifying and working on problem areas.
- Sing the piece through using solfège and hand signs or numbers with full ensemble.
- Divide into sections and re-cite the text rhythmically for each voice part.
- Sing the piece through with text as a full ensemble.

4. Add choreography.

Have students:

- Add the hand claps at measure 75.
- Make up their own choreography beginning at measure 20.

TEACHING STRATEGY

Phrases

"Over There" has even, well-developed phrases in sets of four. Students should be encouraged to think and sing through each phrase, not breathing until the end, and shaping the phrases so the phrases feel like complete thoughts. Compare these even phrases with those in "A Red, Red Rose," Lesson 2, and discuss the different moods created by even and uneven phrases. Ask: What other musical characteristics contribute to the differences in mood between these two pieces? Would it be good to put one after the other in a musical program? Why? Why not?

Assessment

Informal Assessment

In this lesson, students showed the ability to:

- Sing scale tones, using syncopated rhythms, in different keys using solfège and hand signals.
- In three parts, read melodies in different keys.

Student Self-Assessment

Have students:

- Return to page 21 and read the questions in the How Did You Do? section.
- Answer the questions individually. Discuss them in pairs or small groups, and/or write their responses on a sheet of paper.

Individual Performance Assessment

To further demonstrate accomplishment, have students:

- Point to two different examples of syncopated rhythm in the piece "Over There."
- Identify the keys used in "Over There" by pointing to the key signature and naming the key.

TEACHING STRATEGY

Extra Help with Pitch

Use the Pitch Challenge on page xiii for students who are not experienced at reading pitches using solfège and hand signals. Begin each class with some sight-singing from your hand signs, using scale tones upward, downward, and in skips. Increase complexity as confidence increases. You may want to post large pictures of the hand signs around the room (See page xii.)

there.

there, o- ver there. When the roll is called up yon- der as

Ga- briel plays his horn, _____ I'm a- gon- na lay down my

sor- rows o- ver there, o- ver there. I'm a- gon- na

MUSIC LITERACY
Alla Breve Meter

Have students:
- Review the meter used in "Bound for Jubilee."
- Speak the words in rhythm.
- Point out the pick-up beat. How many beats?

Syncopation

Have students:
- Identify the augmented syncopations, including a hidden one in measure 75.
- Articulate the eighth-dotted quarter rhythm everywhere it occurs. This is also a form of hidden syncopation.

Form

Have students:
- Analyze the phrase structure of each section. What are the similarities and differences in text, rhythm, and melody?
- Analyze the coda section, measure 94. How does the composer lead the performer to the ending?

TEACHING STRATEGY
Understanding Syncopation

One simple way to explain syncopation is to begin by writing ♩ ♫ on the board and clapping it several times. Change the ♫ to ♪♪ and clap again several times. It sounds the same. Finally, take one ♪, and move it ahead of the ♩ to create ♪ ♩ ♪ You might use words to help, finding a one-syllable word for the quarter note, and a two-syllable word for the two eighths. When the eighths get divided, so does the word, for example: *hat sweat-er* becomes *sweat -hat er.*

Extension

More Practice Singing and Reading Pitches

Place a scale on the board in a comfortable key chosen by the group. Have one student point to one pitch at a time in random order, as the group sings the pitches with syllable name and hand sign or number. At first, move slowly from one pitch to the other, increasing speed as confidence increases. Allow several students to act as leaders, changing the key signature with each new leader.

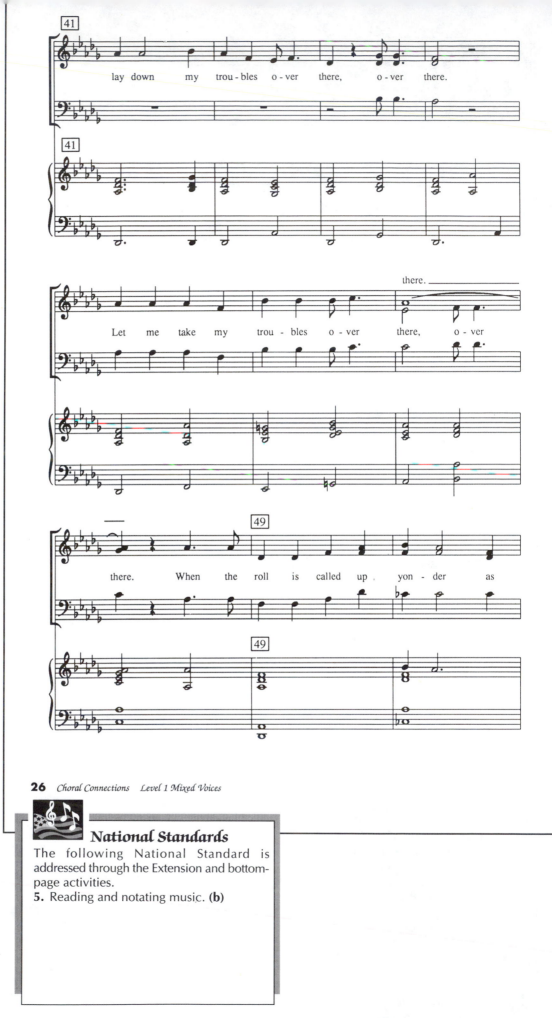

lay down my trou-bles o-ver there, o-ver there.

Let me take my trou-bles o-ver there, o-ver there, o-ver there.

there. When the roll is called up yon-der as

National Standards

The following National Standard is addressed through the Extension and bottom-page activities.

5. Reading and notating music. **(b)**

Ga - briel plays his horn, _____ I'm a-gon - na

lay down my trou-bles o - ver there, o - ver there.

O - ver there, gon - na lay my bur - dens

The Cambiata Voice

As a boy's voice changes, it reaches a stage called the *cambiata voice.* In this stage, the voice begins to stretch lower, but is still able to reach the higher pitches. It is important not to stretch this voice too low, as it can become strained. It is fascinating for young men to track their development through the year as they are able to sing lower and lower.

Over There **27**

down. O - ver there, when I

hear that trum-pet sound. O - ver there, but

not be - fore my time. _____ When the

trum-pet sounds for me will be just fine. _____ I'm a-gon-na

(All hand clap)
75
(Continue hand claps to 94)

lay down my {1. wor - ries / 2. bur - dens} o - ver, lay my {wor-ries / bur - dens}

75
I will lay, will

down. Let me take my {wor - ries / bur - dens} o - ver

there. _____ Lay down my bur-dens

way o-ver there. Lay down my bur-dens

way o-ver there. Lay down my bur-dens

Dare to Dream!

COMPOSER: *Niel Lorenz*
TEXT: *Mary Lynn Lightfoot*

CHORAL MUSIC TERMS
staggered entrances
stepwise movement

VOICING
SAB

PERFORMANCE STYLE
With feeling
Accompanied by piano

FOCUS
• Read stepwise passages with solfège and hand signals.
• Recognize and sing staggered entrances.

Warming Up

Vocal Warm-Up
Sing each scale and the tonic chord using solfège syllables and hand signs or numbers. Repeat each, moving up by half steps. Be sure to assume singing posture, take a deep breath, and sing with an open tone.

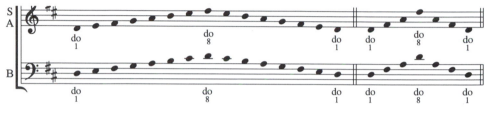

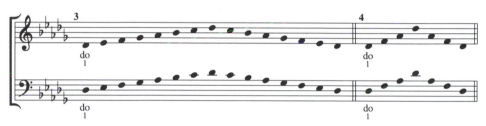

TEACHER'S RESOURCE BINDER
Blackline Master 6, *Stepwise Movement and Thirds,* page 80

National Standards
Through involvement with this lesson, students will develop the following skills and concepts:
1. Singing, alone and with others, a varied repertoire of music. **(d)**
5. Reading and notating music. **(c)**

LESSON 4

Dare to Dream!

COMPOSER: Niel Lorenz
TEXT: Mary Lynn Lightfoot

Focus

OVERVIEW
Stepwise movement; staggered entrances.

OBJECTIVES
After completing this lesson, students will be able to:
• Read stepwise passages with solfège and hand signs or numbers.
• Recognize and sing staggered entrances.

CHORAL MUSIC TERMS
Define the Choral Music Terms for students, providing correct pronunciation, and answering any questions that may arise.

Warming Up

Vocal Warm-Up
This Vocal Warm-Up is designed to prepare students to:
• Sing a scale and its tonic chord.
• Sing in stepwise motion.
• Sing in unison.
Have students:
• Read through the Vocal Warm-Up directions.
• Sing, following your demonstration.

Sight-Singing

This Sight-Singing exercise is designed to prepare students to:

- Sight-sing using solfège and hand signs or numbers.
- Sing in D major.
- Identify and sing staggered entrances.

Have students:

- Read through the Sight-Singing exercise directions.
- Read each part rhythmically, using rhythm syllables.
- Sight-sing through each part separately.
- Sing all parts together.

Singing: "Dare to Dream!"

Introduce staggered entrances with a game.

Have students:

- Read the text in the Singing section on page 34.
- Follow the directions for the game, without any help from you, until they can do the activity together.
- Define staggered entrances as one section doing something, with other sections entering later, imitating the first entrance.
- Repeat the game to watch the visual staggered entrances.

Sight-Singing

Sing this phrase using solfège and hand signs. Notice the staggered entrance. Where does the melody move stepwise in your part?

Singing: "Dare to Dream!"

What is your dream? Do you work to make it come true?

Developing skills requires hard work and practice. Whether you are practicing creative writing, sports, or sight-singing, you have to keep working and trying if you're going to succeed.

A Staggered Entrance Game

Count from 1 to 10. Sopranos stand on 1, 5, and 10. Altos stand on 2 and 6. Baritones stand on 3 and 9. Sit on all other numbers. Can you tell what a *staggered entrance* might be?

Now turn to the music for "Dare to Dream!" on page 35.

HOW DID YOU DO?

It is important to dream about your goals in life. However, if you really have the dream of becoming a good musician, it takes practice. Think about your experiences with "Dare to Dream!"

1. What can you tell about this piece?
2. At which skills are you improving? How do you know?

3. Can you sight-sing your part to "Dare to Dream!"? Which part is easy? Where is it difficult? What do you do differently during the difficult passages than the easy ones?
4. Did you recognize where your staggered entrance occurs?
5. What did you enjoy most about this lesson?

Mary Lynn Lightfoot

In addition to her responsibilities as the choral editor for Heritage Music Press, Mary Lynn Lightfoot has published over 100 choral compositions. Named the Outstanding Young Woman of America in 1984, she was also the 1994 recipient of the Luther T. Spayde Award for Missouri Choral Conductor of the Year, presented by the Missouri American Choral Directors Association. When not busy with her composing and editorial duties, Mary Lynn frequently travels throughout the United States as a guest conductor and clinician.

Dare to Dream!

Niel Lorenz
Mary Lynn Lightfoot

Three-part Mixed Chorus and Piano

Dare to Dream! **35**

Suggested Teaching Sequence

1. Review Vocal Warm-Up.
Identify stepwise movement through the Vocal Warm-Up. Have students:

- Read the directions for the Vocal Warm-Up scale exercise on page 33.
- Identify appropriate singing position and how to breathe.
- Sing the scale and tonic chord exercise, moving upward on each repetition.
- After reviewing Blackline Master 6, *Stepwise Movement and Thirds*, identify scalewise passages as stepwise movement, and the tonic chord as skipwise movement.

2. Review Sight-Singing with solfège and hand signs or numbers.
Help students identify staggered entrances.
Have students:

- Read the directions for the Sight-Singing exercise on page 34.
- Sight-sing the exercise on pitch syllables, using hand signs.
- Identify any difficulties.
- Identify the staggered entrance at the beginning and where each part moves stepwise.
- Look at the beginning of "Dare to Dream!" and tell how the beginning relates to the Sight-Singing exercise.

3. Sight-sing "Dare to Dream!" using solfège and hand signs or numbers.

Have students:

- Read the text through together, noticing when the parts are together, when sections sing individually, and when there are staggered entrances. (Challenge each section to work carefully to fulfill the dream of being able to sight-sing this piece.)
- Divide into voice sections (SAB) and read each part rhythmically, using rhythm syllables.
- Still in sections, sing with solfège and hand signs or numbers, identifying and working on problem areas.
- Sing the piece through using solfège and hand signs or numbers with full ensemble.
- Divide into sections and recite the text rhythmically for each voice part.
- Sing the piece through with text as a full ensemble.

MUSIC LITERACY

To help students expand their music literacy, have them:

- Speak the words in rhythm, with precision on dotted quarter notes, notes with ties, and augmented syncopations.
- Review *alla breve* written as 2/2.

- Analyze the cadential process in measures 16-19. Ask: How does the composer create excitement by repeating the same words?

VOCAL DEVELOPMENT

To encourage vocal development, have students:

- Sustain phrases with no breath in the middle of the phrase.
- Sing a resonating *oo* on the words *you, do,* and *through.*
- Sing a resonating *oh* on the words *go* and *know.*
- Energize all long notes with more breath support and a slight crescendo, holding out the full note value.
- Pay close attention to diphthongs in *try* and *fly* on the sustained notes.

CURRICULUM CONNECTIONS
Creative Writing

What's the message? The following can be done as a creative writing or journal assignment, in small group discussions, or as a whole group. Perhaps students will want to write their own philosophies down in poetic style, then set them to stepwise melodies.

Have students:
- Read the text of "Dare to Dream!"
- Tell what the message is in their own words, and whether they believe in it.
- Give the pros and cons of believing the message, and relate their own experiences to convey their feelings about it.

Informal Assessment

In this lesson, students showed the ability to:

- Sing the scale and tonic chord with pitch syllables and hand signs or numbers.
- Visually identify the first staggered entrance in "Dare to Dream!"
- Identify and work through problems with sight-singing in "Dare to Dream!"

Student Self-Assessment

Have students:

- Return to page 34 and read the How Did You Do? section.
- Answer the questions individually. Discuss them in pairs or small groups, and/ or write their responses on a sheet of paper.

Individual Performance Assessment

To further demonstrate accomplishment, have students:

- Point to notation that shows stepwise movement in three different places in "Dare to Dream!"
- In a double trio, accurately perform staggered entrances as marked in measures 49–63 in "Dare to Dream!"

Dare to Compare

Staggered entrances have similarities to rounds and canons. Have students:

• Sing a familiar round, such as "Row, Row, Row Your Boat."

• Compare the round to the staggered entrances in "Dare to Dream!" Ask: How are rounds and staggered entrances the same? How are they different?

• Sing the scale in three groups, with staggered entrances every two pitches. Is this demonstration an example of staggered entrances, a round, or both?

Dare to Dream! **41**

National Standards

The following National Standards are addressed through the Extension and bottom-page activities:

6. Listening to, analyzing, and describing music. **(c)**

8. Understanding relationships between music, the other arts, and disciplines outside the arts. **(a, b)**

The Tiger

COMPOSER: Sherri Porterfield

TEXT: William Blake
(1757-1827)

Focus

OVERVIEW
Rhythms in 6/8 meter; repetitive entrances.

OBJECTIVES
After completing this lesson, students will be able to:
- Read rhythms in 6/8 meter.
- Locate repetitive entrances.

CHORAL MUSIC TERMS
Define the Choral Music Terms for students, providing correct pronunciation, and answering any questions that may arise.

Warming Up

Rhythm Drill
This Rhythm Drill is designed to prepare students to:
- Keep a steady beat in 6/8 meter.
- Read 6/8 meter.
- Keep a steady beat reading in various parts.

Have students:
- Read through the Rhythm Drill directions.
- Perform the drill.

Vocal Warm-up
This Vocal Warm-Up is designed to prepare students to:
- Sing in the key of E♭.
- Sing using solfège and hand signs or numbers.
- Tune in unison.

Have students:
- Read through the Vocal Warm-Up directions.
- Sing, following your demonstration.

LESSON 5

The Tiger

COMPOSER: *Sherri Porterfield*

TEXT: *William Blake* (1757–1827)

CHORAL MUSIC TERMS
repetitive entrances
6/8 meter
symbol

VOICING
| SAB

PERFORMANCE STYLE
| With intensity
Accompanied by piano

FOCUS
- Read rhythms in 6/8 meters.
- Locate repetitive entrances.

Warming Up

Rhythm Drill
Clap each line separately. Choose a sound for each line, for example: line 1, stand and step in place; line 2, pat your legs; line 3, clap; line 4, "sizzle the rhythm" using a *ts* sound. Each group starts on one of the lines, then reads through the whole piece twice and stops.

TEACHER'S RESOURCE BINDER

National Standards

Through involvement with this lesson, students will develop the following skills and concepts:
5. Reading and notating music. **(a)**
8. Understanding relationships between music, the other arts, and disciplines outside the arts. **(a)**

Vocal Warm-Up

Sing the exercise below using solfège.

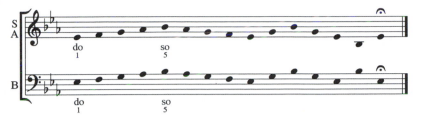

Sight-Singing

Sing this phrase using solfège and hand signs. Notice the symbol for "no breath."

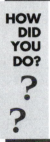

Singing: "The Tiger"

A symbol is something that represents something else. Notation is a symbol system, and so are words.

What do you think the tiger symbolizes in William Blake's poetry, "The Tiger" page 44? Does everyone have the same idea, or are symbols personal and individual?

Now turn and perform the music for "The Tiger" on page 44.

HOW DID YOU DO?

A tiger can be considered a symbol of destruction, or a bold and daring creature. Which were you during this lesson? Think about your experiences with "The Tiger."
1. Do you understand 6/8 meter?
2. How was your sight-singing? What did you do really well? What still needs more practice?

3. Do you think the composer did a good job of setting William Blake's poem "The Tiger"? What musical tools did she use effectively? Would you have done anything differently?

Sight-Singing

This Sight-Singing exercise is designed to prepare students to:
- Sing in three-part harmony.
- Sing three parts written on two staves.
- Identify the "no breath" sign.

Have students:
- Read through the Sight-Singing exercise directions.
- Read each part rhythmically, using rhythm syllables.
- Sight-sing through each part separately.
- Sing all parts together.

Singing: "The Tiger"

Introduce the tiger as a symbol. Have students:
- Read the Singing section on page 43.
- Discuss their thoughts about the two questions. (These are opinion questions and have no right or wrong answers, although some answers will be more appropriate and thoughtful than others.)
- Make a list of words and/or phrases and their symbolic representatives. (cold as ice, soft as down.)

William Blake

William Blake, born in London, England, in 1757, was trained as an artist. Even though he began to write poetry at age twelve, as an adult he made a modest living by running his own print shop. Blake wrote many kinds of poetry, but some of his most famous are included in *Songs of Innocence* (1789) and *Songs of Experience* (1794), which includes "The Tiger." He provided the illustrations for both collections, as well as for the books of his own favorite poet, John Milton, and many others.

As Blake became older, his poems increased in length and complexity. Toward the end of his life, Blake's visions of human triumph often reached epic proportions. Characteristic of the nineteenth century and much of the art it produced, Blake's poetry was not appreciated by many during his lifetime. In fact, he died after years of poverty.

Suggested Teaching Sequence

1. Review Rhythm Drill.

You may need to assist students at first, but let them discover through practice how to make the Rhythm Drill work.

Have students:

- Review the directions for the Rhythm Drill on page 42 and identify 6/8 meter.
- Practice each line separately, deciding upon a sound for each.
- Review the patterns until the drill can be performed smoothly.

2. Review Vocal Warm-Up.

Singing in three-part harmony, identify the no-breath symbol and practice it.

Have students:

- Sing the Vocal Warm-Up exercise on page 43 using solfège and hand signs or numbers.
- Identify the key as E♭, and find the low *so*.
- Read the directions and sing the exercise.

3. Review Sight-Singing.

Have students:

- Read the directions on page 43 and sight-sing the exercise.
- Identify which line of the Rhythm Drill each measure came from. (The dotted half note is not represented in the Rhythm Drill.)
- Identify the no-breath symbol, and sing once again, being certain not to take a breath.

The Tiger

COMPOSER: Sherri Porterfield
TEXT: William Blake (1757–1827)

Three-part Mixed, Accompanied

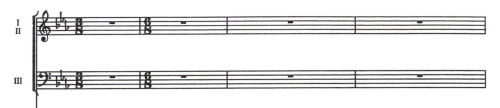

Ti - ger! Ti - ger! burn-ing bright - ly in the for - ests

4. Sight-sing "The Tiger" using solfège and hand signs or numbers.

Have students:

- Look at "The Tiger," identifying the meter (6/8—but occasionally 3/8), and the key (E♭ major).
- Look through the piece to find familiar rhythms, and speak the text in rhythm.
- Look at the pitches of the first sung measure, and find other measures which contain the same rhythm and pitches. (measure 9—women only, measure 13, measure 29—women only; measure 33, measure 49-women only; measure 54 in a new key; measure 61-women only; measure 63-women only)
- Identify these as repetitive entrances.
- Divide into voice sections (SAB) and read each part rhythmically, using rhythm syllables.
- Still in sections, sing with solfège and hand signs or numbers, identifying and working on problem areas.
- Sing the piece through using solfège and hand signs or numbers with full ensemble.
- Divide into sections and recite the text rhythmically for each voice part.
- Sing the piece through with text as a full ensemble.

TEACHING STRATEGY
Reading Rhythms in 6/8 Meter

If students are not familiar with the rhythmic notation for 6/8 meter, return to the introductory pages and find the Rhythm Challenge in 6/8 Time on page x. Have students:

- Construct a rhythm challenge together, beginning with just one or two of the rhythms, and gradually adding more challenging combinations.

- Keep track of how well students are doing on the rhythm challenge by graphing the measure on which they made their first mistake.
- Track and graph this information over 15 trials. By the end of these trials, the students should be ready to work in 6/8 meter.

VOCAL DEVELOPMENT

To encourage vocal development, have students:

- Take a prep breath on the rest when it occurs on the first beat, for precision.
- Note diphthongs on words like *night*, *eye*, *skies*, *fire*, and *aspire*.
- Listen for the *r* consonant in words like *Tiger*, *burning*, *forests*, *immortal*, *fire*, *furnace*, *spears*, *tears*, and *burnt*. Determine what modifications need to be made for the *r* sound to avoid the emphasis on the unpleasant *err* sound in singing.

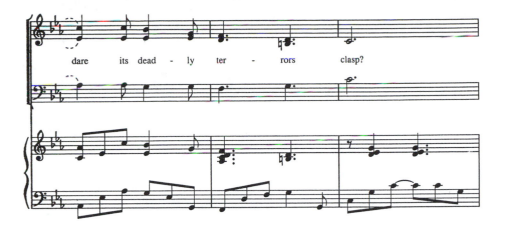

dare   its   dead - ly   ter - rors   clasp?

When the   stars   threw down   their   spears_____   and

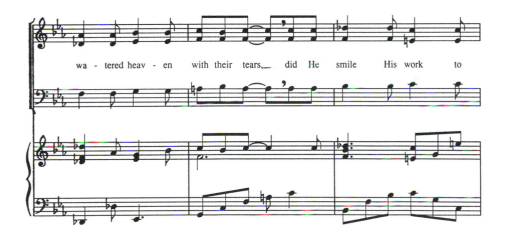

wa - tered heav - en   with their tears,_   did He   smile   His   work   to

The Tiger **47**

MUSIC LITERACY

The 6/8 meter is new. Introduce it with a known song, such as "Row, Row, Row Your Boat." Have students:

- Identify the meters of 3/8 and 6/8 in the familiar round.
- Identify the different patterns of 6/8 contained in "The Tiger." Tap the beat and speak or sizzle the rhythm.
- Discover conducting 6/8 time in 6 and 2 to feel the differences. Ask: Which feels best?
- Recognize that 3/8 time is new. Discover how it is conducted.
- Alternate conducting in 6/8 and 3/8.
- Note the rests in the first two measures of the text. Speculate about why the composer began with a rest.

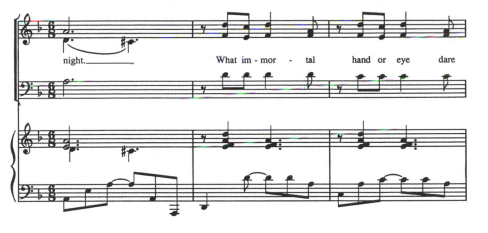

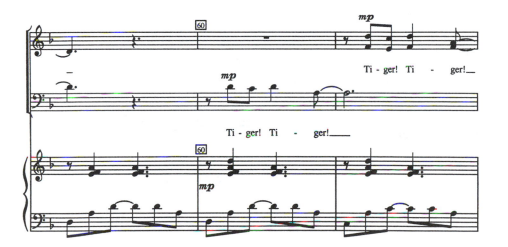

Assessment

Informal Assessment
In this lesson, students showed the ability to:
- Read 6/8 rhythms in the Rhythm Drill.
- Sight-sing in three parts using solfège and hand signs or numbers.
- Locate repetitive entrances in "The Tiger."

Student Self-Assessment
Have students:
- Return to page 43 and read the How Did You Do? section.
- Answer the questions individually. Discuss them in pairs or small groups, and/or write their responses on a sheet of paper.

Individual Performance Assessment
To further demonstrate accomplishment, have students:
- Perform the Rhythm Drill in groups of four, with each group beginning on a different line.
- Point to four repetitive entrances in the music for "The Tiger."

Extension

Interpretation

"The Tiger" is a piece that sets a mood. The text and rhythm build a certain tension that can be enhanced by attending to diction, articulation, and dynamics. Have students:

- Make suggestions of how to increase the tension in this piece, and try out their ideas.
- Together assess the effectiveness of each idea, refining the performance until it effectively represents the mood they desire.

Blake's Poetry

For students who enjoyed the text of "The Tiger," have them:

- Read other Blake poems. If they find one especially appealing, have them set it either in rhythmic speech or to a melody. Playing with the text of a poem can be profound and contagious, and some students might find that they have an interest in composition through this type of activity.
- Another possibility is to write a poem in the style of Blake.

Ti - ger! Ti - ger! burn-ing so bright-ly

Ti - ger! Ti - ger!

in   the   night!

(whisper)   Ti - ger!

(whisper)

National Standards

The following National Standards are addressed in the Extension and bottom-page activities:

4. Composing and arranging music within specified guidelines. **(a)**
6. Listening to, analyzing, and describing music. **(c)**
7. Evaluating music and music performances. **(b)**
8. Understanding relationships between music, the other arts, and disciplines outside the arts. **(b)**

Shalom, My Friends

Based on a traditional Hebrew melody
TEXT: Douglas E. Wagner

CHORAL MUSIC TERMS
la tonal center
minor mode
relationships between
   parts
tuning chords

VOICING
SAB

PERFORMANCE STYLE
Moderate
Accompanied by piano

FOCUS
• Sight-sing pitches in D minor.
• Describe different relationships between vocal parts.
• Sight-sing a piece in three parts, using solfège or text.

Warming Up

Vocal Warm-Up
Sing these examples using solfège syllables and hand signs or numbers, listening for balance, tuning, and blend. Is *do* the tonal center in each of these examples?

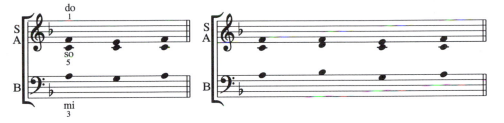

TEACHER'S RESOURCE BINDER

National Standards
Through involvement with this lesson, students will develop the following skills and concepts:
1. Singing, alone and with others, a varied repertoire of music. **(c)**
6. Listening to, analyzing, and describing music. **(c)**

Shalom, My Friends

Based on a traditional Hebrew melody
TEXT: Douglas E. Wagner

Focus

OVERVIEW
La tonal center (minor mode); relationships between parts.

OBJECTIVES
After completing this lesson, students will be able to:
• Sight-sing pitches in D minor.
• Identify different relationships between vocal parts.
• Sight-sing a piece in three parts using solfège and hand signs or text.

CHORAL MUSIC TERMS
Define the Choral Music Terms for students, providing correct pronunciation, and answering any questions that may arise.

Warming Up

Vocal Warm-Up
This Vocal Warm-Up is designed to prepare students to:
• Sing chords using solfège and hand signs or numbers.
• Hear the difference between *do* and *la* as tonal center. (major and minor)
• Sing in tune.
• Blend voices and chords.
Have students:
• Read through the Vocal Warm-Up directions.
• Sing, following your demonstration.

Sight-Singing

This Sight-Singing exercise is designed to prepare students to:
- Sight-sing using solfège and hand signs or numbers.
- Recognize pitches in the key of D minor.
- Sing in three parts.
- Identify relationships in three parts.

Have students:
- Read through the Sight-Singing exercise directions.
- Read each part rhythmically, using rhythm syllables.
- Sight-sing through each part separately.
- Sing all parts together.

Singing: "Shalom, My Friends"

Compare working with friends to relationships between soprano, alto, and baritone parts.
Have students:
- Discuss where they have heard the word *Shalom*, giving their definitions. (*Shalom* is a Hebrew word meaning hello, good-bye, and peace.)
- Read the Singing section on page 52, brainstorming ways that soprano, alto, and baritone lines might work like the examples of friends. (unison, two different parts that work together, canon)

Sight-Singing

Sight-sing the exercise using solfège syllables and hand signs or numbers. Which pitch is the tonal center? Find the *mi-la* skips. Describe how the three parts work together in this exercise.

Singing: "Shalom, My Friends"

There are many different ways to work with a friend. Sometimes you both do the same job together, in unison. Sometimes you may do one part of the task and have your friend do the other part.

Think about how a piece of music might demonstrate these different ways of working with a friend. How might the parts be divided for performance?

Now turn to the music for "Shalom, My Friends" on page 53.

HOW DID YOU DO?

You and your friends worked together to perform "Shalom, My Friends."
1. Describe how the parts worked together at different points in the piece.
2. Can you sing from the beginning to measure 13 with two friends—each one from another section of the choir?

3. Describe what it means when a melody is minor rather than major. Do you like this sound? Why? Why not?

CULTURAL CONNECTIONS
Jewish Musical Tradition

Jewish musical tradition evolved from three major migratory groups around A.D. 1000, the eastern group comprising Yemen, Iraq, Syria, Persia, Palestine; the Sephardic tradition from Spain, North Africa, Italy, Greece, Turkey, and Holland; and the Ashkenazic tradition of Germany, Austria, Eastern Europe, and America. While each group's music reflected the countries and cultures of their origin, all three music traditions are represented in modern Israel.

Unifying features of Jewish music tradition include the use of the same Biblical texts in Hebrew and the similarity of music for festivals and religious observances.

A Jewish cantor leads singing in the synagogue, and is the guardian, interpreter, and transmitter of Jewish music traditions.

Shalom, My Friends

Traditional
Douglas E. Wagner
Based on a traditional Hebrew melody

Three-part Mixed Chorus and Piano

Shalom, My Friends **53**

Suggested Teaching Sequence

1. Review Vocal Warm-Up.
Identify *do* and *la* tonal centers. Have students:

- Read the directions and sing the Vocal Warm-Up on page 51.
- Decide what the tonal center is for each example. (F [*do*] for the first two, D [*la*] for the last two)
- Listen as you describe *la* tonal center and the minor scale.

2. Review Sight-Singing.
Practice reading and singing in *la* tonal center. Have students:

- Read the directions and sing the Sight-Singing exercise using solfège and hand signs or numbers.
- Recognize D (*la*) as the tonal center, identifying this as a minor key.
- Point to the *mi-la* skips. (beginning and measure 6)
- Describe how the three parts work together. (two or three different melodies that work together to create melody and chords)

MUSIC LITERACY

Signing in music is the use of hand signals to represent relative sounds of pitches. The signs were used by Reverend John Curwen from a method developed by Sarah Glover of Norwich in the nineteenth century. The *do* is movable and was intended to teach beginners to sing accurate pitches. The system has been adopted by the Kodaly approach and Tonika-Do system in Germany.

3. Sight-sing "Shalom, My Friends" using solfège and hand signs or numbers.

Have students:

- Divide into voice sections (SAB) and read each part rhythmically, using rhythm syllables.
- Remaining in voice sections, look through the piece for different relationships between parts including unison (beginning, measure 16—soprano and alto), different complementary parts (measures 8–9, measures 12 and 13, end of piece), and canon (measures 25–33—soprano and alto).
- Still in sections, sight-sing with solfège and hand signs or numbers, identifying and working on problem areas.
- Sing the piece through using solfège and hand signs or numbers with full ensemble.
- Divide into sections and recite the text rhythmically for each voice part.
- Sing the piece through with text as a full ensemble.

VOCAL DEVELOPMENT

To encourage vocal development, have students:

- Sing the word *Shalom* with tall, open *ah* and *oh* vowels. Mouth shape should remain consistent with sound focused in the center rather than forward.
- Carry the phrases without noticeable breath to avoid "choppiness" of the text.
- Create a dynamic arch for each phrase with crescendo and decrescendo.

TEACHING STRATEGY
"Shalom, My Friends"

The original Hebrew words to this song are:
Shalom, cha-ve-rim, shalom cha-ve-rim,
   Shalom, Shalom.
Le-hit-ra-ot, le-hit-ra-ot,
Shalom, Shalom
Translation: Shalom—farewell
              chaverim—my friends
              l'hitraot—until we meet again

Informal Assessment
In this lesson, students showed the ability to:
• Sight-sing in *la* tonal center (D minor) in the Sight-Singing exercise.
• Identify and perform different ways that parts work together, including unison, independent parts, and canon.
• Sight-sing "Shalom, My Friends" using solfège and hand signs or text.

Student Self-Assessment
Have students:
• Return to page 52 and read the How Did You Do? section.
• Answer the questions individually. Discuss them in pairs or small groups, and/ or write their responses on a sheet of paper.

Individual Performance Assessment
To further demonstrate accomplishment, have students:
• Sing the Vocal Warm-Up or a segment of "Shalom, My Friends," using solfège and hand signs or numbers, into a tape recorder in a secluded area.
• Write an essay comparing the relationships between the soprano, alto, and baritone parts in "Shalom, My Friends" to the ways friends work together on a task.

Shalom, My Friends **55**

Minor Sound

If students seem interested in the minor sound, place a staff on the board and write both the F major scale and the D minor scale. They both have the same key signature. Minor scales have three possibilities: natural, melodic, and harmonic. There are also minor modes. Have the students find out more about minor scales and modes in a theory text, then learn to play each one. They might improvise or compose short minor melodies using mostly stepwise motion.

Extension

Working Together in D Minor Pentatonic

Students can improvise melodic patterns that work together by using D minor pentatonic: *la, do, re, mi, so,* and *la.* After reading from your hand signs until they have the pitches firmly in mind, have small groups create short patterns using any or all of these pitches. Encourage some rhythmic variation and creation of patterns eight beats long, so there is some variety. Some patterns should have lots of "space" (silence) in them. Have each group share its pattern, then combine the patterns by singing one after another, or singing each over and over, layering them one over the other.

National Standards

The following National Standards are addressed in the Extension and bottom-page activities:

3. Improvising melodies, variations, and accompaniments. **(b)**

9. Understanding music in relation to history and culture. **(a)**

sha - lom, sha - lom,   my   friends. _____

lom,   sha - lom,   my   friends. _____

lom,   sha - lom,   my   friends. _____

Whisper! Whisper!

COMPOSER: Jay Althouse
TEXT: Jay Althouse

CHORAL MUSIC TERMS
block chords
broken chord
solo and response
tonic chord

VOICING
Three-part mixed

PERFORMANCE STYLE
Spirited
A cappella

FOCUS
• Distinguish between broken and block versions of the tonic chord.
• Perform call-and-response segments of a choral piece.

Warming Up

Vocal Warm-Up
Read these examples with solfège syllables and hand signs. Where do you hear and see the broken tonic chord? Where do you hear and see scalewise motion?

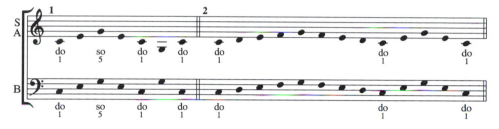

Rhythm Drill
Choose one line or the other and sight-read these rhythms. Clap each line alone, then combine them. How do the parts relate to one another? How would you make this a call and response?

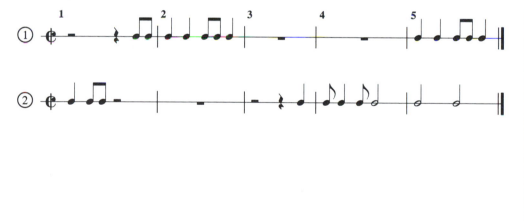

Lesson 7: Whisper! Whisper! **59**

TEACHER'S RESOURCE BINDER

National Standards
This lesson addresses the following skills and concepts:
1. Singing, alone and with others, a varied repertoire of music. **(d)**
4. Composing and arranging music within specified guidelines. **(c)**
5. Reading and notating music. **(c)**
6. Listening to, analyzing, and describing music. **(c)**
7. Evaluating music. **(b)**

LESSON 7

Whisper! Whisper!

COMPOSER: Jay Althouse
TEXT: Jay Althouse

Focus

OVERVIEW
Tonic triad in broken and block style; call and response.

OBJECTIVES
After completing this lesson, students will be able to:
• Distinguish between broken and block versions of the tonic chord.
• Perform call-and-response segments of a choral piece.

CHORAL MUSIC TERMS
Define the Choral Music Terms for students, providing correct pronunciation, and answering any questions that may arise.

Warming Up

Vocal Warm-Up
This Vocal Warm-Up is designed to prepare students to:
• Read and sing the broken tonic chord.
• Distinguish between the broken tonic chord and scalewise movement.
• Read pitches using solfège and hand signs or numbers.
Have students:
• Read through the Vocal Warm-Up directions.
• Sing, following your demonstration.

Rhythm Drill

The Rhythm Drill on page 59 is designed to prepare students to:

- Review how to read known rhythms.
- Review how to read known rests.
- Read call-and-response segments, where parts "take turns."

Have students:

- Read through the Rhythm Drill directions.
- Perform the drill.

Sight-Singing

This Sight-Singing exercise is designed to prepare students to:

- Sight-sing in C major with solfège and hand signs or numbers.
- Sing block chords in three parts.
- Identify and hear the tonic chord.

Have students:

- Read through the Sight-Singing exercise directions.

Singing: "Whisper! Whisper!"

Introduce the concept of call and response through school cheers. Have students:

- Read the Singing section on page 60.
- Cheer as one or a few volunteers lead.
- Identify the sequence as a solo leader, then a response by the whole group.

Sight-Singing

Sight-sing these chords using solfège syllables and hand signs or numbers. The tonic chord includes the syllables *do*, *mi*, and *so*. Can you find which chords in this example are tonic chords?

Singing: "Whisper! Whisper!"

Do you know any school cheers? Have someone lead the class in a cheer! Next, try the same cheer, but whisper the words. Compare how you felt performing it both ways.

Now turn to the music for "Whisper! Whisper!" on page 61.

HOW DID YOU DO?

?
?

Sometimes sections of a choir take turns being the leader, and sometimes they all work together. Sometimes pitches of a chord take turns, being heard one after the other, and sometimes they are all heard at once. Think about your activities with "Whisper! Whisper!" and answer these questions:

1. What have you learned about chords during this lesson?
2. Are you better at reading rhythms or pitches?
3. Can you and two friends from other sections of the choir demonstrate a tonic chord, both broken and as a block chord?

Composer Jay Althouse

One of the country's experts on choral music, Jay Althouse has devoted his career to composing, arranging, and promoting the choral art form. As a composer, Althouse is the originator of a composition. As an arranger, he takes a composition written by someone else and arranges each part of the music and each musical part in an original way. He has over 300 titles in print and has

won several special awards for his compositions.

Besides working as a composer and arranger, Althouse has worked for music publishers to make sure that people obtain the rights of ownership to their original works. Althouse has traveled throughout the United States to conduct clinics and seminars, sharing his appreciation and knowledge of choral music with others.

Whisper! Whisper!

Words and Music by
JAY ALTHOUSE

Three-part Mixed Voices, A cappella*

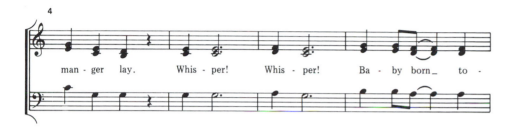

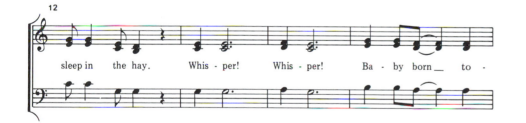

*Also available for S.A.T.B. voices (5796)

Whisper! Whisper! **61**

Suggested Teaching Sequence

1. Review Vocal Warm-Up.
Distinguish between the broken tonic chord and scalewise motion.
Have students:
- Read the directions, then sing the Vocal Warm-Up exercise on page 59 with solfège and hand signs or numbers.
- Identify the solfège in the first example (*do, mi*, and *so*) as the tonic chord. Decide why it is called "broken."
- Distinguish between scalewise and broken tonic chord segments of the second example. (scalewise—first nine pitches; tonic chord—last six pitches)
- Sing the exercise once again.

2. Sight-sing "Whisper! Whisper!" using solfège and hand signs or numbers.
Have students:
- Divide into voice sections (SAB) and read each part rhythmically, using rhythm syllables.
- Still in sections, sing with solfège and hand signs or numbers, identifying and working on problem areas.
- Sing the piece through using solfège and hand signs or numbers with full ensemble.
- Divide into sections and re-cite the text rhythmically for each voice part.
- Sing the piece through with text as a full ensemble.

3. Review Rhythm Drill.

Identify call and response. Have students:

- Read the directions, then clap the Rhythm Drill on page 59.
- Identify the structure as one part leading, the other part responding, or taking turns. (It is important to have a sense of the whole phrase, however, even though each group is performing only part of the phrase.)
- Discuss how to create a call and response by having one person perform the lower line, and then have volunteers clap the top part individually.
- Look at "Whisper! Whisper!" measures 17–25, identifying and singing the call and response.

4. Review Sight-Singing.

Practice identifying the tonic chord and sing block chords. Have students:

- Read the directions and sight-sing the exercise on page 60.
- Describe the difference between these block chords and the broken tonic chords sung during the Vocal Warm-Up.
- Review the tonic chord as including *do, mi,* and *so.*
- Find the tonic chords in the example. (chords 1, 2, 6, 7, 8, 9, 10, 12, 13, and 18)
- Sing the exercise again to hear the tonic chords.
- Look at "Whisper! Whisper!" measures 1–8, identifying and singing the block chords with syllable names and hand signs or numbers.

CULTURAL CONNECTIONS
Gospel Style

Gospel music is a genre of the twentieth century, originating with sacred songs used in Black American Protestant churches. The gospel singer takes simple melodies and vocally embellishes them in radical ways, such as using full and falsetto voices, shouting, humming, growling, moaning, whispering, crying, and screaming. Fancy melismas, syncopations, blue notes, glissandi, and repeated fragments of the text are musical ways of improvising in a gospel song.

Gospel songs are used in religious and commercial settings and can be sung or performed by many different performers, such as the

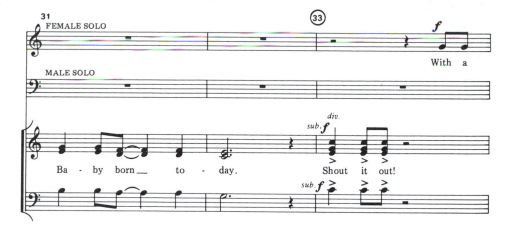

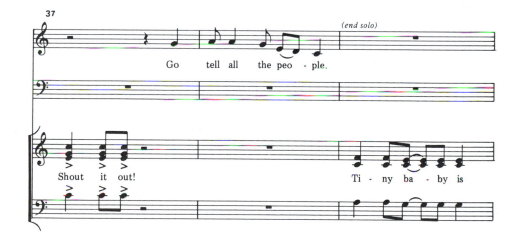

preacher, barbershop ensembles, soloists, or choirs. Accompaniment can include piano, organ, bass, drums, and tambourine.

The gospel repertoire grew out of the eighteenth- and nineteenth-century hymns, spirituals, blues, ragtime, pop, country/western, and jazz music. It forms the basis for rhythm and blues and soul styles found in pop music.

VOCAL DEVELOPMENT

To encourage vocal development, have students:

- Use their upper head register when singing a low tessitura with a soft dynamic.
- Use energy and breath support on soft passages. Make a difference in the sound of *p, mp, pp,* and *ppp.*
- Sing diphthongs correctly on the words *shout, out, tiny, today, lay,* and *hay.*
- Sing the *r* consonant correctly on words such as *whisper, born, Lord,* and *glory.*
- Understand that sudden *f* passages with accented notes should be carefully sung with full-bodied, supported sound. Avoid tensing and forcing of vocal chords to sing the accented notes.
- Get the correct sound production by singing *whoo* with full connection of the breath, using the head tone and tall, open mouth space.

Assessment

Informal Assessment

In this lesson, students showed the ability to:

- Distinguish between scale-wise and broken tonic chord patterns in the Vocal Warm-Up exercise.
- Identify and perform call-and-response style in "Whisper! Whisper!" measures 17–25.
- Identify and perform block tonic (and other) chords in the Sight-Singing exercise and "Whisper! Whisper!" measures 1–16.

Student Self-Assessment

Have students:

- Return to page 60 and read the How Did You Do? section.
- Answer the questions individually. Discuss them in pairs or small groups, and/or write their responses on a sheet of paper.

Individual Performance Assessment

To further demonstrate accomplishment, have students:

- In quartets, with one person singing the solo, demonstrate call-and-response by singing "Whisper! Whisper!" from measures 17–25 or 69–84.
- In a trio or sextet, demonstrate the difference between broken and block tonic chords using their choice of lesson materials.

Whisper! Whisper! **65**

Extension

Dynamics in "Whisper! Whisper!"

Have students:

- Look through the piece for dynamic markings.
- Perform the piece with the contrasts between soft and loud.
- Tape record the performance.
- Together, assess whether the performance was effective.
- Discuss the concept of a group getting louder by each individual getting only a little louder.
- Also discuss the balance between solo and group during the louder section. The group must still balance with the soloist.
- Make suggestions for improving the overall balance and contrast, and rehearse several times until the performance matches the planned effect.

National Standards

The following National Standards are addressed through the Extension and bottom-page activities:

3. Improvising melodies, variations, and accompaniments. **(c)**
7. Evaluating music and music performances. **(a, b)**
9. Understanding music in relation to history and culture. **(a)**

Whis - per! Whis - per! Ba - by born __ to -

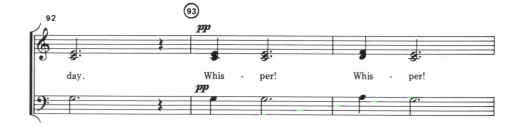

day. Whis - per! Whis - per!

Ti - ny ba - by, he sleep in the hay. Whis - per!

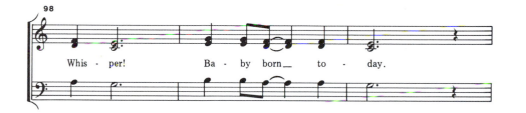

Whis - per! Ba - by born __ to - day.

Whis - per! Whis - per! Mm

Improvising on the Tonic Chord

The pitches of the tonic chord are a wonderful place to start improvising in many styles. The teacher or a student establishes an ostinato bass line using only the tonic pitch. This pattern should remain steady, and provide a solid foundation for the singers. It can have a jazzy rhythm, be in 3/4 meter, or whatever other style you wish to explore. Once the bass is firmly established, have the singers:

- Begin by improvising rhythms on the tonic pitch, using whatever neutral syllable they choose. *(loo, lie, dah-bah, etc.)*
- Next improvise rhythmically on the third, then the fifth.
- Finally, move between the tonic, third, and fifth (adding high *do* and low *so* if they wish) as they are comfortable. By limiting the pitches and providing a solid foundation, and everyone singing at once, a safe environment is created for exploring the world of improvisation.

Echo Clap

Have students:

- Volunteer to be a leader (call).
- Choir will echo leader's claps (response).

Whisper! Whisper! **67**

Mansions in the Sky

COMPOSER: Carl Strommen

TEXT: Carl Strommen

Focus

OVERVIEW

Three-part singing; unison and chords; stepwise and skipwise melodies.

OBJECTIVES

After completing this lesson, students will be able to:

- Read and sing in three parts.
- Distinguish between and sing in unison and in chords.
- Distinguish between and sing stepwise and skipwise melodic movement.

CHORAL MUSIC TERMS

Define the Choral Music Terms for students, providing correct pronunciation, and answering any questions that may arise.

Warming Up

Vocal Warm-Up

This Vocal Warm-Up is designed to prepare students to:

- Read and sing in three parts, using solfège and hand signs or numbers.
- Read on three staves.
- Identify unison and chord tones between parts.
- Tune chords.
- Sing in 3/4 meter.

Have students:

- Read through the Vocal Warm-Up directions.
- Sing, following your demonstration.

Mansions in the Sky

CHORAL MUSIC TERMS
a tempo
mezzo forte (mf)
mezzo piano (mp)

VOICING
Three-part mixed

PERFORMANCE STYLE
Gently
Accompanied by piano

FOCUS

- Read and sing in three parts.
- Distinguish between and sing unison and chords.
- Distinguish between and sing stepwise and skipwise melodic motion.

Warming Up

Vocal Warm-Up

Sing these chords using solfège. Notice the pitches where all three parts are in unison, and those that have different chord tones.

TEACHER'S RESOURCE BINDER
Blackline Master 7, *Rhythm Challenge*, page 81

National Standards

This lesson addresses the following National Standards:

1. Singing a varied repertoire of music. **(d)**
5. Reading and notating music. **(e)**
6. Listening to, analyzing, and describing music. **(c)**
7. Evaluating music and music performances. **(a)**
8. Understanding relationships between music and the other arts. **(b)**

Sight-Singing

Read and sing this exercise using solfège. Where does each melody move in steps or skips? Which is easier to sing?

Singing: "Mansions in the Sky"

People say your wishes and dreams are like mansions in the sky.

When you dream, you help build your mansion.
When you wish, your mind imagines your mansion.
When you work hard, you move closer to achieving your dreams.

Read the text of "Mansions in the Sky." What does the little bird represent?

Now turn to the music for "Mansions in the Sky" on page 70.

HOW DID YOU DO?

?

?

If you set your sights on learning a new piece and work hard, you should see positive results.

Think about your preparation and performance of "Mansions in the Sky."

1. What was easy about reading the music of "Mansions in the Sky"? What was hard?

2. Describe the difference between stepwise and skipwise melodic movement. How can this help you read music?

3. Describe the difference between unison and chord tone singing. Which is easier? Which do you like better?

4. How well did you perform "Mansions in the Sky"? How well did the choir do? What criteria did you use to make this evaluation?

Sight-Singing

This Sight-Reading exercise is designed to prepare students to:

- Sight-sing in three parts on three staves.
- Sing using solfège.
- Distinguish between step-wise and skipwise melodic movement.
- Read in 3/4 meter.

Have students:

- Read through the Sight-Singing exercise directions.
- Read each part rhythmically, using rhythm syllables.
- Sight-sing through each part separately.
- Sing all parts together.

Singing: "Mansions in the Sky"

Identify imagery.
Have students:

- Read the Singing section on page 69.
- Read the text of "Mansions in the Sky," discussing what the little bird may represent. (Accept all reasonable answers.)

Suggested Teaching Sequence

1. Review Vocal Warm-Up.

Identify unison and chord tone singing.
Have students:

- Review the Vocal Warm-Up on page 68.
- Identify the unison measures, (1, 2, 8, 9, and 10) and the chord measures (3–7).
- Sing again, raising a hand on the unison measures and lowering it for the chords.
- Look at the notation for "Mansions in the Sky," identifying parts of the piece that are written in unison. Notice measures 21–23, where the soprano and alto are in unison while the baritone sings harmony.

2. Review Sight-Singing.

Distinguish between stepwise and skipwise melodic movement.
Have students:

- Review the Sight-Singing exercise on page 69, using solfège and hand signs or numbers.
- Tell whether each interval in their part moves stepwise or skipwise.
- Read measures 25–28 of "Mansions in the Sky," identifying all the stepwise movement in the three parts.
- Discuss why it is important to read the notes as well as the text.
- Sing the exercise again, holding extended fingers together for steps and apart for skips.

Mansions in the Sky

Words and Music by
CARL STROMMEN

Three-part Mixed Voices and Piano*

* Also available for S.A.T.B. (5770) and S.S.A./2-part voices (5772).

3. Sight-sing "Mansions in the Sky" using solfège and hand signs or numbers.

- Divide into voice sections and read each part rhythmically, using rhythm syllables.
- Still in sections, sing with solfège and hand signs or numbers, identifying and working on problem areas.
- Sing the piece through using solfège and hand signs or numbers with full ensemble.
- Divide into sections and recite the text rhythmically for each voice part.
- Sing the piece through with text as a full ensemble.

VOCAL DEVELOPMENT

Breath Support

"Mansions in the Sky" requires legato—smooth singing and long flowing phrases. Both techniques need good breath support and control. Have students:

- Sing long, seamless phrases using a staggered breathing technique.
- "Lift" the octave leap each time it occurs. Breath support and a precise sense of the octave sound are necessary.
- Avoid any sliding or scooping in a song of this character.
- Sing diphthongs correctly: *nigh, sky, away, high, day,* and *beyond*.
- Sing the *r* consonant correctly on *bird, morning,* and *hour*. Feel an uplifted, unstressed *r* rather than a heavy, stressed *r*.

Composer Carl Strommen

A background in music and education led Carl Strommen to become a teacher, then a high school choir director. His love of teaching and choral music originated in the 1970s when he began arranging music for a high school choir. Since then, he has had a prolific career writing and arranging music for school choirs and bands. Currently the Band Director at a New York high school, Strommen is highly respected by his students, peers, and audiences for his articulate words and choral arrangements.

MUSIC LITERACY

To help students expand their music literacy, have them:
- Review the 3/4 meter and conduct in 3.
- Conduct and speak the text in rhythm.

21

man - sions in the sky. _____ Swift - ly

man - sions in the sky. _____ Swift - ly

man - sions in the sky. _____ Swift - ly

25 *mf*

now, a - way the morn - ing is nigh, to

now, a - way the morn - ing is nigh, _____ to

now, a - way the morn - ing is nigh, to _____

wing, the glow of first light. This

wing, the glow of first light. This

wing, the glow of first light. This

shin - ing hour, this break of day, to

shin - ing hour, this break of day, to

shin - ing hour, this break of day, to

Informal Assessment

In this lesson, students showed the ability to:

- Distinguish between unison and chords in the Vocal Warm-Up.
- Distinguish between step-wise and skipwise melodic movement in the Sight-Singing exercises.
- Read and sing in three parts in "Mansions in the Sky."

Student Self-Assessment

Have students:

- Return to page 69 and read the How Did You Do? section.
- Answer the questions individually. Discuss them in pairs or small groups, and/or write their responses on a sheet of paper.

Individual Performance Assessment

To further demonstrate accomplishment, have students:

- Sing "Mansions in the Sky," raising a hand on the unison parts, and lowering it for the chords.
- Sing measures 8–32 in a trio, correctly demonstrating unison singing.
- Sing measures 25–28, holding extended fingers together for steps and apart for skips.

Mansions in the Sky **73**

Extension

Phrases in "Mansions in the Sky"

This piece offers a nice opportunity to work on phrasing and extending breath support. Have students:

- Identify a phrase as a complete musical thought.
- Sing through the piece, marking phrases with arcs in the air.
- Discuss their ideas, noticing that there are short phrases that seem to come in pairs to create a longer phrase.
- Look for the breath marks in the notation, for example, in measure 16.
- Sing the song, breathing deeply at the beginning of each phrase, and controlling the breath so it lasts through to the end.
- Work on using a crescendo in the first part of the phrase, and a decrescendo in the second part, to add some shape to the phrase.

National Standards

The following National Standards are addressed in the Extension:

3. Improvising melodies, variations, and accompaniments. **(c)**
7. Evaluating music and music performances. **(a, b)**

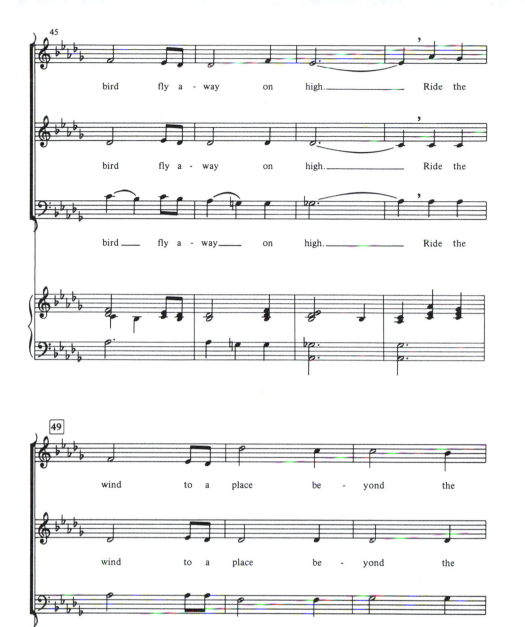

Composing with Steps and Skips

Have students:

* Write short melodies that have both steps and skips in C major.
* Share these melodies with one another, identifying the steps and skips in each other's compositions.
* Listen and decide what combinations of steps and skips are especially good, and tell why.
* Make a list of recommendations for a future composer of step/skip combinations.

Add a Percussion Accent

Have students:

* Decide as a class when the accent should be played and when it should not.

Ask volunteers to:

* Take turns playing finger cymbals on each strong beat during some parts of the piece.

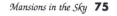

Mansions in the Sky **75**

LESSON 9

Down by the Riverside

Traditional, Spiritual
ARRANGER: Brad Printz

CHORAL MUSIC TERMS
key change
part independence
syncopation

VOICING
Three-part mixed

PERFORMANCE STYLE
Spiritual
Accompanied by piano

FOCUS
- Read and clap syncopated rhythms.
- Sing in two parts with independent melody and rhythm lines.

Warming Up

Rhythm Drill
Clap the following exercise. After you feel secure, clap the three parts together. There's syncopation in the Rhythm Drill, and syncopation makes the rhythm swing.

Can you find three places where there is syncopation?

Use scat syllables to make these rhythms swing! Use any combination of these sounds: *dah, dah-bah, shoo, boop,* etc. Just make it up as you go along. Working in a group, make up your own scat pattern using the best ideas of group members.

Vocal Warm-up
Use the tonic triad—*do, mi, so*—in the key of G major to sing the Rhythm Drill. Use *do* for Line 1, *so* for Line 2, and *mi* for Line 3. Sing each line separately, then all together.
Now try using scat syllables to make these rhythms swing! Use any combination of these sounds: *dah, dah-bah, shoo, boop,* etc. Just make it up as you go along. Working in a group, make up your own scat pattern using the best ideas of group members.

Lesson 9: Down by the Riverside **77**

TEACHER'S RESOURCE BINDER
Blackline Master 8, *Syncopated Rhythms,* page 82

National Standards
Through involvement with this lesson, students will develop the following skills and concepts:
1. Singing, alone and with others, a varied repertoire of music. **(c, d)**
5. Reading and notating music. **(c)**

LESSON 9

Down by the Riverside

Traditional, Spiritual
ARRANGER: Brad Printz

Focus

OVERVIEW
Syncopated rhythms; part independence.

OBJECTIVES
After completing this lesson, students will be able to:
- Read and clap syncopated rhythms.
- Sing in two parts with independent melody and rhythm lines.

CHORAL MUSIC TERMS
Define the Choral Music Terms for students, providing correct pronunciation, and answering any questions that may arise.

Warming Up

Rhythm Drill
This Rhythm Drill is designed to prepare students to:
- Read and clap rhythms in 2/2 meter containing syncopation.
- Combine parts with different rhythm patterns.
- Sing parts with different rhythm patterns.
Have students:
- Read through the Rhythm Drill directions.
- Perform the drill.

Sight-Singing

This Sight-Singing exercise is designed to prepare students to:

- Sight-sing in the key of D major using solfège and hand signs or numbers.
- Sing vocal lines with contrasting motion.
- Sight-sing in 2/2 meter.

Have students:

- Read through the Sight-Singing exercise directions.
- Read each part rhythmically, using rhythm syllables.
- Sight-sing through each part separately.
- Sing all parts together.

Singing: "Down by the Riverside"

Introduce key change and the concept of change in music. Have students:

- Review "Over There," page 20 (Lesson 3).
- Read the text in the Singing section on page 78.
- Discuss possible answers to the questions. (A key change indicates a new tonal center and new placement of *do.* It may require the melody to move to a new part. It may provide interest for the listener. A composer might also change the tempo, dynamics, rhythm, accompaniment, etc.)
- Listen to "Down by the Riverside," and then identify any of these changes they heard or found.

 Sight-Singing

Sight-sing these parts using solfège syllables or numbers. These two parts have melodies in contrasting motion. Look at the parts and decide how you can tell when there is contrasting motion.

 ## Singing: "Down by the Riverside"

Change is important in music, and in life. When changes are made, we have to adjust. In "Over There" (Lesson 3), there are several key changes.

Explain what a key change is in your own words.

How might a key change affect a piece of music for the singer? For the listener? What other changes might a composer make in a piece of music?

Now turn to the music for "Down by the Riverside" on page 79.

HOW DID YOU DO?

Think about your performance of the Rhythm Drill, Sight-Singing, and "Down by the Riverside."

1. How well did you perform the syncopated rhythms?

2. How well are you sight-singing? With what do you need help?

3. Can you sing measures 73–78 with just a trio—one student performing each part? Choose another short segment of "Down by the Riverside," and perform it as a trio.

4. The song "Down by the Riverside" is about a change from war to a world of peace. How do you feel about this message?

 CULTURAL CONNECTIONS

The Beginning of the Spiritual

The enslaved Africans brought music with the following elements to the New World: syncopation, polyrhythm, pentatonic and gap scales, and body movement to accompany song text.

Out of the suffering that came from being forcibly removed from their homelands and subjugated by another race, Africans created a new genre, the *spiritual* or religious folk song. This music revealed their unhappiness, taught facts, sent messages, provided a common language, and gave solace in their slavery.

Down by the Riverside

Traditional, Spiritual
BRAD PRINTZ

Three-part Mixed Chorus and Piano*

Duration: approx. 2:45
*Also available for Two-part (15/1012).

  Special TRAK-PAK 16 (99/1027) also available.

Reproduced by permission. Permit # 275772.

Down by the Riverside **79**

Suggested Teaching Sequence

1. Review Rhythm Drill.
Identify syncopation. Try scat singing.
Have students:

- Review the Rhythm Drill on page 77.
- Identify syncopated rhythm as a type of rhythm in which stressed sounds occur between beats.
- Perform the Rhythm Drill again as you keep the steady beat, identifying the three different syncopated rhythms. (part 1, measures 1 and 2; part 2, measures 1 and 2; part 3, measures 3 and 4).
- Try saying the Rhythm Drill using "scat" syllables.
- Work in groups to create a scat syllable version of their rhythm line, and then combine the three.

2. Sight-sing "Down by the Riverside" using solfège and hand signs or numbers.
Have students:

- Divide into voice sections (SAB) and read each part rhythmically, using rhythm syllables.
- Still in sections, sing with solfège and hand signs or numbers, identifying and working on problem areas.
- Sing the piece through using solfège and hand signs or numbers with full ensemble.
- Divide into sections and recite the text rhythmically for each voice part.
- Sing the piece through with text as a full ensemble.

TEACHING STRATEGY
Extra Help: Snapping Off-Beats

If the students are having difficulty snapping the offbeats, have them do a step-snap pattern, with the step on the beat. Have them say "yes, sir" and "yes" with the steps, and "sir" with the snaps. Eventually they will just whisper the words, then think them as they step-snap. Finally, remove the steps, leaving only the snaps on the offbeats.

3. Review Sight-Singing.

Sing in solfège. Identify contrasting melodic motion.

Have students:

- Review the Sight-Singing exercise, reading through each part with solfège and hand signs or numbers.
- Sight-sing both parts together.
- Read the text and identify the visually contrasting motion in the notation of the two parts.
- Look at measures 74–78 of "Down by the Riverside," identifying the connection to the Sight-Singing exercise.
- Identify the alto part as the solo line, having an independent rhythm and melody.
- Sing measures 73–78 in three parts.

CHOREOGRAPHY

Have students:

- Identify the main sections of the piece.
- Determine the characteristics of those sections.
- Then devise movement to highlight those characteristics. For example:

measures 0–20	snap with one hand, using reserved motion
measures 20–37	**Part III:** stand **Parts I and II:** sway with hands left then right at shoulder height
measures 37–52	**All Parts:** stand, join hands and sway

MUSIC LITERACY

To help students expand their music literacy, have them:

- Conduct the alla breve meter and speak the text in rhythm. Be precise on tied notes, syncopations, and pick-up beats.
- Use new solfège on altered notes. Practice singing and identifying the difference in the major 2nd and minor 2nd interval. (whole and half steps)
- Contrast legato chords at measure 21 with articulated melody in part III.
- Note the broken chord patterns in contrasting motion at the key change. (measure 73)

measures 52–68	more exaggerated snaps, perhaps using two hands
	Part III: stand
measures 69–88	**Parts I and III:** sit down, no movement
measures 89–107	all stand, clap alternating left and right, shoulder height

measures 107–end snaps—one group sit down after each two measures of spoken text

Practice movements until they are done with accuracy and precision.

 CULTURAL CONNECTIONS
Spirituals

Spirituals, originating between the voyages of the slave traders to America and the post-Civil War Reconstruction era, tell the history and treatment of the African American. Topics included fate, emotions, everyday life, faith, and freedom.

Spirituals have different styles—the melodic, the call and response, and the syncopated. The melodic spiritual is a slow-to-moderate tempo, plaintive song with long, sustained melodic phrases. The ballads "Nobody Knows the Trouble I've Seen" and "Deep River" are two examples of the melodic spiritual. Call-and-response style characteristically exhibits a fast

This piece would be excellent for celebrations of Martin Luther King Jr.'s birthday, Black History Month, or World Peace celebrations.

Down by the Riverside **83**

and fiery tempo with short, punctuated melodic phrases. "Go Down Moses" and "Cert'nly Lord" are call-and-response spirituals with a lead soloist making a statement and the choir responding. Syncopated style is usually a fast tempo with an incomplete or fragmented melodic phrase and highly punctuated syncopation, often eliciting a body response. "I Got a Robe" and "Shout All Over God's Heaven" are examples of the syncopated spiritual.

TEACHING STRATEGY
Extra Help

If students have difficulty reading syncopated rhythm, use Blackline Master 8, *Syncopated Rhythms,* for extra explanation and practice. The beat bars on the Blackline Master provide a visual representation of sounds that fall "off" the beat.

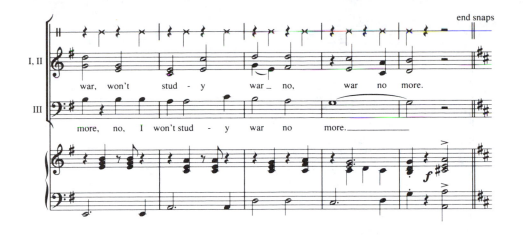

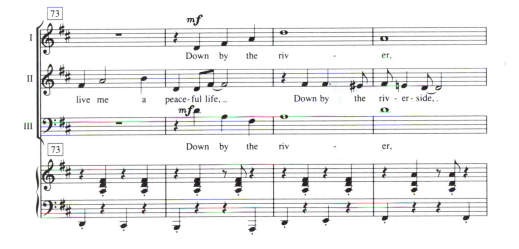

CURRICULUM CONNECTIONS

History

The events leading to the Civil War, 1861–1865, began much earlier with laws like the Fugitive Slave Law, books like *Uncle Tom's Cabin,* the Dred Scott Case, and furious debates between Northern Abolitionists and Southern slave owners in the Senate and the House of Representatives.

On October 16, 1859, John Brown led a raid and seized the federal arsenal at Harpers Ferry, Virginia, taking hostages and trying to incite a slave uprising. He wanted to arm local slaves and spread his uprising across the South.

Have students research to find out what motivated John Brown to take such drastic steps and what happened to him after Harpers Ferry. Ask volunteers for a short verbal report at the beginning of their next class period.

Informal Assessment

In this lesson, students showed the ability to:

- Read rhythms with syncopation during the Rhythm Drill.
- Sight-sing melodic lines in contrasting motion in the Sight-Singing exercise.
- Sight-sing contrasting melodic lines with an independent melody in measures 73–78 in "Down by the Riverside."

Student Self-Assessment

Have students:

- Return to page 78 and read the How Did You Do? section.
- Answer the questions individually. Discuss them in pairs or small groups, and/ or write their responses on a sheet of paper.

Individual Performance Assessment

To further demonstrate accomplishment, have students:

- Clap the Rhythm Drill alone, and then point out three different examples of syncopation.
- Sing a segment of "Down by the Riverside" with two others, forming a trio.

Down by the Riverside **87**

Singing with Scat Syllables

Jazz singers frequently use scat syllables. There's no "right way" to sing them, you just have to feel it. Try playing some Sarah Vaughn or Mel Torme recordings as models. Tell students:

- It's just like talking without words. They have to tell the story using the scat syllables and musical kinds of expression.
- Sometimes it's best not to think too much, but just try it and see what happens.
- If they all try in a large group, no one will be too embarrassed.
- Then let volunteers share with the class individually or in small groups.

Extending the Rhythm Exercise

If students enjoy the Rhythm Drill on page 77, extend the exercise by choosing different body percussion for each line, for example: clap line 1, stamp line 2 (stand up to do this), and pat line 3 with alternating hands. Have each group begin on a different line simultaneously, then read through the exercise three times without stopping. For example, the group that starts on line 2 will clap lines 2, 3, 1, 2, 3, 1, 2, 3, and 1. This will result in a canon of sorts, with one group standing on each phrase. You might consider assigning each line to a different unpitched instrument, for example: drums, play line 1; cow bell, play line 2; sticks, play line 3.

Down by the Riverside **89**

National Standards

The following National Standards are addressed through the Extension and bottom-page activities:

4. Composing and arranging music within specified guidelines. **(b)**

6. Listening to, analyzing, and describing music. **(a)**

8. Understanding relationships between music, the other arts, and disciplines outside the arts. **(a)**

9. Understanding music in relation to history and culture. **(a)**

Something Told the Wild Geese

COMPOSER: *Sherri Porterfield*
TEXT: *Rachel Field* (1894–1942)

CHORAL MUSIC TERMS
cadence
chords
composer
mood
phrase
3/4 meter
tuning

VOICING
Three-part mixed

PERFORMANCE STYLE
With anticipated motion
Accompanied by piano

FOCUS
- Perform correctly shaped musical phrases.
- Demonstrate good intonation while singing with two other parts.

Warming Up

 Rhythm Drill

In music, a phrase is a complete thought. How can you clap the A section below so it feels like a phrase? Clap each line keeping a steady 3/4 beat. Then together as a group clap the A section, and divide into three parts for the B section. Try the Rhythm Drill this way: A, BI, A, BI and BII, A, BI and BII and BIII, A. Do you feel each phrase acts as a complete thought?

Vocal Warm-Up

Sing the following chords, using solfège and hand signs. Listen to each chord and tune it before moving to the next. One sharp in the key signature could mean G major or E minor. Are these examples in G or E? How do you know?

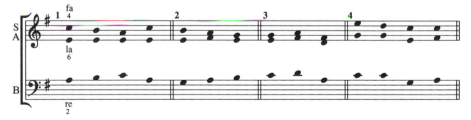

Lesson 10: Something Told the Wild Geese **91**

TEACHER'S RESOURCE BINDER

National Standards

Through involvement with this lesson, students will develop the following skills and concepts:
1. Singing, alone and with others, a varied repertoire of music. **(a, c)**
5. Reading and notating music. **(a, c)**

LESSON  10

Something Told the Wild Geese

COMPOSER: Sherri Porterfield
TEXT: Rachel Field (1894-1942)

Focus

OVERVIEW
Phrasing; tuning.

OBJECTIVES
After completing this lesson, students will be able to:
- Perform correctly shaped musical phrases.
- Demonstrate good intonation while singing with two other parts.

CHORAL MUSIC TERMS
Define the Choral Music Terms for students, providing correct pronunciation, and answering any questions that may arise.

Warming Up

Rhythm Drill
This Rhythm Drill is designed to prepare students to:
- Read and clap rhythms in 3/4 meter, in unison and in parts.
- Shape phrases.
Have students:
- Read through the Rhythm Drill directions.
- Perform the drill.

Vocal Warm-Up
This Vocal Warm-Up is designed to prepare students to:
- Sing using solfège syllables and hand signs.
- Sing in unison and three-part harmony.
- Practice altering intonation to tune chords.

Have students:
- Read through the Vocal Warm-Up directions.
- Sing, following your demonstration.

Sight-Singing
This Sight-singing is designed to prepare students to:
- Sight-sing in unison and harmony using solfège and hand signs or numbers.
- Sing in tune while singing with two other parts.
- Sing phrases.

Have students:
- Follow the exercise directions.
- Read each part rhythmically, using rhythm syllables.
- Sight-sing through each part separately.
- Sing all parts together.

Singing: "Something Told the Wild Geese"

Introduce "Something Told the Wild Geese."
Discuss mood.
Have students:
- Read the text in the Singing section on this page.
- Discuss possible answers.
- Listen to you sing "Something Told the Wild Geese," and then answer the questions.

Sight-Singing
Sight-sing these parts using solfège syllables or numbers. Where are there chords? Tune the chords carefully as you sing. Practice shaping the phrases.

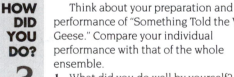

Singing: "Something Told the Wild Geese"

When geese begin flying south, it's a sign that summer is over, and winter is near. What mood might you feel as you see the geese flying? When the geese fly, each individual becomes part of a larger group. Compare this to when you sing, you add your individual voice to the group.

Listen to "Something Told the Wild Geese." What mood did the composer convey? Was it similar to your mood? How did the composer convey her imagined mood?

Now turn to the music for "Something Told the Wild Geese" on page 93.

HOW DID YOU DO?

Think about your preparation and performance of "Something Told the Wild Geese." Compare your individual performance with that of the whole ensemble.

1. What did you do well by yourself? How did the group do?

2. Where do you need more work? Where does the group need more work?

3. Did you work together to build phrases? What did you do?

4. How did you enhance the mood of the piece through your performance?

Poet/Author Rachel Field

Born in New York City in 1894, Rachel Field was an American author and poet. Best known for her books and poetry for children, she won the Newbery Medal in 1929 with her story *Hitty, Her First Hundred Years*. The story was based on the adventures of an early American wooden doll. Rachel Field lived in Beverly Hills, California, and died there in 1942.

TEACHING STRATEGY
Phrases and Teamwork

The concept of phrasing is one that requires teamwork and collaboration. Each student and each part must be listening to all other parts so the phrase builds together. This idea of individuals as part of a group is a very satisfying aspect of the choral experience, and can be compared to being part of a team. The team consists of individual members who work together toward a common goal.

Something Told the Wild Geese

Sherri Porterfield
Rachel Field (Used by Permission)

Three-part Mixed Chorus

Duration: approx. 2:00      Special TRAK-PAK 16 (99/1027) also available.

*Also available for Two-part (H5890).

Something Told the Wild Geese **93**

Suggested Teaching Sequence

1. Sight-sing "Something Told the Wild Geese" using solfège and hand signs or numbers.

Have students:

- Divide into voice sections (SAB) and read each part rhythmically, using rhythm syllables.
- Still in sections, sing with solfège and hand signs or numbers, identifiying and working on problem areas.
- Sing the piece through using solfège and hand signs or numbers with full ensemble.
- Divide into sections and re-cite the text rhythmically for each voice part.
- Sing the piece through with text as a full ensemble.

2. Review Rhythm Drill.

Read rhythms in 3/4 meter. Clap in unison and in three parts. Identify phrase.

Have students:

- Review the Rhythm Drill on page 91, rehearsing rhythms in 3/4 meter.
- Identify the A section as unison and the B section as three separate parts.
- Read the text defining the term *phrase,* and then explore ideas for enhancing the feeling of phrase. (Sing toward the "peak" note, clapped louder or stronger, which is in each phrase. Get louder then softer, or use more energy toward the middle of the phrase to build tension and release. Put a phrase of words with the rhythm and feel the phrase, using one breath as they clap to get the feeling of singing a phrase with one breath)
- Practice the piece using the form suggested, rising slowly from their chair as the phrase starts, coming to a full stand at the peak of the phrase, and slowly going back to a sitting position by the end of the phrase.

MUSICAL CONSIDERATIONS

- Meter in 3/4.
- Minor mode—use solfège warm-ups in minor.
- Chords—use solfège to tune.
- Entrance measure 25—precise rhythm, flow.

TEACHING STRATEGY
Extra Rhythm Help

If students are unfamiliar with the rhythms in 3/4 meter, have them practice the rhythms until they can be clapped smoothly and are familiar.

- Look at "Something Told the Wild Geese," finding the rhythms from the A section (measures 25–28, bass melody line), and the B section (measures 45–48, I for soprano and alto, II for bass, III for piano).
- Read and clap through the rhythm of "Something Told the Wild Geese."
- Find the phrases in measures 7–24 of the song, then sing each phrase, standing and sitting as directed above to show the phrases.

3. Review Vocal Warm-Up.

Sing with solfège in three parts. Tune chords with correct intonation. Have students:

- Review the Vocal Warm-Up on page 92 using solfège and hand signs or numbers.
- Identify the key of E minor, and *la* as the tonal center.
- Listen to each chord and tune it before moving to the next.
- Read and sing each phrase in "Something Told the Wild Geese," measures 7–24, on *loo*.
- Slowly sing measures 7–24 together on *loo*, tuning pitches carefully and keeping the *oo* vowel matched between singers.
- Switch to singing the vowels of the text—checking for vowel unification (unified vowels).
- Add consonants for clarity, keeping vowels pure.

4. Review Sight-Singing.

Sing with solfège and hand signs or numbers. Identify unison and three parts. Practice tuning chords and shaping phrases. Have students:

- Review the Sight-Singing exercise on page 92, reading through each part with solfège and hand signs or numbers.

 TEACHING STRATEGY

Extra Help—Tuning Chords

To help students listen to one another, have one student in each group choose a pitch and hold it out until everyone in the group is singing the same pitch, using a neutral syllable such as *oo* or *ah*. Point to one student from one of the groups. That student changes the group's pitch, and everyone must listen and move to that pitch. Continue to point to individual students in each of the three groups, waiting each time until the group has tuned to the new pitch. The chords will be very interesting and sometimes dissonant, which requires even more careful listening. Encourage soft singing and very careful listening within and between groups.

- Sight-sing all three parts together.
- Identify unison (phrase 1) and chords in three parts (phrase 2).
- Practice tuning chords during phrase 2.
- Shape the phrases using strategies explored during the Rhythm Drill.
- Compare the Sight-Singing exercise to measures 7–14 in the song. (same rhythms, some different pitches, different ending.)
- Read through measures 7–14.

5. Find, sing, and identify cadences.

Have students:
- Sing measures 13 and 14, 22 and 23, and 31 and 32, tuning each carefully.
- Sing these three segments in consecutive order.
- Discuss the differences in each voice part.
- Identify these phrase endings as cadences, resting points at the end of a phrase.

VOCAL DEVELOPMENT

To encourage vocal development, have students:
- Sing legato, carrying the full phrase without a breath.
- Sense the "moving forward feeling" of conducting in 1.
- Energize with a slight crescendo on sustained notes of *go* and *snow.*
- Notice that two-syllable words tend to be stressed on the second part. Practice measure 16, "stirring" with a circular arm movement to show loud to soft.
- Practice diphthongs on *fly, cry, ice,* and *spice.*

CURRICULUM CONNECTIONS
Expressive Writing

The poem "Something Told the Wild Geese" is a very expressive text, which can be set many ways. Have students write the poem out on the board or paper, and then in groups compose their own settings using expressive language. Remind them to consider rhythm, phrasing, dynamics, tempo, vocal tone color, solo and group possibilities, and so on, to create a unique mood. Have the groups perform for one another, then assess their own work and the work of others by telling: 1) what they heard (facts); 2) some things they liked (opinions), and why; and finally, 3) what they might have improved or changed the next time.

Assessment

Informal Assessment

In this lesson, students showed the ability to:

- Read rhythms in 3/4 meter during the Rhythm Drill.
- Show phrases by slowly standing and sitting during the Rhythm Drill and measures 7–24 of "Something Told the Wild Geese."
- Demonstrate good intonation by tuning chords in the Vocal Warm-Up and measures 7–24 of "Something Told the Wild Geese."
- Sight-sing "Something Told the Wild Geese" using solfège and hand signs or numbers.

Student Self-Assessment

Have students:

- Return to page 92 and read the questions in the How Did You Do? section.

Individual Performance Assessment

To further demonstrate accomplishment, have students:

- While being videotaped, demonstrate by gradually standing and sitting, the correct shape of the phrases in measures 25–32.
- Demonstrate good intonation while singing measures 39–49 in a double trio.
- Assess their own performance on videotape using correct terminology and appropriate analysis of phrase interpretation and intonation.

TEACHING STRATEGY

Individual Performance Assessments

If students are not ready to undertake the rigorous assessments in this lesson, have them choose some section of the piece with which they are comfortable to demonstrate their understanding of the concept or skill.

PERFORMANCE TIP

The author tells of the anticipation of the coming of winter and the urgency of the geese to fly to a warmer climate. The students should strive for phrasing that works toward the feeling and expression of the natural rise and fall of each phrase. Effort should be given to the correct word and syllabic emphasis, so that the singers will musically portray the feelings that describe the poem.

MUSIC LITERACY

Have students:

- Review meter in 3/4.
- Conduct and speak rhythms on lyrics.
- Perform precisely the distinctive dotted rhythm at measures 25 and 27 for rhythmic contrast.
- Review the minor scale, noting the altered pitch on *si* and *fi*.

Extension

Rhythm Exercise

Have students:

- Transfer the rhythms in the Rhythm Drill to everyday sounds or unpitched instruments, such as triangles for part I, wood blocks for part II, and drums for part III.
- Decide on dynamics, phrasing techniques, and how to play the instruments to get the appropriate duration for the long notes.
- Decide whether all will play the A section, or whether another instrument, for example tambourine, should play that part.

Directing Game

Have students:

- Observe as you silently conduct measures 7–14 in "Something Told the Wild Geese." (exaggerate the breath break, the crescendo/ decrescendo, fermata, etc.)
- Find the place in the music they think you directed. Speak the words to the phrase they suggest, following your conducting, and decide whether that section fits your gestures.
- Recognize the 3/4 conducting pattern, and how to indicate dynamics and the fermata, and then try it along with you.

 **TEACHING STRATEGY**

Cadences

Cadences are the few chords indicating points of rest at the end of phrases. Some cadences are only half cadences, providing some sense of pause, but not a final resting point. You might compare these to the difference in feeling represented by a comma or period at the end of a phrase.

National Standards

The following National Standards are addressed through the Extension and bottom-page activities:

3. Improvising melodies, variations, and accompaniments. **(a)**
4. Composing and arranging music within specified guidelines. **(a)**
6. Listening to, analyzing, and describing music. **(a)**
7. Evaluating music and music performances. **(b)**
8. Understanding relationships between music, the other arts, and disciplines outside of music. **(b)**

LESSON 11

Praise Ye the Lord, All Nations

COMPOSER: Johann Sebastian Bach (1685-1750)

ARRANGER: Arnold B. Sherman

Focus

OVERVIEW
Part independence; read rhythms in 3/4 meter including half, quarter, and eighth notes.

OBJECTIVES
After completing this lesson, students will be able to:
- Sing their part independently with the other two parts.
- Read notation in 3/4 meter including half, quarter, and eighth notes.

CHORAL MUSIC TERMS
Define the Choral Music Terms for students, providing correct pronunciation, and answering any questions that may arise.

Warming Up

Vocal Warm-Up
This Vocal Warm-Up exercise is designed to prepare students to:
- Sing in three-part harmony using solfège and hand signs or numbers.
- Read and sing half, quarter, and eighth notes.

Have students:
- Read through the Vocal Warm-Up directions.
- Sing, following your demonstration.

LESSON 11

Praise Ye the Lord, All Nations

CHORAL MUSIC TERMS
allegro
cantata

COMPOSER: *Johann S. Bach (1685–1750)*
ARRANGER: *Arnold B. Sherman*

VOICING
SAB

PERFORMANCE STYLE
Allegro
Accompanied by keyboard

FOCUS
- Sing your part independently with the other voice parts.
- Read notation in 3/4 meter including half, quarter, and eighth notes.

Warming Up

Vocal Warm-Up
Sing these parts using solfège. Describe the musical features of this Vocal Warm-Up including as many of the following as possible: rhythms, meter, key, and melodic and structural features.

Sight-Singing
Sight-sing the following exercise on *loo*. Work toward singing the entire phrase using only one breath. Be sure not to strain your voice. Sizzle the rhythms, using a *tss* sound, to make them accurate and crisp. Now try singing the exercise using different vowels, for example: *na, ne, ni, no,* and *nu*. Use the long, pure vowel sounds, like the vowels are saying their own names.

TEACHER'S RESOURCE BINDER

National Standards
This lesson addresses the following National Standards:
1. Singing, alone and with others, a varied repertoire of music. **(a, c, d)**
5. Reading and notating music. **(a)**
6. Listening to, analyzing, and describing music. **(b)**
7. Evaluating music and music performances. **(a, b)**

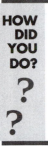

Singing: "Praise Ye the Lord, All Nations"

Sometimes a performance captivates an audience, regardless of the type of music being sung or played.

What are some reasons an audience might become captivated by the music? What are the musical elements that make a performance appealing?

Now turn to and perform the music for "Praise Ye the Lord, All Nations" on page 100.

HOW DID YOU DO?

A strong choir needs to perform as a team comprising strong, independent players who work together toward a common goal.

1. Are you a strong, independent singer? How do you know?

2. Were you able to sight-sing "Praise Ye the Lord, All Nations"?

3. Are you a strong contributing member of the team when you perform? How do you know?

4. Was the choir able to sight-sing "Praise Ye the Lord, All Nations"?

5. What did you practice to make your performance better?

This Sight-Singing exercise is designed to prepare students to:

- Sight-sing using a neutral syllable.
- Blend their voices, vowel sounds, and parts.
- Breathe correctly in order to sing long phrases.
- Sing with part independence.

Have students:

- Read through the Sight-Singing exercise directions.
- Read each voice part rhythmically, using a *tss* sound to sizzle the rhythms.
- Sight-sing through each part separately on *loo*.
- Sing all parts together.

Singing: "Praise Ye the Lord, All Nations"

Discuss reasons for audience interest.

Have students:

- Read the text in the Singing section on this page.
- Discuss possible answers, encouraging opinions as well as facts.
- Determine whether teamwork in a choir has any impact on the audience response.

Present a challenge.

Because this piece is fairly easy to sight-sing, challenge the students to sight-sing it right away, before reviewing warm-ups or practicing individual parts.

Composer J.S. Bach

Johann Sebastian Bach created masterpieces of choral and instrumental music and wrote both sacred and secular music. His music is regarded as the high point of the Baroque era, which lasted from 1600 to 1750. Bach married twice and was the father of 20 children. Several of his children became well-known composers. He died July 28, 1750.

Suggested Teaching Sequence

1. Review Vocal Warm-Up.
Describe musical features.
Have students:

- Review the Vocal Warm-Up exercise on page 98, reading in three parts.
- Identify the musical features, including those listed.
- Identify the meter as 4/4, and the notes as half, quarter, and eighth notes.
- Read and sing the exercise again with solfège and hand signs or numbers.

2. Review Sight-Singing.
Sing with solfège in three parts. Practice reading rhythms in 3/4 meter. Build breath support. Blend vowels.
Have students:

- Review the Sight-Singing exercise on page 98, reading through each part with *loo*, then combining all three parts.
- Sizzle the rhythms using a *tss* sound.
- Read the directions for using different pure vowel sounds, and then read the exercise through once for each vowel sound.
- Discuss the placement of the vowels, and how to listen to one another and blend the sound.
- Find the Sight-Singing exercise notation in "Praise Ye the Lord, All Nations." (measures 14–15)

Praise Ye the Lord, All Nations

Psalm 117, Adapted by A.B.S.

Johann S. Bach

Arranged by Arnold B. Sherman

SAB Chorus with Keyboard Accompaniment

Bass line may be supported by appropriate bass instrument (Cello, Bassoon, etc.).

100 *Choral Connections Level 1 Mixed Voices*

3. Sight-sing "Praise Ye the Lord, All Nations" using solfège and hand signs or numbers.

Have students:

- Divide into voice sections (SAB) and read each part rhythmically, using rhythm syllables.
- Still in sections, sing with solfège and hand signs or numbers, identifying and working on problem areas.
- Sing the piece through using solfège and hand signs or numbers with full ensemble.
- Divide into sections and recite the text rhythmically for each voice part.
- Sing the piece through with text as a full ensemble.

♫ MUSIC LITERACY

To help students expand their music literacy, have them:

- Review meter in 3 with a fast tempo and conduct in 1 while speaking the rhythm of the text.
- Point out the numerous melismas.
- Perform the dotted quarter rhythms precisely.
- Identify imitations and sequences in the different voice parts.
- Experience the hemiola effect at four bars before number 4 on page 102 and from the end of page 102 to the beginning of page 103.

To encourage vocal development, have students :

• Articulate the slurred notes and melismas by holding the vowel sound with a slight *h* sound on each note.

• Sing the *r* sound correctly on *mercy, endure, Lord,* and *earth*.

• Vary the dynamics and intensity on text that repeats.

CURRICULUM CONNECTIONS
Visual Arts

Bach wrote many pieces of music, and although they were varied, they all had characteristics of Baroque music. Have students discover what these characteristics are, and find out the titles of some of Bach's masterpieces. Then make a collage of the titles, showing the characteristics of Baroque music in some visual way. For example, students might represent a canon by placing the same title three times, one below the other, with each slightly to the right of the one above it. Think about how they might visually represent melody and accompaniment, block chords, ornamentation, and so on.

National Standards

The following National Standards are addressed through the Extension and bottom-page activities:

8. Understanding relationships between music, the other arts, and disciplines outside the arts. **(a, b)**

9. Understanding music in relation to history and culture. **(b, c)**

Assessment

Informal Assessment

In this lesson, students showed the ability to:

- Read rhythms in 4/4 meter including half, quarter, and eighth notes in the Vocal Warm-Up.
- Read rhythms in 3/4 meter including half, quarter, and eighth notes in the Sight-Singing exercise.
- Sight-sing known rhythms and pitches in "Praise Ye the Lord, All Nations."

Student Self-Assessment

Have students:

- Return to page 99 and read the How Did You Do? section.
- Answer the questions individually. Discuss them in pairs or small groups, and/or write their responses on a sheet of paper.

Individual Performance Assessment

To further demonstrate accomplishment, have students:

- Sing, in a trio, measures 28–31 with part independence, and measures 46–49 with correct note values.

Extension

A Visit with Bach

Have students think of questions they might ask Bach if they met him today. They can research information about him, how his contemporaries felt about him and his work, the times in which he lived, and the music he wrote. Then role play an interview with J.S. Bach. Set it in the past, but conduct it like a television interview, with several students alternating the roles of Bach and the interviewer, and others helping out with questions and answers.

VOCAL DEVELOPMENT

Breathing Correctly

Deep, controlled breathing is required to sustain long phrases in one breath.

Posture is a critical feature in breath support. The body should be relaxed, but the backbone must be straight. Bending over and straightening several times helps to stretch out the back, and prepare the rib cavity without unnecessary raising of the shoulders.

When sitting, the students should sit toward the front edge of their chairs with two feet on the floor and backbone straight. When standing, one foot should be slightly ahead of the other, with equal balance and slightly bent knees.

To inhale, the breath should expand the lungs outward and downward, pushing the diaphragm down. This must be done inaudibly. One image to suggest is that students: imagine taking a "cool sip" of air through a straw.

To control the outgoing stream of air, have the students hold one finger in front of their mouth, about 6 inches away from the lips. Imagine that this is a birthday candle, and blow hard enough to bend the flame, but not hard enough to blow it out. See who can make their breath last the longest.

peo - ples on earth. Ex - tol him, ex - tol him, all peo - ples on

earth. Ex - tol him, ex - tol him, all

peo - ples on earth! Ex - tol him, all peo - ples on earth!

TEACHING STRATEGY

Cultural Context

Some students may question the appropriateness of this text in a school setting. "Praise Ye the Lord, All Nations" was written for performance in church, as was most of the music of the Baroque period. Bach was hired to write music for the church services, as were most of his talented contemporaries. It was the custom of the time. However, this piece has been chosen for its musical characteristics. It also has a more general message of loving kindness, gentleness, and mercy, as universal human qualities which might be sought and valued.

LESSON 12

Wiegenlied

COMPOSER: *Johannes Brahms* (1833–1897)
ARRANGER: *Sherri Porterfield*
ENGLISH TEXT: *Sherri Porterfield*

CHORAL MUSIC TERMS
chord building
dynamics
I, IV, and V chords
phrase

VOICING
Three-part mixed

PERFORMANCE STYLE
With tenderness
Accompanied by piano

FOCUS
- Sing, demonstrating an understanding of phrase.
- Use correct German pronunciation for the song text.
- Build I, IV, and V chords in the key of E♭ major.

Warming Up

Rhythm Drill
Clap the phrases of rhythm softly, shaping each phrase so it sounds like part of a story you are telling with your hands. Notice the dynamic markings (< >) and the breath (ʼ) mark. Where does the second phrase start? How do you know? Compare the two phrases. How are they the same? How are they different? Divide your class into two groups. Have Group 1 clap phrase 1 as a question; have Group 2 clap phrase 2 as an answer.

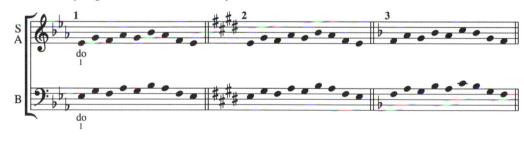

Vocal Warm-Up
Sight-sing using solfège syllables and hand signs or numbers. Repeat each exercise one step higher or lower on each repetition.

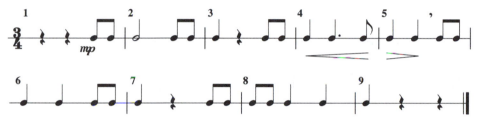

TEACHER'S RESOURCE BINDER
Blackline Master 9, *Chord Building,* page 83
Blackline Master 10, *"Wiegenlied" Pronunciation Guide,* page 84

National Standards
This lesson addresses these National Standards:
1. Singing, alone and with others, a varied repertoire of music. **(c)**
5. Reading and notating music. **(a)**
6. Listening to, analyzing, and describing music. **(c)**
7. Evaluating music. **(a, b)**
9. Understanding music in relation to history and culture. **(b)**

LESSON 12

Wiegenlied

COMPOSER: Johannes Brahms (1833-1897)
ARRANGER: Sherri Porterfield

Focus

OVERVIEW
Phrase building; I, IV, and V chords; German language.

OBJECTIVES
After completing this lesson, students will be able to:
- Sing, demonstrating an understanding of phrasing.
- Use correct German pronunciation for the song text.
- Build a I, IV, and V chord in the key of E♭.

CHORAL MUSIC TERMS
Define the Choral Music Terms for students, providing correct pronunciation, and answering any questions that may arise.

Warming Up

Rhythm Drill
This Rhythm Drill is designed to prepare students to:
- Read and clap rhythms in 3/4 meter.
- Clap phrases expressively through the use of dynamics and flow.
- Relate one phrase to the next.

Have students:
- Read through the Rhythm Drill directions.
- Perform the drill.

Vocal Warm-Up

This Vocal Warm-Up is designed to prepare students to:
- Sing ascending and descending patterns in steps and thirds using solfège and hand signs or numbers.
- Tune while singing in unison.
- Identify key changes.

Have students:
- Read through the Vocal Warm-Up.
- Sing, following your demonstration.

Sight-Singing

This Sight-Singing is designed to prepare students to:
- Sing unison and chords.
- Identify various chords.
- Sing in the German language.

Have students:
- Read through the Sight-Singing exercise directions.
- Read each voice part rhythmically, using rhythm syllables.
- Sight-sing through each part separately.
- Add the German text and focus on vowel sounds.
- Sing all parts together.

Singing: "Wiegenlied"

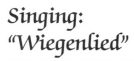

Review phrase building.

Have students:
- Read the text in Singing on this page.
- Discuss possible answers. Ask volunteers to share favorite lullabies.
- Listen to a few volunteers speak, especially watching for evidence of phrasing. (dynamics, a complete idea, pause at the end.)
- Review ways of building phrases while singing. (crescendo to high point, then decrescendo, connect notes to express one idea, relate one phrase to the next to keep the momentum of the piece going, one breath per phrase)

106

Sight-Singing

Sight-sing these examples using solfège and hand signs. Add the German text, focusing on vowel sounds. Notice that a chord is built in each second measure.

Singing: "Wiegenlied"

Have you ever heard or watched adults try to put babies to sleep? How do they move? What do they say? Do they sing? What are the characteristics of the music, language, or movement you would use to get a baby to go to sleep?

Now turn to the music for "Wiegenlied" on page 107.

Read the new translation of the German text. Do you think these words would soothe a crying baby or small child? Why?

HOW DID YOU DO?

? ?

"Wiegenlied" is one of the most famous and loved lullabies in Western music.
1. What characteristics of "Wiegenlied" do you think make it so valued?
2. Was your performance of "Wiegenlied" a convincing lullaby? How do you know?
3. Discuss how phrase is important in "Wiegenlied," and how you used the idea of phrase in your planning of the performance of the piece.

4. How difficult or easy was it to sing in German?
5. Can you point to examples of I, IV, and V chords in E♭ in "Wiegenlied"? Can you write examples of these chords?

Composer Johannes Brahms

In 1833 Brahms was born into a very poor musical family. He studied with Remenyi, a violinist, and toured Europe with him as his accompanist. He met the famous composers Joachim, Liszt, and Schumann on the tour. He became acquainted with gypsies, their culture, and their music. After his tour he concentrated on learning the classics composed by Beethoven and Bach.

His music reflected these earlier influences. He wrote every kind of music except opera: symphonies, concerti, overtures, variation, piano compositions, sonatas, intermezzi, rhapsodies, caprices, ballads, waltzes, and lieder. Brahms was a conservative in the Romantic era, writing pure or absolute music.

Wiegenlied

COMPOSER: Johannes Brahms
ARRANGER: Sherri Porterfield
ENGLISH TEXT: Sherri Porterfield

Three-part Mixed, Accompanied

Gu-ten A-bend, gut' Nacht, mit Ro-sen be-
Go to sleep, lit-tle one, with a blan-ket of

pedal simile throughout

Copyright © 1994 STUDIO 224, c/o CPP/BELWIN, INC., Miami, FL. 33014
International Copyright Secured   Made in U.S.A.   All Rights Reserved

Wiegenlied **107**

Phrases

Many times in music, phrases are paired as a question and an answer. Although they are related to one another, and the answer has some elements of the question, they are also different. Have students ask themselves a question in words, then give themselves an answer that is the same length. Listen to a few volunteers, and identify the similarities and differences between questions and an-swers. (Questions end without resolution; answers have a feeling of finality.)

Clap the Rhythm Drill, thinking of phrase 1 as a question and phrase 2 as the answer. Then you clap phrase 1, and the students each clap their own improvised answer for phrase 2. There are lots of possible "right" answers, as long as they are the same length, stay in 3/4 meter, and are related to Phrase 1 by imitating or contrasting rhythm, dynamics, or clapping style.

Suggested Teaching Sequence

1. Review Rhythm Drill.
Review 3/4 meter. Practice phrase building.
Have students:
- Review the Rhythm Drill on page 105, emphasizing phrase building strategies.
- Read the text.
- In two groups, clap the phrases, being sure that they seem like a question and an-swer related to one another.
- Look at the first two phrases of "Wiegenlied," identifying them as having the same rhythm as the Rhythm Drill.
- Clap these first two phrases, reading the text expressively.

2. Review Vocal Warm-Up.
Identify different keys.
Have students:
- Review the Vocal Warm-Up on page 105, using solfège and hand signs or numbers.
- Identify the three different keys as E♭, A, and F.
- Look at "Wiegenlied" and identify where the key signature is located (beginning of each line), what key the piece is in (E♭), and whether there is a key change (there is not).

3. Review Sight-Singing.
Practice German language sounds.
Have students:
- Review the Sight-Singing exercise on page 106, reading through each part with solfège and hand signs or numbers, then singing it through together.
- Study the pronunciation guide, Blackline Master 10, *"Wiegenlied" Pronunciation Guide*, then read the German lyrics slowly.
- Speak the German lyrics in rhythm.
- Sing the Sight-Singing exercise again, carefully pronouncing the text.

4. Build I, IV, and V chords.

Have students:

- Follow the directions on Blackline Master 9, *Chord Building*, discovering how to build I, IV, and V chords in E♭.
- Write I, IV, and V chords on the Blackline Master or the board.
- Look at measures 5-13 in "Wiegenlied" and identify examples of the I, IV, and V chords.

5. Sight-sing "Wiegenlied" using solfège and hand signs or numbers.

Have students:

- Divide into voice sections (SAB) and read each part rhythmically, using rhythm syllables.
- Still in sections, sing with solfège and hand signs or numbers, identifying and working on problem areas.
- Sing the piece through using solfège and hand signs or numbers with full ensemble.

TEACHING STRATEGY

Performance Tip

This piece is a lullaby. Have students work on smooth and connected phrasing that creates the suggestion of sweetness and tenderness.

VOCAL DEVELOPMENT

Have students:

- Use a fully resonant *ooo* tone throughout for a flowing lullaby style.
- Use tall, open Italian vowels.
- Feel the lilt of 3/4 tempo that follows the word stresses—flow gently into each phrase, sustaining as much as possible.
- The flow of the music intensifies on repeated notes and leads up to the accented, long, or high notes. Give it a shape. Keep the intensity when singing softly.

Ask students: Where are these places in the music? Does this treatment contribute to the emotion and feeling of the piece? What kind of energy is needed for forte (*f*) dynamics? What kind of energy is needed for piano (*p*) dynamics? How long can you hold a soft sound without changing the intensity?

Music score with the following lyrics:

weckt!
sun.
Gu-ten A — bend, gut' Nacht.
Go to sleep and good night.

Gu-ten A — bend, gut' Nacht, von
Go to sleep and good night. May the

Eng-lein be-wacht. die zie-gen im Traum dir
An-gels watch o'er you. They will show you in your dreams a

Christ-kind-leins Baum; Schlaf' nun se — lig und süss, schau im
spe-cial Christ-mas tree. Close your eyes my sweet child and be-

Assessment

Informal Assessment

In this lesson, students showed the ability to:

- Clap two phrases in 3/4 meter, demonstrating phrase building skills, during the Rhythm Drill.
- Sing in German, using correct pronunciation, in the Sight-Singing exercise.
- Identify I, IV, and V chords by pointing to the notation of "Wiegenlied."

Student Self-Assessment

Have students:

- Return to page 106 and read the How Did You Do? section.
- Answer the questions individually. Discuss them in pairs or small groups, and/ or write their responses on a sheet of paper.

Individual Performance Assessment

To further demonstrate accomplishment, have students:

- Perform individually the first two phrases of "Wiegenlied" on audiotape, demonstrating phrasing and proper German pronunciation.
- Using Blackline Master 9, individually build I, IV, and V chords in the key of E♭.

Wiegenlied **109**

CULTURAL CONNECTIONS

African Lullabies

Adults in all world cultures sing lullabies, but some of them are not peaceful and calm. Some African lullabies, for example, are very rhythmic and bounce the baby to sleep. There is probably no one "right" way to put a baby to sleep, but the combination of a familiar melody or rhythm, the sound of a familiar voice, and some movement seem to be common elements between cultures. Encourage students to research and find out more about characteristics of lullabies around the world.

Extension

Improvising Phrases

Once students understand the concept of question/answer phrases being related, they can work in pairs to improvise question/answer phrases. As a class, determine the meter and phrase length, for example; two measures of 4/4 meter. You establish the steady beat with a very strong pattern on a drum, or a bass line on the piano, for example:

(Change the pattern according to style, but keep it very basic, with some interest to give a feeling of the complete phrase length.)

Now partners each improvise, alternating questions and answers, over your bass line. Switch roles after about four sets. Continue to refine the interactions between questions and answers by encouraging the answerer to listen carefully and either take something from the question or contrast with the question. The question should eventually flow right into the first beat of the answer, and the answer should end with a sense of finality.

Who was Johannes Brahms?

On the board write an obituary notice that states, "Johannes Brahms, composer/musician, (1833-1897)." Have students assume the role of investigative reporters. Tell them you are the newspaper editor in chief. You found this obituary, but you know there is really more to this man than this small bit of information. Have them investigate Johannes Brahms and prepare a newspaper article or multimedia presentation that will let you know more about Brahms.

National Standards

The following National Standards are addressed through the Extension and bottom-page activities:

3. Improvising melodies, variations, and accompaniments. **(b)**
6. Listening to, analyzing, and describing music. **(c)**
8. Understanding relationships between music, the other arts, and disciplines outside the arts. **(b)**
9. Understanding music in relation to history and culture. **(b, c)**

Nightfall

COMPOSER: *Lou Williams-Wimberly*
TEXT: *Henry Wadsworth Longfellow (1807–1882)*

CHORAL MUSIC TERMS
breathing mechanics
staccato
legato

VOICING
SATB

PERFORMANCE STYLE
Slow
A cappella

FOCUS
- Describe and demonstrate correct breathing mechanics.
- Describe and demonstrate legato singing style.

Warming Up

Vocal Warm-Up

Sing this exercise using solfège syllables or numbers. Listen carefully and tune to the group. Each note is related to the ones beside it, and to others in the phrase. Sing the exercise with separated, staccato tones. Be sure to keep in tune. Sing the exercise again with legato, attached tones.

TEACHER'S RESOURCE BINDER
Blackline Master 11, *Breathing Checklist,*
page 86

National Standards

This lesson addresses the following National Standards:
1. Singing, alone and with others, a varied repertoire of music. **(a, d)**
5. Reading and notating music. **(c)**
6. Listening to, analyzing, and describing music. **(a)**
7. Evaluating music. **(b)**
9. Understanding music in relation to history and culture. **(a)**

Nightfall

COMPOSER:
Lou Williams-Wimberly
TEXT: Henry Wadsworth
Longfellow (1807-1882)

Focus

OVERVIEW
Breathing technique; legato singing.

OBJECTIVES
After completing this lesson, students will be able to:
- Describe and demonstrate correct breathing mechanics.
- Describe and demonstrate legato singing style.

CHORAL MUSIC TERMS
Define the Choral Music Terms for students, providing correct pronunciation, and answering any questions that may arise.

Warming Up

Vocal Warm-Up
This Vocal Warm-Up is designed to prepare students to:
- Read and sing in F major using solfège and hand signs or numbers.
- Sing in unison and harmony, tuning carefully to the group.
- Sing legato, attached tones.
Have students:
- Read through the Vocal Warm-Up directions.
- Sing, following your demonstration.

Sight-Singing

This Sight-Singing exercise is designed to prepare students to:

- Sight-sing in three parts using solfège and hand signs or numbers.
- Use proper breathing mechanics.
- Sing legato.

Have students:

- Read through the Sight-Singing exercise directions.
- Read each voice part rhythmically, using rhythm syllables.
- Sight-sing through each part separately.
- Practice correct breathing mechanics.
- Sing all parts together.

Singing: "Nightfall"

Compare the rise and fall of a feather to a musical phrase.
Have students:

- Read the text in the Singing section on this page.
- Do the simulation exercise with the feather or use a real feather if you have one.
- Compare the rise and fall of the feather to that of a musical phrase.
- Review how dynamics and singing from pitch to pitch can build a heightened sense of phrase.

Sight-Singing

Sight-sing the parts below using solfège syllables or numbers. What are the characteristics of "good breathing"? Use them when you sing this exercise. Decide where you might take a breath in this piece. Try several places. Can you sing it all on one breath without straining your voice?

Singing: "Nightfall"

Imagine a feather on your hand. Blow it gently up into the air, and watch its imaginary path. Describe the path your imaginary feather took. Compare that path to the "rise and fall" of musical phrases.

Now turn to the music for "Nightfall" on page 113.

HOW DID YOU DO?

Think about your performance of "Nightfall."

1. Can you sight-sing the pitches and rhythms? When do you feel most confident?
2. Describe the mechanics of good breathing, then sing a phrase to demonstrate your ability.

3. Describe legato singing, and sing a phrase to demonstrate your description.
4. What musical tools did the composer use to convey the feeling of "Nightfall"?

Composer Lou Williams-Wimberly

Born and educated in Texas, Lou (Ann) Williams-Wimberly's passion for music has lasted throughout her career as a teacher and choir director in several Texas cities, including Plano, where she was born. Her published works include her arrangements of religious pieces "The Incarnation," "Carol of Adoration," and "Angels We Have Heard on High," a collaboration with Jim Leininger. Combining her love of music with her fondness for students and teaching, she continues to teach high school in Plano.

Nightfall

Lou Williams-Wimberly
Henry Wadsworth Longfellow

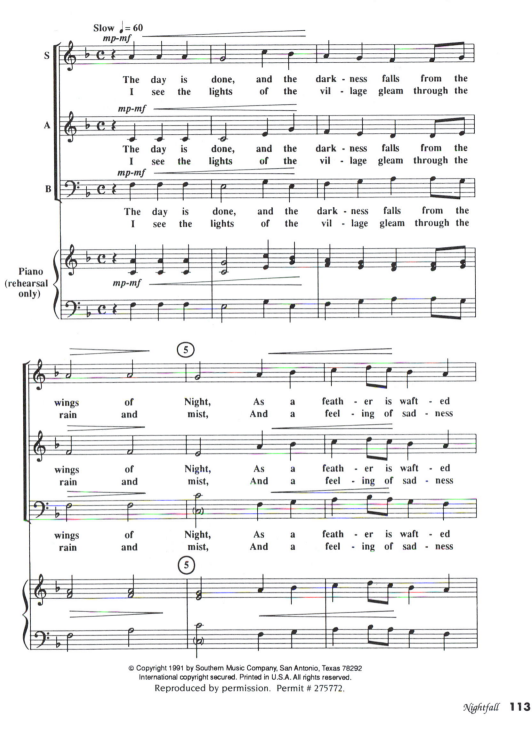

Nightfall **113**

1. Review Vocal Warm-Up.
Identify and practice legato singing.
Have students:

- Review the Vocal Warm-Up on page 111.
- Read the text, and sing the exercise first staccato, then legato, being sure to stay in tune.

2. Sight-sing "Nightfall" using solfège and hand signs or numbers.
Have students:

- Divide into voice sections (SAB) and read each part rhythmically, using rhythm syllables.
- Identify the beginning of each new phrase, locate dynamic markings, and review legato singing.
- Still in sections, sing with solfège and hand signs or numbers, identifying and working on problem areas.
- Sing the piece through using solfège and hand signs or numbers with full ensemble.
- Divide into sections and recite the text rhythmically for each voice part.
- Sing the piece through as a full ensemble, demonstrating proper breathing and legato singing.

3. Review Sight-Singing with solfège in three parts.

Identify and practice mechanics of good breathing.

Have students:

- Review the Sight-Singing exercise on page 112, reading through each part with solfège and hand signs or numbers.
- Read all the text.
- Using the Blackline Master 11, *Breathing Checklist*, identify and practice the characteristics of good breathing.
- Read the exercise again, choosing different places to breathe.
- Decide on one good solution (either half way through, or the whole phrase) and sing, demonstrating proper breathing mechanics.
- Sing measures 5–9 of "Nightfall," first clapping every beat, then moving hand and arm in a large circular motion. Repeat with measures 12–20.
- Discuss the differences between the two performances.

 MUSIC LITERACY

To help students expand their music literacy, have them:

- Perform the basic rhythms and sight-singing.
- Review meter of C, 4/4.
- Sing long, sustained phrases with arched dynamics.
- Point to the new element—a repeat sign in the first and second endings.
- Sing I, IV, V chords. Use solfège warm-ups in three parts to tune and identify.

SC 360

Gravity, the Feather, and the Phrase

Students will discover that even a feather is affected by gravity. As it has momentum from the breath it can move upward, but it eventually is taken over by the force of gravity and falls to the ground. The musical parallel to the pull of gravity is the pull of the tonic or home tone in a key. Usually melodies end on *do* in major, or *la* in minor. Harmonic compositions usually end on the tonic chord. Have students try to write short melodies that end somewhere other than the tonic, and then have them sing the melodies to experience this aural feeling of no gravity.

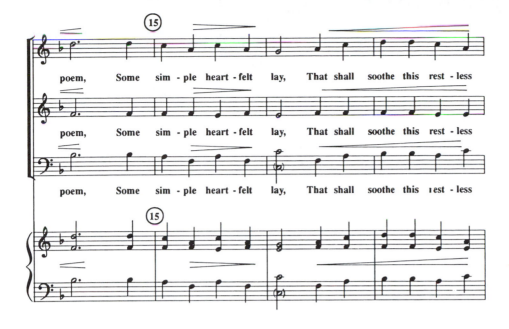

poem, Some sim-ple heart-felt lay, That shall soothe this rest - less

poem, Some sim-ple heart-felt lay, That shall soothe this rest - less

poem, Some sim-ple heart-felt lay, That shall soothe this rest - less

feel - ing And ban-ish the thoughts of day. And then the

feel - ing And ban-ish the thoughts of day. And then the

feel - ing And ban-ish the thoughts of day. And then the

SC 360

Nightfall **115**

Informal Assessment

In this lesson, students showed the ability to:

- Sing legato during the Vocal Warm-Up.
- Use proper breathing mechanics during the Sight-Singing exercise.
- Sing in legato style using proper breathing mechanics in "Nightfall."

Student Self-Assessment

Have students:

- Return to page 112 and read the How Did You Do? section.
- Answer the questions indi-vidually. Discuss them in pairs or small groups, and/ or write their responses on a sheet of paper.

Individual Performance Assessment

To further demonstrate accom-plishment, have students:

- Check a partner's breathing by using Blackline Master 11, *Breathing Checklist*.
- Sing in a trio measures 15–20, demonstrating good breathing mechanics and use of legato style.

Extension

Reviewing I, IV, and V Chords

The Vocal Warm-Up provides an opportunity for students to review the chord tones in the I, IV, and V chords. Have students identify these chord tones, writing them as block chords on the board. If resonator bells are available, distribute all bells that have pitches in the F major scale, and then have each student decide which chords contain their spe-cific pitch. Point to the chords in random order, as students play once on their chord. Create a

(continued on page 116)

SC 360

simulated legato effect by holding your finger on one chord for a sustained period. During this time, students with bells in that chord continue striking their bells gently and very quickly to attain a sustained chord. Discuss how this technique is different from legato, and why it is necessary with the bells but not with their voices.

Composing with I, IV, and V Chord Tones

Have students compose their own short melodies to sing using chord tones from the I, IV, and V chords. First decide on the meter and number of measures. Then decide which chords will be used in which measures. Finally, construct the melody using chord tones that are correct for each measure. Read and perform the song, changing it until it is satisfying to the composer.

Setting a Longfellow Poem

Have students read several of Longfellow's poems, and then choose one to arrange using a sound carpet, instruments on key words, a vocal speech piece, or a composed melody. The treatment will depend on the poem chosen, and deciding upon the appropriate treatment will be a source for exploring musical elements and discussing points of view.

Getting to Know Henry Wadsworth Longfellow

Have students research more about Henry Wadsworth Longfellow, and then write a paper describing what they have learned. Have them include several of the their favorite Longfellow poems. The student might give an oral presentation of the paper, reading the poetry interspersed with factual information.

116 *Choral Connections   Level 1 Mixed Voices*

National Standards

The following National Standards are addressed through the Extension and bottom-page activities:
4. Composing and arranging music within specified guidelines. **(a)**
8. Understanding relationships between music, the other arts, and disciplines outside the arts. **(b)**

Riu, Riu, Chiu

Anonymous Spanish Carol (1556)
ARRANGER: Linda Steen Spevacek
ENGLISH TEXT: Linda Steen Spevacek

CHORAL MUSIC TERMS
doubling
F minor
la tonal center
meter changes
3/2 meter

VOICING
| SAB

PERFORMANCE STYLE
| Rhythmically, with a lilt
| A cappella
| Optional: Tambourine and Hand Claps

FOCUS

- Read in F minor, using solfège syllables and hand signs or numbers.
- Perform correct meter changes from 2/2 to 3/2 and back.
- Use correct Spanish pronunciation.

Warming Up

Vocal Warm-Up

Sing these chord drills on *loo* to become familiar with the key of F minor. Is *do* or *la* the tonal center of each exercise below? How do you know?

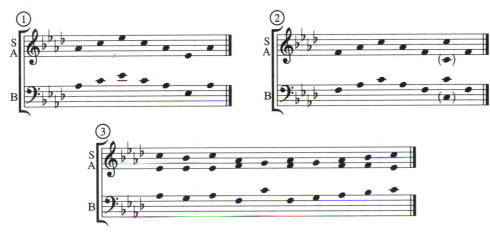

Rhythm Drill

Clap the following exercise. Notice the time change. What type of note gets one beat in 2/2 meter? Have a beat keeper play on every beat. When you get to 3/2 meter, there will be an extra beat in each measure. In 2/2 meter, every other beat is strong. In 3/2 meter every third beat is strong.

Lesson 14: Riu, Riu, Chiu **117**

TEACHER'S RESOURCE BINDER
Blackline Master 12, *Rhythm Challenge,* page 87
Blackline Master 13, *Spanish Pronunciation Guide,* page 88

National Standards
This lesson addresses:
1. Singing, alone and with others, a varied repertoire of music. **(b, c)**
5. Reading and notating music. **(c)**
6. Listening to, and analyzing, and describing music. **(c)**
7. Evaluating music and music performances. **(a, b)**
9. Understanding music in relation to history and culture. **(a)**

Riu, Riu, Chiu

Anonymous Spanish Carol
(1556)
ARRANGER and ENGLISH TEXT:
Linda Steen Spevacek

Focus

OVERVIEW
La tonal center; meter changes; Spanish language.

OBJECTIVES
After completing this lesson, students will be able to:
- Read in F minor using solfège and hand signs or numbers.
- Perform correct meter changes from 2/2 to 3/2 and back.
- Use correct Spanish pronunciation.

CHORAL MUSIC TERMS
Define the Choral Music Terms for students, giving correct pronunciation, and answering any questions that may arise.

Warming Up

Vocal Warm-Up
This Vocal Warm-Up is designed to prepare students to:
- Sing in F minor using solfège and hand signs or numbers.
- Distinguish between *do* and *la* tonal centers in A♭ major and F minor.
- Sing in tune.
Have students:
- Read through the Vocal Warm-Up directions.
- Sing, following your demonstration.

Rhythm Drill

This Rhythm Drill is designed to prepare students to:

- Read rhythms in 2/2 and 3/2 meter.
- Read parts that change meter.
- Combine lines with different entrances and rhythmic patterns.

Have students:

- Read through the Rhythm Drill directions.
- Perform the drill.

Sight-Singing

This Sight-Singing exercise is designed to prepare students to:

- Sight-sing in F minor using solfège and hand signs or numbers.
- Sing staggered entrances.
- Sing in harmony.
- Identify and describe doubling.

Have students:

- Read through the Sight-Singing exercise directions.
- Read each part rhythmically, using rhythm syllables.
- Sight-sing through each part separately.
- Sing all parts together.
- Identify the chord formed on the first beat of each measure.

Singing: "Riu, Riu, Chiu"

Identify musical change and repetition.

Have students:

- Read the text in the Singing section on this page.
- Identify the changes in the exercises (tonal center/key, meter), and predict these changes in "Riu, Riu, Chiu."
- Listen as you sing "Riu, Riu, Chiu," identifying the key as F minor, the meter changes from 2/2 to 3/2, and the repetition of the melody over and over.
- Discuss how to keep the piece musically interesting with so much repetition.

Sight-Singing

Sight-sing the parts below using solfège syllables or numbers. Sometimes pitches are doubled in a chord. Then you might only hear two pitches. Name the chords that are suggested on the first beat of each measure. What mood or feeling does this doubling give?

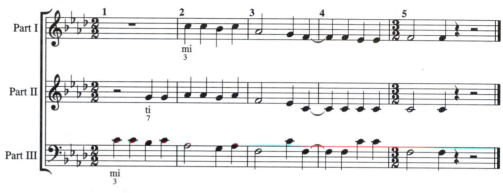

Singing: "Riu, Riu, Chiu"

Sometimes musical interest is created by change. Sometimes it can be created through repetition. Look at the three exercises you have read, and predict what types of changes you might expect in "Riu, Riu, Chiu." Listen to "Riu, Riu, Chiu" and tell how musical interest is maintained. Now turn to the music for "Riu, Riu, Chiu" on page 119.

HOW DID YOU DO?

"Riu, Riu, Chiu" has lots of repetition.
1. Tell how you kept the piece interesting.
2. Explain how the meter changes from 2/2 to 3/2 works, using the words *beat* and *strong beats*. Then sing measures 1–8 to demonstrate your understanding.
3. What is the tonal center of this piece? Choose and sing a phrase in solfège that shows the tonal center.

4. How was your Spanish pronunciation?
5. Tape record the group performing "Riu, Riu, Chiu," then write a critique describing what you heard. Tell what you liked and what could be improved.

MORE ABOUT...

"Riu, Riu, Chiu"

Why is there so much repetition? This song may have been part of the procession used during the Spanish Christmas celebration, or as a processional in the church service. Processionals are found in many cultures around the world, and usually have a strong sense of beat at a walking tempo, and lots of repetition so the group can stay together as they walk. Once the students know the piece well, plan a procession for entering a space as they sing. It could be used as a beginning or ending piece during a performance. You might want to find some other examples of processionals from other cultures.

Riu, Riu, Chiu

Anonymous Spanish Carol (1556)
Arranged by Linda Steen Spevacek
Original English text by L.S.S.

Three-part Mixed Chorus, A cappella,
and Optional Tambourine, Hand Claps, and Spanish text

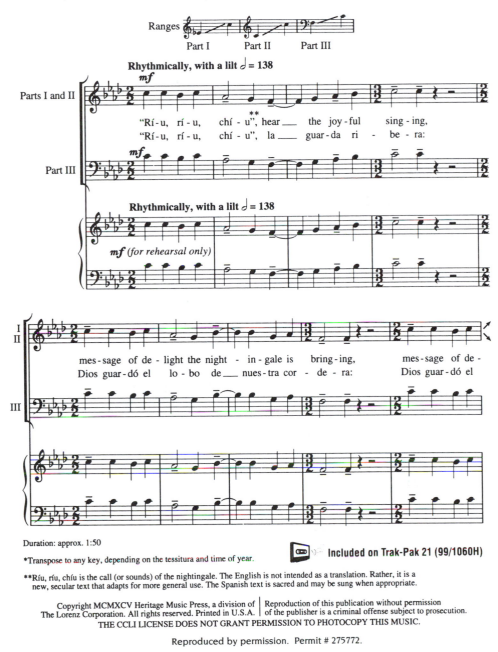

Duration: approx. 1:50

*Transpose to any key, depending on the tessitura and time of year.

**Ríu, ríu, chíu is the call (or sounds) of the nightingale. The English is not intended as a translation. Rather, it is a new, secular text that adapts for more general use. The Spanish text is sacred and may be sung when appropriate.

Included on Trak-Pak 21 (99/1060H)

Riu, Riu, Chiu **119**

Suggested Teaching Sequence

1. Review Vocal Warm-Up.
Identify F minor as a tonal center.
Have students:
- Review the Vocal Warm-Up on page 117, singing with solfège and hand signs or numbers.
- Read the question and answer for each example. (A♭ major, F minor, F minor)

2. Review the Rhythm Drill.
Identify and practice changing from 2/2 to 3/2 meter.
Have students:
- Review the Rhythm Drill on pages 117–118.
- Read the text, and then perform the exercise again with someone keeping the beat.

3. Review Sight-Singing with solfège.
Read in F minor tonal center. Identify chord tones and doubling.
Have students:
- Review the Sight-Singing exercise, reading through each part with solfège and hand signs or numbers.
- Sight-sing all three parts together.
- Read the text, and then identify the chord tones at the beginning of each measure.
- Discuss the open, folk-like quality that results from the doubling of chord tones and incomplete chords.

4. Sight-sing "Riu, Riu, Chiu" using solfège and hand signs or numbers.

Have students:

- Divide into voice (SAB) sections and read rhythmically from measures 1–56, using rhythm syllables.
- Still in sections, sing with solfège and hand signs or numbers, identifying and working on problem areas.
- Sing the piece through using solfège and hand signs or numbers with full ensemble.
- Repeat the above three steps with measures 57–116.

5. Learn Spanish lyrics.

Have students:

- Study the pronunciation guide on Blackline Master 13.
- Read the Spanish lyrics slowly.
- Read the Spanish lyrics in rhythm.
- Discuss and practice any problem areas.
- Divide into voice sections again and recite the text rhythmically for each voice part.
- Sing the piece through with text as a full ensemble.

MUSIC LITERACY

To help students expand their music literacy, have them:

- Find the mixed meters and conduct and speak the words.
- Analyze the form of the piece using lower-case letters a, b, and c to designate different sections.

Ask them: How will this exercise help you visualize the sections?

Riu, Riu, Chiu **121**

CULTURAL CONNECTIONS
Help with Spanish Lyrics

It will be very helpful for students to imitate a native Spanish speaker to learn the pronunciation of this text. If you have a Spanish teacher at your site, ask for help. Perhaps there is a Spanish-speaking parent or community member who will help. Tape record the session so the students can refer back to it. This is one way to reach out into the community and recognize community members in your school.

Informal Assessment
In this lesson, students showed the ability to:
- Identify by sight those exercises written in F minor in the Vocal Warm-Up.
- Perform meter changes from 2/2 to 3/2 in the Rhythm Drill.
- Sight-sing in F minor using solfège and hand signs or numbers in the Sight-Singing exercise, changing meters correctly.
- Speak the Spanish lyrics to "Riu, Riu, Chiu" with correct pronunciation.
- Perform "Riu, Riu, Chiu" using correct Spanish pronunciation, singing in F minor, and changing meters correctly.

Student Self-Assessment
Have students:
- Return to page 118 and read the How Did You Do? section.
- Answer the questions individually. Discuss them in pairs or small groups, and/or write their responses on a sheet of paper.

Individual Performance Assessment
To further demonstrate accomplishment, have students:
- Perform either of the exercises within a small, randomly selected group of two sopranos, two altos, and two basses.

Riu, Riu, Chiu **123**

COMMUNITY ACTION

Understanding the Text

Have students read the English lyrics out loud, and then discuss the meaning of the text in their own words. There is a challenge in the text to carry the good will and message of peace beyond this song into the world. Discuss how they might do this with words, actions, tolerance, and, also, where they might perform this song to bring its message to others. Some possibilities are to other classes within the school, elementary schools, homes for the elderly, malls, and so on. Put together a short program to spread the message of good will through song.

Remembering Other Musical Changes

Have students review "Over There," Lesson 3, to remember the many key changes. Remind students that key change is another way to add musical interest.

Riu, Riu, Chiu **125**

National Standards

The following National Standards are addressed through the Extension and bottom-page activities.

8. Understanding relationships between music, the other arts, and disciplines outside the arts. **(a)**
9. Understanding music in relation to history and culture. **(c)**

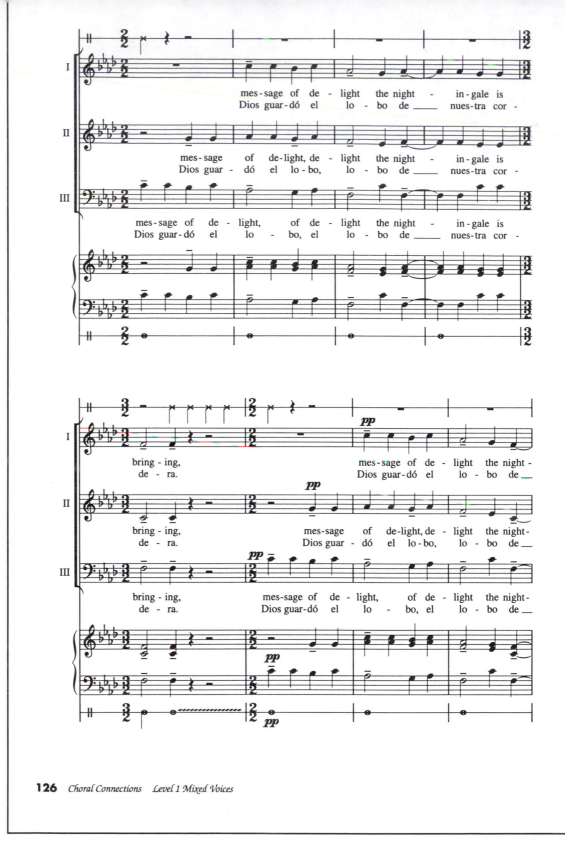

- in-gale is bring-ing.
__ nues-tra cor - de - ra.

- in-gale is bring-ing.
__ nues-tra cor - de - ra.

- in-gale is bring-ing.   Hear the song of love he sings __ to all cre -
__ nues-tra cor - de - ra.   Yo vi mil gar - ço - nes que an - da-van can -

bring-ing joy to   all at this time of cel-e-bra-tion. For the sea-son
por a - quí bo - lan-do, ha - zien-do mil __ so - nes; di - zien-do a gas -

a - tion,
tan - do,

now stands for   love and hope and   peace, __   car-ry it be - yond, nev-er
co - nes, "Glo - ria se a en el   cie - lo,   y paz en el   sue - lo ques

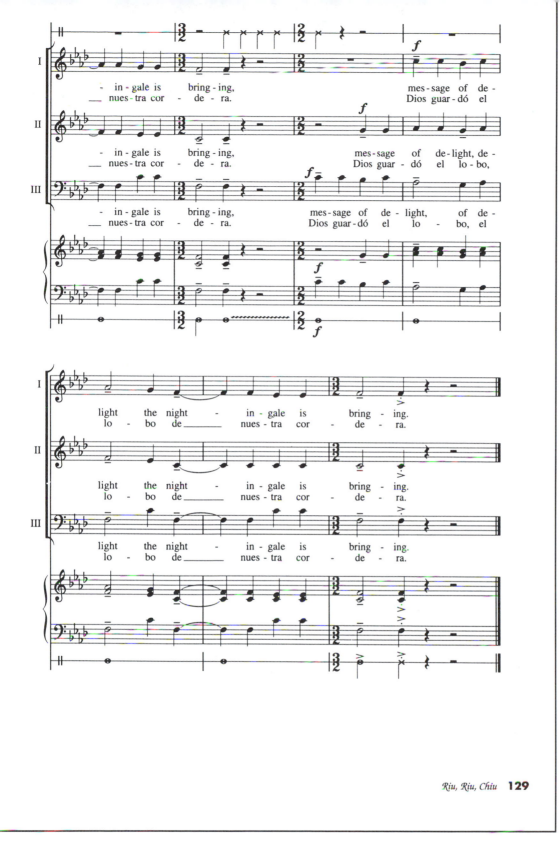

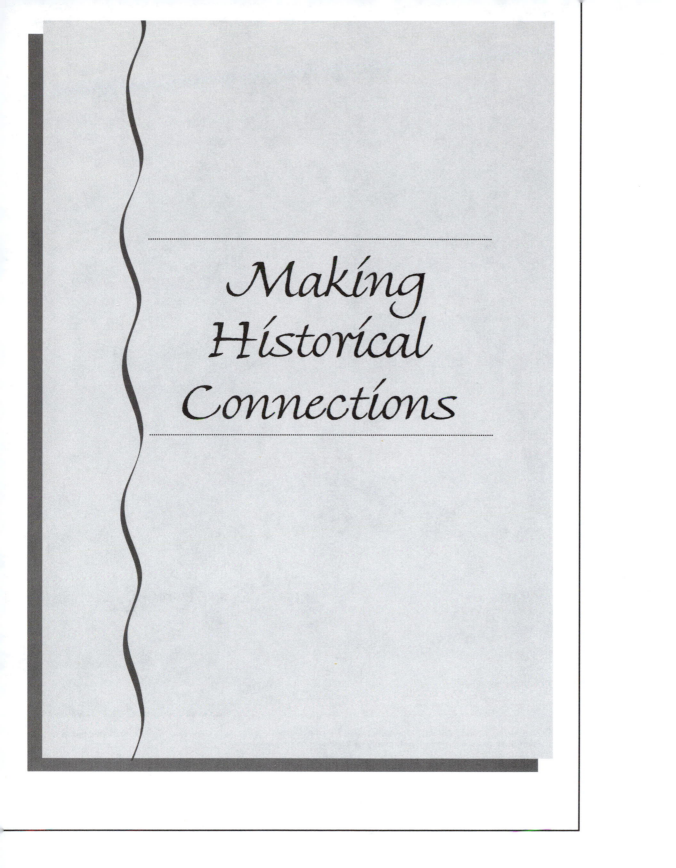

Making Historical Connections

Renaissance Period

Focus

OVERVIEW

Understanding the development of choral music during the Renaissance period.

OBJECTIVES

After completing this lesson, students will be able to:

- Describe some developments that took place during the Renaissance period.
- Describe some changes in sacred and secular music that occurred during the Renaissance period.
- Compare characteristics of the Renaissance to characteristics of today.
- Define *madrigal* and *polyphony*.

CHORAL MUSIC TERMS

Define the Choral Music Terms for students, providing correct pronunciation, and answering any questions that may arise.

Introducing the Lesson

1. Introduce the Renaissance through visual art.

Point out the art, *Madonna and Child*, by Giovanni Bellini, that appears on this page, and St. Peter's Basilica on page 134. Have students:

- Look at the works of art. Explain to students that the changes that took place in music during the Renaissance have a direct correlation to visual art. Paintings and sculpture began to reflect the humanistic, realistically proportioned, rounded

The *Madonna and Child* by Giovanni Bellini (c. 1430–1516) expresses a calm and idyllic mood. This mood is similar to the quiet, devotional quality of Renaissance religious music.

c. 1470–75. Giovanni Bellini. *Madonna and Child.* Tempera and oil on wood panel. 82 x 58 cm (32³⁄₈ x 22¾"). Kimbell Art Museum, Fort Worth, Texas.

132 *Choral Connections Level 1 Mixed Voices*

TEACHER'S RESOURCE BINDER

Fine Art Transparency 1, *Madonna and Child*, by Giovanni Bellini

National Standards

This historical lesson addresses the following National Standards:

6. Listening to, analyzing, and describing music. **(c)**
8. Understanding relationships between music, the other arts, and disciplines outside the arts. **(a, b)**
9. Understanding music in relation to history and culture. **(a, b, c)**

Renaissance Period

After completing this lesson, you will be able to:

- *Describe the developments that took place in music during the Renaissance period.*
- *Compare the differences in sacred music between the Middle Ages and the Renaissance.*
- *Define* madrigal, Renaissance, *and* polyphony.

Think of recent discoveries that have changed your life. Due to advances in technology and communications, you are living in a time of great change. Sophisticated computers and telecommunications systems affect how you receive and process information. Explorers are traveling into space and deep into the ocean. New scientific discoveries are making life better on Earth, and better *for* Earth. New art and music styles are being created. Some people say that we live in a very exciting time, because we are only now realizing the range of possibilities before us.

The Renaissance—a Time of Rebirth

The fifteenth and sixteenth centuries were a similar time in history. This period has become known as the **Renaissance,** which means *rebirth* or *renewal*. During the Renaissance period (c. 1430–1600), tremendous growth and discoveries took place. Great achievements occurred in music, art, and literature.

At the same time, explorers traveled to new continents and experienced very different cultures. Scientists such as Copernicus, Galileo, and da Vinci explored the idea that the Earth was not the center of everything, but perhaps revolved around the sun. In the early 1500s, the Protestant Reformation, led by Martin Luther, began and brought about other important developments in religion, politics, and music.

One of the most important contributions of the Renaissance, however, is attributed to Johann Gutenberg, who perfected the printing press in the mid-1400s. The invention of movable type accelerated opportunities to learn. Before that time, books were rare and expensive and had to be copied by hand. With the printing press came mass-produced books, and many more people were able to learn the arts of reading both words and music.

Looking Back

Most written music during the Middle Ages (eleventh to the fifteenth centuries) was composed for and performed in church. Many of the texts were taken mainly from the Book of Psalms

Renaissance Period **133**

COMPOSERS

Guillaume Dufay (1400–1474)
Josquin Desprez (c. 1440–1521)
William Cornysh (c. 1465–1523)
Christopher Tye (c. 1500–c. 1572)
Giovanni Pierluigi da Palestrina
   (c. 1525–1594)
Orlande de Lassus (1532–1594)
Luca Marenzio (1553–1599)
Michael Praetorius (c. 1571–1621)
Thomas Weelkes (1575–1623)

ARTISTS

Donatello (1386–1466)
Giovanni Bellini (c. 1430–1516)
Leonardo da Vinci (1452–1519)
Michelangelo (1475–1564)
Raphael (1483–1520)
Titian (c. 1488–1576)

AUTHORS

Martin Luther (1483–1546)
Sir Walter Raleigh (c. 1552–1618)
Sir Philip Sidney (1554–1586)
William Shakespeare (1564–1616)

CHORAL MUSIC TERMS

madrigal
polyphony
Renaissance
sacred music
secular music

---

images that displayed depth—very much like the ancient classical art created by Greek and Roman artists more than a thousand years previously.

2. Compare works of art.
Explain that while much of the visual art was still commissioned by the Catholic Church, secular paintings also began to appear as well. Artists throughout Europe painted portraits of royal personages, military heroes, and wealthy merchants as well as landscapes and scenes of everyday life.

Suggested Teaching Sequence

1. Examine the Renaissance.
Have students:

- Read the text on student pages 133 to 135.
- Read, discuss, and answer the questions individually, in pairs, or in small groups.
- Discuss their answers with the whole group, clarifying misunderstandings.

2. Examine the Renaissance in historical perspective.
Have students:

- Turn to the time line on pages 134–135 and read the citations.
- Discuss why these are considered important dates during the Renaissance period.
- Devise a one- or two-sentence statement that describes the Renaissance based on one of the events in the time line. (For example: The Renaissance spirit grew because of the invention of the printing press. Through this press, everyday people were exposed to new ideas, and could write their ideas down and even have them printed for wider dissemination, if they wished.)

Gutenberg press;
beginning of modern printing

c. 1435

Sistine Chapel construction begins

1473

Columbus lands in
West Indies/Americas

1492

1465
First printed music appears

1480
Sistine Chapel finished

- Devise one additional sentence that tells how this Renaissance event is related to the student's world. (For example: Today, we can read about events, people, and ideas from around the world, sent to us through newspapers, radio, television, and computer terminals.)

3. Define the musical aspects of the Renaissance.

Have students:
- Review the changes in music during the Renaissance.
- Define *madrigal* and *polyphony*.

Extension

Distinguishing Between Sacred and Secular Music

To help students distinguish between sacred and secular music, have them brainstorm a one-sentence definition for each. (For example: Sacred music is music that is used to glorify God and is usually performed in a church or for church-related activities. Secular music has nonreligious text, and is performed in settings outside of church for many purposes, including work songs, celebration songs, sharing experiences, telling stories, or just enjoyment. Have students:

- Make a list of five times or places in our present day where they could hear secular music. (radio, television, concerts, musical plays, CDs or tapes)
- List five times or places they could hear sacred music. (radio, television, live performances, CDs or tapes, church or temple)

in the Old Testament of the Bible. The music was chanted in unison in Latin, with accompaniment. This musical form is called Gregorian chant, and it marks the beginning of Western art music. Many of these chants, as well as popular folk melodies, became the basis for two-, three-, or four-part compositions. Since the voices used were of equal ranges and vocal quality, the sound of vocal groups during the Middle Ages lacked a full choral range. During the Middle Ages, however, scales, solfège, and the beginnings of musical notation were developed.

▲ The artists and architects of the Renaissance rediscovered classical antiquity and were inspired by what they found. In 1547, Michelangelo (1475–1564) became chief architect for the replacement of the original basilica of Old St. Peter's. Architect Giacomo della Porta finished the dome 26 years after Michelangelo's death.

1546–64. Michelangelo. Exterior view, St. Peter's. St. Peter's Basilica, Vatican State, Rome, Italy. (Dome completed by Giacomo della Porta, 1590.)

Music and Art

The Renaissance was a time when scholars and artists became interested in the study of Greek and Roman art, architecture, and philosophy. The major artists of the period, such as Leonardo da Vinci, Raphael, Titian, Michelangelo, Bellini, and Donatello began to capture the new feeling of individuality and human achievement that was emerging. You will notice that their art celebrates the lifelike and realistic appearance of the individual.

New art and music styles emerged. **Sacred music,** or *hymns, chorales,* and *early masses,* also changed. Eventually, the equal-voice quality of the music of the Middle Ages developed into the full choral range of the present-day choir. Imitative forms continued to develop, with more and more independence of parts. Now the music could be printed, distributed, and read. Instruments such as organs, strings (lute and viol), and winds (recorder, shawm) began to be used with voices in processions and other ceremonies. Martin Luther believed that languages other than Latin were suitable for worship, so he translated the Bible into German. He then composed hymns in German so everyone could sing parts of the church services.

134 *Choral Connections   Level 1 Mixed Voices*

Magellan begins voyage around the world | 1519   Composer William Byrd born | 1543

1517
Protestant Reformation begins in Germany with Luther's 95 Theses

1584
Sir Walter Raleigh discovers Virginia

1522
Magellan's crew ends voyage around the world

of the church services.

Secular music, *any music that is not sacred,* also flourished during the Renaissance. For the first time in history, musicians traveled throughout Europe, bringing new styles from one country to another. Popular songs and madrigals were common and were frequently fused to create even newer styles. A **madrigal** is *a secular vocal form written in several imitative parts.* Each part is equally important, and the parts weave together to form polyphony. **Polyphony** means that *each voice part begins at a different place, is independent and important, and sections often repeat in contrasting dynamic levels* (poly—many, phony—sounds).

Choral music became more and more complex. Because more people were reading and singing composed songs, the range and depth of expression expanded. While polyphony existed during the Middle Ages, it was developed during the Renaissance, causing this period to frequently be called "the golden age of polyphony." People sang polyphony in church, at home, and for celebrations.

A Modern Renaissance

You also live in an age of great change, combined with tremendous possibilities. This time could be compared to that of the Renaissance. Perhaps your creativity and imagination will inspire you to be one of the new explorers, inventors, artists, or musicians who will discover new ways to look at the world.

Check Your Understanding

Recall

1. Describe some of the nonmusical changes that occurred during the Renaissance.

2. How did sacred music change from the Middle Ages to the Renaissance?

3. How did secular music change during the Renaissance?

4. Define a madrigal.

5. Describe polyphony.

Thinking It Through

1. Compare the influence of the printing press during the Renaissance to the development of the computer today. What modern changes are similar to the changes that occurred during the Renaissance?

2. What new skills did people need to learn in order to participate in music

Renaissance Period **135**

ANSWERS TO RECALL QUESTIONS

1. Answers may include the printing press and movable type.
2. Full choral range imitative forms were developed, instruments were used with voices in ceremonies, and hymns were composed in languages other than Latin.
3. Musicians traveled, new styles were invented, choral music became more complex.
4. A secular vocal form written in several imitative parts.
5. Each voice part begins at a different place, is independent and important, and sections often repeat in contrasting dynamic style.

Assessment

Informal Assessment

During this lesson, students showed ability to:
- Identify characteristics of the Renaissance period and music of the Renaissance.
- Describe significant events of the Renaissance period.
- Compare the Renaissance period to today's world.
- Define *madrigal* and *polyphony*.

Student Self-Assessment

Have students:
- Review the questions in Checking Your Understanding.
- Write a paragraph describing what they understand about the development of music during the Renaissance.

Individual Performance Assessment

To further demonstrate accomplishment, have students:
- Learn more about one aspect of music during the Renaissance period.
- Share their findings with the class in a creative way, such as a poster, demonstration, design for the cover of a CD or video, and so on.

RENAISSANCE CONNECTIONS

Listening to...
Renaissance Music

This feature is designed to expand students' appreciation of choral and instrumental music of the Renaissance period.

Choral Selection: "Cantate Ninfe" by Marenzio

Have students:

- Read this page to learn more about "Cantate Ninfe."
- Study the Blackline Master, Listening Map 1.

Using the Listening Map

Start in the upper left-hand corner and follow the melodic lines. Note that parts often begin phrases independently and end singing all together. Parts sung independently are represented by lines, and parts sung together are represented by stacked circles or dots.

Have students:

- Read the English translation of "Cantate Ninfe" and predict which words might be treated in a special way.
- Follow their listening map as you show how the music reinforces the meaning of the text. For example, high voices are used for "laughing cupid," chordal singing is used at "everyone," and smooth lines are used at "grace" and "beautiful." Tell students that this technique is called text painting.
- Listen as you play the first phrase or two from the CD, and identify, along with you, where the singers are performing independently and where the voices end phrases singing together.
- Listen to "Cantate Ninfe" and follow their listening map.

Listening to...
Renaissance Music

CHORAL SELECTION

Marenzio — "Cantate Ninfe"

Luca Marenzio (1553–1599) composed "Cantate Ninfe," a light and airy piece that is a worthy representative of Renaissance music. In this composition, Marenzio's use of "text painting" coupled with independent parts moving to chords and cadences create a texture typical of Renaissance music. "Cantate Ninfe" provides a reliable example of music that comes from the period in history in which Europe transitioned from the Middle Ages to more modern classical and humanistic concepts.

INSTRUMENTAL SELECTION

Anonymous — "Saltarello"

The word *saltarello* is a broad term for swift Italian folk dances. These dances involve jumping and are usually in triple meter. Generally, a saltarello consists of several repeated melodies with each melody having a different ending. The origin of these dances is unknown, but the earliest recorded use of saltarello as a musical term is in the late fourteenth and early fifteenth centuries. Saltarellos were popular throughout several different musical periods because of their authentic folk-dance quality.

TEACHER'S RESOURCE BINDER
Blackline Master, Listening Map 1
Blackline Master, Listening Map 2

Optional Listening Selections:
The Norton Recordings, 7th edition
"Cantate Ninfe": Vol. I, CD 1, Track 44
"Saltarello": Vol. I, CD 1, Track 21

National Standards
This lesson addresses the following National Standard:
6. Listening to, analyzing, and describing music. **(b)**

Introducing...
"Kyrie Eleison"

Antonio Lotti

Setting the Stage

Translated to mean "Lord, have mercy upon us," the "Kyrie Eleison" is customarily the first prayer of the Ordinary of the Mass. It is suitable for both church and concert use. Its polyphonic textures and imitative melodies are a perfect example of Renaissance religious music, as well as many other forms of the time. The time signature and bar lines would not have been written during this time period, therefore they are additions to the music. This rendition includes both the Greek text and the English translation. Let this piece transport you back to a time long ago.

Meeting the Composer
Antonio Lotti (c. 1667–1740)

Antonio Lotti began his musical career as a singer in a Venetian choir and later became the lead organist. Lotti's opera career began to flourish in 1692 when his work Il Trionfo dell' Innocenza was performed in Venice. It wasn't until between 1706–1717, however, that Lotti became the most productive in composing operas, when at least 16 of his original works were staged. Lotti's works were usually composed in the style of the late Baroque period, but he also would sometimes follow the contrapuntal style of the Renaissance composer, Palestrina.

Instrumental Selection: "Saltarello"
Have students:
- Read the information on page 136 to learn more about "Saltarello."
- Study the Blackline Master, Listening Map 2.

Using the Listening Map
Begin at section A on the pick-up. You may follow the beat (arrows) or the melody line (icons). Be careful—this piece is fast!
Have students:
- Identify the arrow as the strong beat symbol.
- Brainstorm ways to show varying phrase lengths. (See the directions on your listening map for color-coding the listening map.)
- Prepare to listen for how the music changes slightly as preformers begin to improvise on the first themes, just as jazz artists might add more trills. Discuss how the music invites dance and movement.
- Listen to "Saltarello" as they follow their listening map.

INTRODUCING . . . "Kyrie Eleison"
This feature is designed to introduce students to the Renaissance Lesson on the following pages.
Have students:
- Read Setting the Stage on this page to learn more about "Kyrie Eleison."
- Read Meeting the Composer to learn more about Antonio Lotti.
- Turn the page and begin the Renaissance Lesson.

ASSESSMENT
Individual Performance Assessment

To further demonstrate understanding of Renaissance music, have students:
- In small groups, develop lists of adjectives that describe the texture and melody of "Cantate Ninfe." (light, energetic, moving) Discuss how they would perform this music to successfully convey these descriptions. (singing lightly, tuning carefully at cadence points)

- In small groups, develop lists of adjectives that describe the melody, tempo, instrumentation, and form of "Saltarello." (jumpy melody, energetic tempo, unusual instruments, rondo form). Have them suggest ways that contemporary performers make their music inviting to dance and movement. (driving beat, syncopated rhythms)

Kyrie Eleison

COMPOSER: Antonio Lotti
(c. 1667–1740)

Focus

OVERVIEW
Polyphonic singing; part independence; Greek pronunciation.

OBJECTIVES
After completing this lesson, students will be able to:
- Sing voice parts independently.
- Visually identify polyphonic textures.
- Demonstrate correct Greek pronunciation.

CHORAL MUSIC TERMS
Define the Choral Music Terms for students, providing correct pronunciation, and answering any questions that may arise.

Warming Up

Vocal Warm-Up
This Vocal Warm-Up is designed to prepare students to:
- Listen and tune when singing in octavos.
- Build an understanding of the cut-time symbol (¢).
- Sing on neutral syllables, internalizing the solfège.

Have students:
- Read through the Vocal Warm-Up directions.
- Sing, following your demonstration.

Kyrie Eleison

COMPOSER: Antonio Lotti (c. 1667–1740)

CHORAL MUSIC TERMS
contrapuntal
cut-time meter (symbol)
Kyrie Eleison
Picardy third

VOICING
SATB

PERFORMANCE STYLE
Prayerfully
A cappella

FOCUS
- Sing your voice part independently.
- Identify polyphonic textures.
- Demonstrate knowledge of correct Greek pronunciation.

Warming Up

Vocal Warm-Up
Sing the following scales in unison. Sing each scale on whole notes, then half notes, then quarter notes.

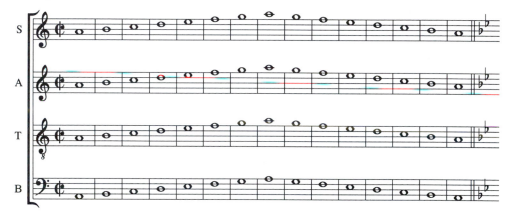

Sight-Singing
Sight-sing these parts using solfège syllables or numbers. Notice the meter signature. It tells you to sing in "cut time," or cut each note value in half. Instead of reading 4/4, you will read 2/2. Each half note gets one beat, and there are two beats in a measure. Count your rests carefully. Can you tell the difference between the parts at the beginning and end of this exercise? Where is there imitative style in this exercise? Where are there chords? What effect does the C♯ have on the last chord?

TEACHER'S RESOURCE BINDER
Blackline Master 14, *Breathing Checklist,* page 90
Blackline Master 19, *Performance Evaluation Rubric,* page 95

National Standards
This lesson addresses the following National Standards:
5. Reading and notating music. **(a, c)**
6. Listening to, analyzing, and describing music. **(b, c)**
7. Evaluating music and music performances. **(b)**
9. Understanding music in relation to history and culture. **(a, b)**

Singing: "Kyrie Eleison"

Can you "row" in two keys?

You know how to sing rounds. Rounds are an example of imitative style. Each part imitates the one before it exactly. The overlapping parts form chords.

What happens when you sing a round in two different keys?

Sing "Row, Row, Row Your Boat" as a round in A major, then A minor. Altos and basses sing the song in D minor.

Sing it as a round: sopranos and tenors in A minor, altos and basses in D minor.

Now turn to the music for "Kyrie Eleison" on page 140.

HOW DID YOU DO? ❓	Think about your performance on the Vocal Warm-Up and "Kyrie Eleison." **1.** How does this relate to the beginning of "Kyrie Eleison"? **2.** Could you sing your part independently? **3.** Could you identify the polyphonic	textures when you heard or saw them? **4.** How was your Greek pronunciation? **5.** What characteristics of Renaissance music did you experience in this piece? **6.** Describe one thing you liked about this piece.

Sight-Singing

This Sight-Reading exercise is designed to prepare students to:

- Visually identify and hear staggered entrances.
- Hear imitative melodies.
- Listen to and sing harmonic and textural sounds of the Renaissance.

Have students:

- Read through the Sight-Singing exercise directions.
- Read each voice part rhythmically, using rhythm syllables.
- Sight-sing each part separately.
- Sing all parts together.

Singing: "Kyrie Eleison"

Introduce round singing in two keys.

Have students:

- Read the text in the Singing section on student page 139.
- Follow the directions as they sing the round in canon first in A major, then A minor.
- Altos and basses sing the song in D minor.
- Sing as a canon, sopranos and tenors as Part I in A minor, altos and basses as Part II in D minor.
- Discuss how different this canon sounds, and whether it was difficult.
- Compare this activity to the first page of "Kyrie Eleison," visually identifying the staggered entrances that show imitative style.

Suggested Teaching Sequence

1. Introduce polyphony.

Have students:

- Recall the definition of *polyphony* from the Renaissance lesson on page 135, or read the definition from the board.
- Discuss whether the Sight-Singing activity created polyphony. (yes)
- Find places where the voices enter separately in "Kyrie Eleison." (measures 1, 2, 36, and 37)
- Find places where the voice parts are all together but do not sing the same words or rhythms. (measures 9, 27, and 39)

2. Review Vocal Warm-Up.

Identify cut time meter.

Have students:

- Review the Vocal Warm-Up on page 138.
- Identify the meter signature as "cut time," and sing again.
- Look at "Kyrie Eleison" to find the same meter signature.
- Sing the exercise on neutral syllables, thinking the solfège.

3. Review Sight-Singing.

Identify staggered entrances.

Have students:

- Review the Sight-Singing exercise on pages 138–139, reading through each part with solfège and hand signs or numbers.
- Sight-sing all four parts together.
- Identify the difference between the first and second halves of the exercise. (staggered entrances, chordal movement)

Kyrie Eleison
(Lord, Have Mercy Upon Us)

Antonio Lotti

Mixed Chorus, SATB, A cappella

From the Liturgy

Antonio Lotti

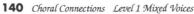

Bel. Oct. 2204 © BELWIN, Inc., 1968, All Rights Reserved Printed in U.S.A. c/o CPP/BELWIN, INC., Miami, Florida 33014

140 *Choral Connections Level 1 Mixed Voices*

Bel.Oct.2204

Kyrie Eleison **141**

4. Learn the Greek pronunciation.

Have students:
- Read the Greek lyrics slowly.
- Speak the Greek lyrics in rhythm.
- Practice problem areas.

5. Sight-sing "Kyrie Eleison."

Have students:
- Divide into voice sections (SATB) and read each part rhythmically, using rhythm syllables and patting the steady beats as they read.
- Read the rhythms as a full ensemble.
- Again in sections, sing their parts using solfège and hand signs or numbers.
- Sing the piece through as a full ensemble.
- Discuss problem areas, working on accurate, secure pitches, correct rhythm at entrances, and any other necessary spots.
- Make a tape of a performance of "Kyrie Eleison."

Performance Tips

This piece should be done in the first part of a concert. Students should be encouraged to use very little vibrato so that it agrees with the style of the period. The phrasing in the musical lines of each part and syllabic stress in the Greek text are very important.

Networking with Your Community

Many towns and cities have performing groups that specialize in Renaissance or early music. They may be vocal groups such as madrigal singers, or instrumental groups such as recorder ensembles or early music ensembles. There may also be dance groups that perform early round dances, Morris dances, or English country dances, including Maypole dances. Groups sometimes are connected with a high school, local college or university, church or local arts council.

Some locations have a Renaissance Festival that is held during the spring and fall. Making a few phone calls and reviewing the events in the newspaper might help you locate a group that would come and perform for your students, giving them a live performance of Renaissance music.

Assessment

Informal Assessment

In this lesson, students showed the ability to:

- Visually identify staggered entrances in the Vocal Warm-Up and "Kyrie Eleison."
- Read staggered entrances in the Sight-Singing exercise.
- Read the Greek text of "Kyrie Eleison."
- Sing staggered entrances, sing parts independently and use correct Greek pronunciation in "Kyrie Eleison."

Student Self-Assessment

Have students:

- Read the How Did You Do? section at the bottom of student page 139.
- Answer the questions individually. Discuss them in pairs or small groups, and/or write their responses on a sheet of paper.

Individual Performance Assessment

To further demonstrate accomplishment, have students:

- Sing their voice parts independently in quartets, graded by the class (on Blackline Master 19, *Performance Evaluation Rubric*) as they perform measures 36 to the end, demonstrating accurate pitches and rhythms.
- Listen and identify polyphonic textures on the audio tape of "Kyrie Eleison" by raising a hand each time a voice part enters.
- Recite the Greek text from measures 1–35 with correct syllabic stress into a tape recorder located in a quiet place. (for example, a practice room)

Bel.Oct.2204

142 *Choral Connections   Level 1 Mixed Voices*

MUSIC LITERACY

To help students expand their music literacy, have them:

- Review the use of alla breve in slow tempo. Conduct and speak the words in rhythm.
- Identify the polyphonic voices and entrances.
- Look for points of imitation and canon.
- Tune up the chromatically altered notes.

Tune carefully when they get to the end. Ask them: Does the movement have a major or minor feel to it? Why didn't the composer include the sharps and flats in the key signature? Compare the tonality of the final chord to the tonal feeling of the entire piece. (The Kyrie ends on a Picardy third. This is a raised third on the final chord in a minor mode piece.)

Bel.Oct.2204

Kyrie Eleison **143**

Creating a New Arrangement

After learning about the Renaissance period and learning "Kyrie Eleison," some students might be interested in arranging the piece by adding unpitched instruments, or playing it on other instruments. Have them research what would be appropriate if they want to do a historically correct rendition. They might also imagine the melody as it might be set today, and apply some of today's compositional techniques.

 VOCAL DEVELOPMENT

Tell students you would like to do a quick experiment. Ask for three volunteers to sing the Greek lyrics with incorrect pronunciation. Have them decide, as a group, the way they will mispronounce the words. Then have all students:

- Sing and listen to the difference in tone and resonance when the volunteer singers alter the pronunciation of the unified *Kyrie*. This points to the importance of pronunciation and singing identical vowel sounds. (You may wish to tape this experiment and a successful rehearsal of this piece and play back the comparisons. The difference should be quite dramatic.)

Have students:

- Think of breath support for the long phrases. The expressive nature of music is affected by the breath moving the music forward with intensity.

National Standards

The following National Standards are addressed through the Extension and bottom-page activities:

2. Performing on instruments, alone and with others, a varied repertoire of music. **(c)**
6. Listening to, analyzing, and describing music. **(b)**
9. Understanding music in relation to history and culture. **(a)**

Baroque Period

Focus

OVERVIEW
Understanding the development of choral music during the Baroque period.

OBJECTIVES
After completing this lesson, students will be able to:
- Describe some developments that took place during the Baroque period.
- Identify some forms and characteristics of Baroque instrumental and vocal music.
- Compare characteristics of Baroque art, architecture, and music.
- Define *cantata, continuo, opera,* and *oratorio.*

CHORAL MUSIC TERMS
Define the Choral Music Terms for students, providing correct pronunciation, and answering any questions that may arise.

Introducing the Lesson

Introduce the Baroque period through visual art.
Have students:
- Look at the artwork on this page, and the architecture illustration, page 146, and note any characteristics that could be described as elaborate or ornamental.

The dramatization observed in this sculpture, *The Ecstasy of St. Teresa* by Gianlorenzo Bernini (1598–1680), demonstrates the Baroque quest for expression and movement. Here the saint floats in space as she receives a vision of heaven. Such drama, movement, and tension are also qualities prominent in the music of the period.

1645–52. Gianlorenzo Bernini. *The Ecstasy of St. Teresa.* Marble. Life-size. Cornaro Chapel, Santa Maria della Vittoria, Rome, Italy.

144 *Choral Connections   Level 1 Mixed Voices*

TEACHER'S RESOURCE BINDER
Fine Art Transparency 2, *The Ecstasy of St. Teresa,* by Gianlorenzo Bernini

National Standards
This lesson addresses:
3. Improvising melodies, variations, and accompaniments. **(b)**
6. Listening to, analyzing, and describing music. **(c)**
8. Understanding relationships between music, the other arts, and disciplines outside the arts. **(a, b)**
9. Understanding music in relation to history and culture. **(a, b, c)**

Baroque Period

After completing this lesson, you will be able to:

- Describe some developments that took place during the Baroque period.
- Identify some forms and characteristics of Baroque instrumental and vocal music.
- Compare characteristics of Baroque art, architecture, and music.
- Define oratorio, cantata, and opera.

Imagine a plain, brick, rectangular building. Notice the plain door and windows. Now begin to create elaboration on the features of this building. Imagine a fancier door, decoration around the door, and ornate columns. Imagine tile work and mosaic patterns over the brick, creating a fancy exterior. Now go through the front door into the hallway to see the gold woodwork, high domed ceilings, and paintings covering the walls and ceilings. You are imagining a building from the **Baroque period** (1600–1750)—*the period of elaboration.* (**Baroque** comes from an Italian word meaning *rocky, irregular.*)

The Baroque Period—a Time of Elaboration

The Baroque period in music developed around 1600. It reached its height and ended with the death of Johann Sebastian Bach in 1750. During this period, Baroque artists and musicians had a style that characteristically had dramatic flair and dynamic movement. The *music became so elaborate toward the end of this period* (*mid-1700s*) that it was termed **Rococo**.

Looking Back

The Renaissance was a period of change, during which there was an increased interest and involvement in cultural activities. The invention of the printing press created a society in which reading and writing were more widely known, and ideas began to be easily shared. Sacred music was written with the increased involvement of everyday people, and secular music began to emerge with strong melody lines.

Music of the Baroque

During the Baroque period, there was a strong desire to classify and assimilate all knowledge. The strength of the individual's spirit and will shaped a very emotional sense of splendor in the arts.

COMPOSERS

Claudio Monteverdi (1567–1643)
Arcangelo Corelli (1643–1713)
Henry Purcell (1659–1695)
Antonio Vivaldi (1678–1741)
Johann Sebastian Bach (1685–1750)
George Frideric Handel (1685–1759)

ARTISTS

El Greco (1541–1614)
Peter Paul Rubens (1577–1640)
Artemisia Gentileschi (1593–1653)
Gianlorenzo Bernini (1598–1680)
Rembrandt van Rijn (1606–1669)
Judith Leyster (1609–1660)

AUTHORS

John Donne (c.1573–1631)
Rene Descartes (1596–1650)
John Milton (1608–1674)
Molière (1622–1673)

CHORAL MUSIC TERMS

Baroque period
cantata
continuo
elaboration
improvised
opera
oratorio
Rococo

Suggested Teaching Sequence

1. Examine the Baroque period.

Have students:

- Read the text on student pages 145–147.
- Read, discuss, and answer the questions in Check Your Understanding, student page 147. They may work individually, in pairs, or in small groups.
- Discuss their answers with the whole group, clarifying misunderstandings.

2. Examine the Baroque period in historical perspective.

Have students:

- Turn to the time line on page 146–147 and read the citations.
- Discuss why these are considered important dates during the Baroque period.
- Compare each of these events to what occurred before and after the Baroque period.

3. Define the musical aspects of the Baroque period.

Have students:

- Review the characteristics of music during the Baroque period.
- Define *cantata, continuo, opera,* and *oratorio.*

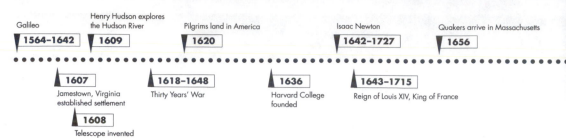

Galileo 1564–1642
Henry Hudson explores the Hudson River 1609
Pilgrims land in America 1620
Isaac Newton 1642–1727
Quakers arrive in Massachusetts 1656

1607 Jamestown, Virginia established settlement
1618–1648 Thirty Years' War
1636 Harvard College founded
1643–1715 Reign of Louis XIV, King of France
1608 Telescope invented

Experimenting with Elaboration

To further explore the concept of elaboration through hands-on activity, have the students sing a scale upward from *do* to *do*. (Write it on the board in whole notes if you wish.) Discuss ways to elaborate upon this scale. Some possibilities are:

- Rhythmically, choose a rhythm pattern and sing each pitch through the pattern.
- Rhythmically, sing each pitch for four beats, improvising different rhythms for each measure.
- Melodically, sing each pitch, then the pitches below and above before moving on.
- Melodically, sing each pitch, then sing two pitches downward and two pitches upward stepwise before moving on. (*do-ti-la, la-ti-do,* and so on)
- Melodically, sing each three pitches upward then begin again one step higher (*do-re mi, re-mi-fa, mi-fa-so,* and so on)
- Think about ways to elaborate harmonically, building chords on each step before moving on.
- Think about articulation (staccato or legato), dynamics (loud or soft), tempo (slow or fast), and form (repetition and contrast).

After brainstorming possibilities, have students form small groups, and then compose short pieces based on the ornamented scale.

The music of the Baroque period reflected the elaborate attitudes of society. Compositions had a strong sense of movement, many times with a *continually moving bass line,* called **continuo.** Melodies were highly ornamental, and more ornamentations were often **improvised,** *invented on the spur of the moment,* during performances. Underneath all the fancy elaboration, however, remained the clear, classical, mathematically precise forms and thinking symbolized by the plain, brick rectangular building you imagined earlier in the example on page 145. The sense of symmetry and planning is clear in the music of the Baroque.

Instrumental Forms

The Baroque period brought about a great interest in instrumental music. Keyboard instruments were refined and elaborated upon, including the clavichord, harpsichord, and organ. The modern string family was dominant, and the trumpet was a favorite melody instrument in the orchestras of the day.

Many new forms of music were developed during the Baroque period. The *suite* usually consisted of several movements, sometimes specific dance rhythms,

▲ **The Baroque period, the period of elaboration, is evident in the detailed exterior of the Palace at Versailles. In 1661, France's King Louis XIV ordered architects to build him the largest, most elaborate palace in the world.**

1682. Louis Le Vau and Jules Hardoin-Mansart. The Cour d'honneur of the Castle at Versailles. Chateau, Versailles, France.

Johann Sebastian Bach		First American newspaper established, *Boston News Letter*		Handel comes to England
1685–1750		**1704**		**1710**

1682
LaSalle explores the Mississippi

1685–1759
George Frideric Handel

1706–1790
Benjamin Franklin

1687
Publication of Newton's *Mathematical Principles*

of contrasting tempos and styles. The *concerto grosso* was a form with several movements composed for a small chamber orchestra. The concerto grosso also contrasted a small musical group with the full orchestra. The pieces featured great clarity of parts, with a moving bass line and elaborate melody.

Vocal and Mixed Forms

Opera was born during the Baroque period, and is considered one of the most important vocal developments of the time. **Opera** is *a combination of singing, instrumental music, dancing, and drama that tells a story*. It was stylized and theatrical, and had effects for their own sakes—all characteristics of Baroque art.

The **oratorio,** *a piece for solo voices, chorus, and orchestra, was an expanded dramatic work on a literary or religious theme presented without theatrical action*. One of the most famous oratorios is George Frideric Handel's *Messiah*, composed in 1741. This piece contains the famous "Hallelujah Chorus."

Another vocal form was the **cantata,** *a collection of vocal compositions with instrumental accompaniment consisting of several movements based on related secular or sacred text segments*. Movements alternated among chorus, solo, duet, and/or trio.

Baroque music is often performed today by orchestras, choirs, and smaller instrumental and vocal ensembles, both in sacred and secular settings. You might explore your community for places where Baroque music is performed.

Check Your Understanding

Recall

1. Describe some major characteristics of the Baroque period, reflected in its music and art.

2. Describe instrumental music during the Baroque period by identifying both popular instruments and some instrumental forms that were composed.

3. Identify three vocal music forms of the Baroque period.

4. Describe an oratorio, and name a famous Baroque oratorio. Who composed it?

Thinking It Through

1. Compare Renaissance and Baroque music by explaining the similarities and differences between both styles.

2. What characteristics of the Baroque period explain why people of this period enjoyed opera? Why do people in today's society still enjoy Baroque operas?

Baroque Period **147**

Assessment

Informal Assessment
During this lesson, students showed ability to:
- Identify characteristics of the Baroque period and music of the Baroque period.
- Describe the impact of the events of the Baroque period.
- Compare the Baroque period to today's world.
- Define *cantata, continuo, opera,* and *oratorio.*

Student Self-Assessment
Have students:
- Review the questions in Checking Your Understanding.
- Write a paragraph describing how much they understand about the Baroque period.

Individual Performance Assessment
To further demonstrate accomplishment, have students:
- Learn more about one aspect of music during the Baroque period.
- Share their findings with the class in a creative way, such as a poster, demonstration, design for the cover of a CD or video, and so on.

ANSWERS TO RECALL QUESTIONS
1. Elaborate decorations, dramatic flair, and dynamic movement.
2. Use of clavichord, harpsichord, organ, and trumpet; development of the suite and concerto grosso.
3. Opera, oratorio, and cantata.
4. A piece for solo voices, chorus, and orchestra; Handel's *Messiah*.

Listening to . . .
Baroque Music

This feature is designed to expand students' appreciation of choral and instrumental music of the Baroque period.

Choral Selection:
"A Mighty Fortress is Our God" by Bach
Have students:

- Read the information on this page to learn more about "A Mighty Fortress is Our God."
- Study the Blackline Master, Listening Map 3.

Using the Listening Map
Start at the top of the page and follow the words. Notice how all four vocal parts and continuo move together. Each chord bar represents one beat.
Have students:

- Identify the four voice parts and bass continuo featured in the chorale.
- Discover that all five parts move together in chords.
- Note that the rhythm for each voice part is indicated in the chord bars.
- Listen as you define a *chorale.* (a hymn tune sung to a German religious text)
- Listen as you describe a church *cantata* from Bach's era. (a work composed for chorus, vocal soloists, organ, and small orchestra whose religious text was meant to reinforce a religious sermon)
- Listen as you define a *cadence.* (a harmonic progression that signals the end of a musical phrase or section) Notice that cadences on the listening map are indicated with a fermata.
- Listen to "A Mighty Fortress is Our God" and follow the listening map, signaling the cadences.

Listening to . . .
Baroque Music

CHORAL SELECTION

Bach — Cantata No. 80 "A Mighty Fortress Is Our God" No. 8

Johann Sebastian Bach (1685–1750) was a devout man of the Lutheran faith. The Lutheran hymn tunes, known as chorales, figured prominently in much of his sacred music. During his time as church organist, Bach wrote more than 140 chorales for organ. His chorale prelude on "A Mighty Fortress Is Our God," composed in 1709 in Weimar, is an extended elaboration on the tune by Martin Luther.

INSTRUMENTAL SELECTION

Bach — *Brandenburg* Concerto No. 2, First Movement

The Brandenburg Concertos were dedicated to the Margrave of Brandenburg in 1721 by Bach, who was in the service of Prince Leopold at the time. The Prince actually played in the court orchestra that Bach conducted. The *concerto grosso* was one of the prominent forms in the eighteenth century. This form revolved around the contrast between a small group of instruments and a larger group of instruments. In *Brandenburg* Concerto No. 2, the small group called a *concertino* included violin, oboe, trumpet, and recorder and the large group or *ripieno* included strings and continuo played by the cello. Sometimes the concertino played by themselves and sometimes they played with the orchestra.

TEACHER'S RESOURCE BINDER
Blackline Master, Listening Map 3
Blackline Master, Listening Map 4
Optional Listening Selections:
The Norton Recordings, 7th edition
"A Mighty Fortress is Our God": Vol. I,
    CD 2, Track 49
Brandenburg Concerto No. 2: Vol. I,
    CD 2, Track 31

National Standards
This lesson addresses the following National Standard:
6. Listening to, analyzing, and describing music. **(a)**

BAROQUE CONNECTIONS

Introducing...

"Alleluia"

Johann Sebastian Bach

Setting the Stage

"Alleluia" is a German chorale written as a hymn with simple rhythms and an unchanging tempo. The texture is homophonic in style and is written above a magnificently ornamented accompaniment This chorale is taken from the Christmas cantata, "For Us a Child Is Born."

Meeting the Composer

Johann Sebastian Bach (1685–1750)

Johann Sebastian Bach, the youngest of eleven children, was born in Eisenach, Germany, in 1685. He is known as one of the greatest composers in Western musical history. When he was nine years old, his parents died and Bach went to live with his brother, Johann Christoph, who was an organist. There he learned the fundamentals of keyboard with his brother and studied composition on his own until 1700.

As an organist and choirmaster for Lutheran churches near his birthplace, Bach devoted his life to composing music for the church service. He wrote wonderful music not only for the organ, but also for choral groups; for clavier and harpsichord, for orchestra, and for small groups of instruments. Bach was the master of *fugue* and he perfected the *choral-prelude*. After devoting his life to music, he died at the age of 65 in Leipzig on July 28, 1750.

As you listen to his music, you will notice the human quality that lies in Bach's music. There is a sense of passion that shines through both his text settings and his instrumental works.

Baroque Connections **149**

Instrumental Selection:
***Brandenburg* Concerto No. 2, First Movement by Bach**
Have students:
- Read the information on page 148 to learn more about Bach's *Brandenburg* Concerto No. 2.
- Study the Blackline Master, Listening Map 4.

Using the Listening Map
Start at the top of page 1 and follow horizontally. Each measure is represented by vertical lines. Each rhythmic motive has a different picture assigned to it. Solo instruments are shown when they are featured.
Have students:
- Clap the five different rhythmic motives for the piece.
- Identify the solo instruments as violin, oboe, trumpet, and recorder.
- Listen as you define a *cadence*. (a harmonic progression that signals the end of a musical phrase or section)
- Listen to the instrumental selection and follow the listening map, signaling the cadences.

INTRODUCING . . . "Alleluia"
This feature is designed to introduce students to the Baroque Lesson on the following pages.
Have students:
- Read Setting the Stage on this page to learn more about "Alleluia."
- Read Meeting the Composer to learn more about Johann Sebastian Bach.
- Turn the page and begin the Baroque Lesson.

ASSESSMENT

Individual Performance Assessment

To further demonstrate understanding of Baroque music, have students:
- Signal when the cadences are heard while listening to Cantata No. 80 without looking at the listening map.
- Define *chorale, cadence,* and *cantata* to another student.

- Signal when the cadences are heard while listening to the First Movement of the *Brandenburg* Concerto No. 2 without looking at the listening map.

BAROQUE LESSON

Alleluia

From the Christmas cantata,
"For Us a Child Is Born"

COMPOSER: Johann Sebastian
Bach (1685-1750)

ARRANGER: Theron Kirk

Focus

OVERVIEW
Breathing techniques; dynamics.

OBJECTIVES
After completing this lesson, students will be able to:
- Sing with proper breathing techniques.
- Define and perform dynamic markings.

CHORAL MUSIC TERMS
Define the Choral Music Terms for students, providing correct pronunciation, and answering any questions that may arise.

Warming Up

Vocal Warm-Up
This Vocal Warm-Up is designed to prepare students to:
- Sing broken tonic chords in C major and A minor, using solfège and hand signs or numbers.
- Tune while singing in octaves.
- Sing block chords.
- Use proper breathing mechanics.

Have students:
- Review the *Breathing Checklist*, Blackline Master 14.
- Read through the Vocal Warm-Up directions.
- Sing, following your demonstration.

BAROQUE LESSON

Alleluia

From the Christmas cantata, "*For Us a Child Is Born*"
COMPOSER: *Johann Sebastian Bach* (1685–1750)
ARRANGER: *Theron Kirk*

CHORAL MUSIC TERMS
breathing techniques
crescendo
decrescendo
dynamics
phrase

VOICING
SAB

PERFORMANCE STYLE
Allegro
Accompanied by piano

FOCUS
- Sing with proper breathing techniques.
- Define and perform dynamic markings.

Warming Up

Vocal Warm-Up

Sing the broken chords on solfège syllables in C major and A minor, holding out the chord in three parts after each broken chord. Review proper breathing techniques as shown on the handout your teacher will provide. Use them when you sing this exercise. Inhale as someone counts to 4, then sing the exercise. Decrease the number of beats allowed for breathing one beat on each repeat, until you breathe in for only one beat.

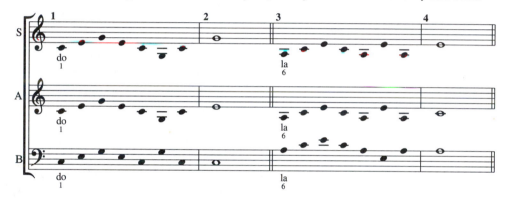

TEACHER'S RESOURCE BINDER
Blackline Master 14, *Breathing Checklist*, page 90
Blackline Master 15, *Music Dynamics*, page 91

National Standards
Through involvement with this lesson, students will develop the following skills and concepts:
1. Singing, alone and with others, a varied repertoire of music. **(a, c, d, e)**
5. Reading and notating music. **(a, b, c)**
9. Understanding music in relation to history and culture. **(a)**

Sight-Singing

Sight-sing these parts using solfège syllables or numbers. Can you sing the whole phrase in one smooth breath? Begin *mezzo forte* and crescendo to the highest point, then decrescendo to the end. Does this change in dynamics change the feeling of the phrase for the performer? For the listener?

Singing: "Alleluia"

Elaboration means adding characteristics to make something more detailed. Think about your breathing—just plain breathing. Now think about how you must elaborate upon your breathing to sing well. Discuss the characteristics of good breathing, and how they contribute to a good vocal performance.

Now turn to the music for "Alleluia" on page 152.

HOW DID YOU DO?

Think about your performance on the Vocal Warm-Up and "Alleluia."

1. Could you sing your part independently?
2. Did you use proper breathing techniques?
3. How well did you follow the dynamic markings? How well did the ensemble do?
4. How was your part different from the accompaniment line?
5. What characteristics of Baroque music did you experience in this piece?
6. Describe one thing you liked about this piece.

Sight-Singing

This Sight-Singing exercise is designed to prepare students to:

- Sing in three-part harmony.
- Read on three staves.
- Sing complete phrases with proper breathing techniques.
- Sing phrases using crescendo and decrescendo.

Have students:

- Read through the Sight-Singing exercise.
- Read through each part rhythmically, using rhythm syllables.
- Sight-sing through each part separately.
- Sing all parts together.

Singing: "Alleluia"

Review proper breathing mechanics. This is an opportunity to reinforce the concept of elaboration. Have students:

- Read the text in the Singing section on this page of their text.
- Discuss proper posture and mechanics of breathing.
- Demonstrate regular breathing, and then elaborate upon it by adding one element at a time, until they are demonstrating correct posture and mechanics for correct breathing.

Suggested Teaching Sequence

1. Review Vocal Warm-Up.

Apply breathing techniques.
Have students:

- Review the Vocal Warm-Up on page 150.
- Read the text and practice inhaling correctly until they can perform the exercise in one beat.
- Discuss difficult aspects of breathing correctly.

2. Review Sight-Singing.

Identify phrases and crescendo/decrescendo. Practice correct breathing techniques.
Have students:

- Review the Sight-Singing exercise on page 151, reading through each part with solfège and hand signs or numbers.
- Sing all three parts together.
- Practice singing the exercise in one breath, using a crescendo and decrescendo.
- Identify the dynamic markings throughout "Alleluia."

Alleluía

From the Christmas Cantata, "For Us a Child Is Born"

Johann Sebastian Bach (1685–1750)
Arranged by Theron Kirk

Mixed Voices, SAB

Pro Oct 2094

TEACHING STRATEGY

Research Baroque Music

Some researchers say that Baroque music is the most mathematically and structurally complex music that has ever been composed, and therefore requires great concentration of the listener. Research done with college students has shown that students who listen to Baroque or Classical music for 15 minutes daily significantly increase their memory capacity and spatial reasoning skills. While this research may be speculative, you might do your own research and see if students are more alert and thoughtful after listening to Bach, Vivaldi, or Mozart for 15 minutes at the beginning of the day, or at another time of the day when their energy starts lagging.

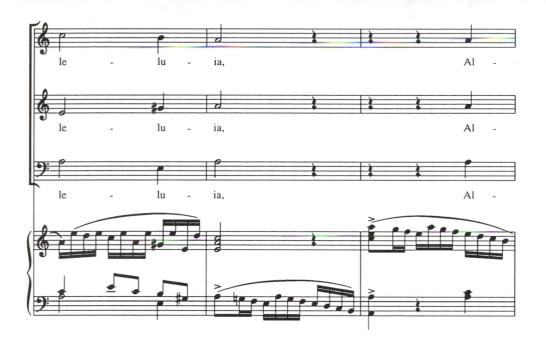

Pro Oct 2094

3. Sight-sing "Alleluia" using solfège and hand signs or numbers.

Have students:

- Divide into voice sections (SAB) and read each part rhythmically, using rhythm syllables or text, patting accurate beats as they read.
- Read the rhythms as a full ensemble.
- Again in sections, sing their part using solfège and hand signs or numbers.
- Sing the piece through as a full ensemble.
- Discuss problem areas, working on accurate pitches, correct breathing, phrasing, and dynamics.

VOCAL DEVELOPMENT

To encourage vocal development, have students:

- Use pure, open Italian vowels in the Latin pronunciatin of *Alleluia*. Each vowel should be pronounced identically by all singers.
- Keep the dropped jaw and a tall, resonance space feeling in the head when singing this cantata movement. Articulation of the diction is mostly with tongue and lips, leaving the dropped jaw as unchanged in shape as possible.
- Listen to the diction of the words. Where are the diphthongs? What vowels should be modified?

TEACHING STRATEGY
Cooperative Learning

Cooperative or collaborative groups are one way to get students engaged in discussing information in order to learn it. Randomly divide the students into groups of not more than five, and divide the task into as many parts as there are group members. Assigning roles within the group helps keep students on task. Randomly assign a reader to read the text, a questioner to ask questions of different group members to see if they are listening, a timekeeper to keep the group on task and let them know how much time is left, a recorder to write answers down, and a checker to ask the questions at the end of the section and moderate the discussions. By assigning roles, everyone has a job and is more responsible to the success of the whole group.

MUSIC LITERACY

To help students expand their music literacy, have them:

- Conduct and speak the rhythms. Then, conduct and speak the words in rhythm.
- Identify the chords and the masterful way Bach leads each voice smoothly in chord progressions.
- Distinguish the hemiola effect at the cadence and at the end. (pages 155 and 157)

Ask them: Why does the composer use this technique?

Pro Oct 2094

154 *Choral Connections Level 1 Mixed Voices*

Networking with Your Community

Many towns and cities have performing groups that perform Baroque music. They may be vocal or instrumental groups connected with a high school, local college or university, church, or local arts council. Many symphony orchestras or professional choirs have outreach programs to the schools, and might arrange a youth concert if there is enough interest, or include a piece from the Baroque period if asked early enough in their planning. Making a few phone calls and reviewing concert programs in the local newspaper might help you locate a live performance for your students.

ff
dim.
mf
with our hearts up - lift - ed.
ff
dim.
mf
with our hearts up - lift - ed.
ff
dim.
mf
with our hearts up - lift - ed.
ff
dim.
f
For God to - day
f
For God to - day
f
For God to - day

Pro Oct 2094

Assessment

Informal Assessment

In this lesson, students showed the ability to:

- Demonstrate correct breathing while singing the Vocal Warm-Up.
- Sing phrases using crescendo and decrescendo during the Sight-Singing exercise.
- Sing complete phrases with correct breathing technique and dynamics in "Alleluia."

Student Self-Assessment

Have students:

- Read the How Did You Do? section on page 151.
- Answer the questions individually. Discuss them in pairs or small groups, and/or write their responses.

Individual Performance Assessment

To further demonstrate accomplishment, have students:

- Check a partner's breathing by using the Blackline Master 14, *Breathing Checklist.*
- Sing measures 17–23 in a double trio, using correct breathing technique and dynamics to perform the phrase.

CURRICULUM CONNECTIONS

History—the Baroque Period

Baroque is a Portuguese word that means "irregular pearl." It came to be used as a slang-like reference to art and music of "corrupt taste." Today the term is applied to denote the flamboyant, highly detailed art, music, and architecture that developed during this period in history. France's reigning monarch, Louis XIV, was the quintessential example of a ruler who left lasting monuments of the age, such as the palace and gardens of Versailles.

has giv'n such joy,

has giv'n such joy,

has giv'n such joy,

cresc.

that we should sing to

cresc.

that we should sing to

cresc.

that we should sing to

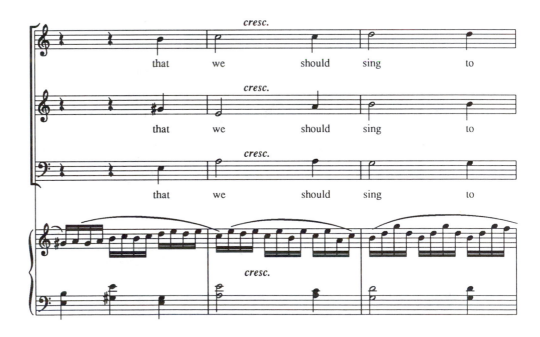

Pro Oct 2094

CULTURAL CONNECTIONS
The Gamelan Sound

The technique of layering a slower moving part over a faster moving one is practiced in the music of many cultures around the world. One example is the Gamelan orchestra of Indonesia, an orchestra consisting of gongs, pitched "pots," and metal xylophones (metallophones). The lower the sound of the instrument, the slower it plays. Parts are layered, with the highest sounding instruments playing very fast patterns. Although the harmonic structure and scales are different than the ones used by Bach, the layering of parts is similar. During the 1930s, a vocal piece was composed using this same layering technique, and evolved into a vocal theater piece for men only called Kecak, with voices imitating the Gamelan style.

Him   our   praise   e   -   ter   -

nal.

nal.

nal.

Pro Oct 2094

Extension

Composing Like J.S. Bach

As students analyze the melody and accompaniment of "Alleluia," one of the most obvious features is that the accompaniment is constantly moving, as the melody has a sustained, rhythmically uncomplicated line. Both parts use chord tones at different speeds. Have students:

• Create a piece for two voices—men and women. Using Bach's 3/4 meter and a key of A minor, decide on a chord scheme using the A minor (i) and E major (V) chords.

• Add any other chords they wish if they check with you first. This two-part piece should have the men's line singing the chord tones slowly, as the women's line is more detached and quickly, but still using chord tones.

• Be sure the women have some time to breathe. Perform these pieces for the class, and analyze how well they do or do not work, and why.

National Standards

The following National Standards are addressed through the Extension and bottom-page activities:

4. Composing and arranging music within specified guidelines. **(a)**
6. Listening to, analyzing, and describing music. **(b, c)**
7. Evaluating music and music performances. **(b)**
8. Understanding relationships between music, the other arts, and disciplines outside the arts. **(b)**
9. Understanding music in relation to history and culture. **(a, b, c)**

Classical Period

Focus

OVERVIEW
Understanding the development of choral music during the Classical period.

OBJECTIVES
After completing this lesson, students will be able to:
- Compare qualities of music written in the Classical and Baroque styles.
- Identify two major composers from the Classical period.
- Define *sonata–allegro form*.

CHORAL MUSIC TERMS
Define the Choral Music Terms for students, providing correct pronunciations, and answering any questions that may arise.

Introducing the Lesson

Introduce the Classical period through visual art and architecture.
Point out the artwork, *The Oath of the Horatii*, on this page, and the architecture example on page 159, Arc de Triomphe. Have students:
- Look at both works, comparing characteristics.

 The Oath of the Horatii reflects Jacques Louis David's (1748–1825) interest in the beauty of Greco-Roman subjects. This interest in idealistic Classical subjects has a parallel in the formal structures of much of the music composed during this period.

1786. Jacques Louis David. *The Oath of the Horatii.* (Detail.) Oil on canvas. 3.35 x 4.27 m (11 x 14'). Toledo Museum of Art, Toledo, Ohio.

158 *Choral Connections   Level 1 Mixed Voices*

TEACHER'S RESOURCE BINDER
Fine Art Transparency 3, *The Oath of the Horatii,* by Jacques Louis David

National Standards
This lesson addresses:
6. Listening to, analyzing, and describing music. **(a)**
7. Evaluating music and music performances. **(a, b)**
8. Understanding relationships between music, the other arts, and disciplines outside the arts. **(a, b)**
9. Understanding music in relation to history and culture. **(a, b, c)**

Classical Period

After completing this lesson, you will be able to:
- Compare qualities of music written in the Classical and Baroque styles.
- Identify two major composers from the Classical period.
- Define sonata form.

Today, we have a fascination with the old. We are excited to climb pyramids or see the ruins of ancient civilizations. We glorify stories that contain archeological subjects. The **Classical period** (1750–1820) was *a time when society began looking to the ancient Greeks and Romans for examples of order and ways of looking at life.*

The Classical Period—a Time of Balance, Clarity, and Simplicity

Baroque music was written with an emotional quality that was rather flamboyant. Embellishments and virtuosity dominated compositions. In comparison, music of the Classical period gave the expression of emotion a more restrained quality. Clarity, repose, and balance took an upper hand in expressing emotion in Classical music.

In the eighteenth century, painters, sculptors, and architects took notice of the ancient Greek and Roman artifacts being excavated in Athens, Pompeii, and other archeological sites. The calmness and simplicity of this ancient, "classical" art inspired logic, symmetry, and balance and guided artists away from the overly decorative, exaggerated ideals of the Baroque.

▲ **The Classical period reflects the renewal of interest once again in the design elements of balance, symmetry, and simplicity of line. Commissioned by Napoleon, the Arc de Triomphe du Carrousel was inspired by the Arch of Septimus Severus in Rome.**

1806. Charles Percier and Pierre F. L. Fontaine. The Arc de Triomphe in the Place du Carrousel. Arc de Triomphe du Carrousel, Paris, France.

COMPOSERS

Franz Joseph Haydn (1732–1809)
Wolfgang Amadeus Mozart (1756–1791)
Ludwig van Beethoven (1770–1827)
Vincento Bellini (1801–1835)

ARTISTS

Francois Boucher (1703–1770)
Jean-Honoré Fragonard (1732–1806)
Francisco Gôya (1746–1828)
Jacques Louis David (1748–1825)

AUTHORS

Voltaire (1694–1778)
Wolfgang Goethe (1749–1832)
Jane Austen (1775–1817)

CHORAL MUSIC TERMS
Classical period
sonata-allegro form

Suggested Teaching Sequence

1. Examine the Classical period.
Have students:
- Read the text on student pages 159–161.
- Read, discuss, and answer the questions individually, in pairs, or in small groups.
- Discuss their answers with the whole group, clarifying misunderstandings.

2. Examine the Classical period in historical perspective.
Have students:
- Turn to the time line and read the citations.
- Discuss why these are considered important dates during the Classical period.
- Compare each of these events to what occurred before and after the Classical period.
- Devise a one- or two-sentence statement that describes the Classical period based on one of the events in the time line. (For example: The excavation of Pompeii reminded people of the clarity and simplicity of the Roman culture. This was reflected by a turn toward simplicity, symmetry, and logic in place of the overly decorated style of the Baroque period.)

Classical Period **159**

Swift writes
Gulliver's Travels
1726

George Washington
1732–1799

Thomas Jefferson

1743–1826

1732–1757
Franklin writes *Poor Richard's Almanac*

3. Define the musical aspects of the Classical period.
Have students:
* Review the changes in music during the Classical period.
* Define *sonata–allegro form*.

Extension

Become a Critic of the Classics

Classical music is performed frequently by live vocal and instrumental groups, on the radio, and on television. Students can find performances by looking in the local newspaper, checking concert programs, radio schedules, and television scheduling.
Have students:
* Begin by listening to just one piece and reviewing it as a concert critic would—facts first, then opinions.
* Read some critiques of movies, concerts, and so on in the local paper. Invite the local music critic to come in to help students understand what a critic does, what the responsibilities are, and what occupational skills are required.

Music of the Classical Period

During the Classical period, people developed an interest in knowing more about the cultural aspects of life, such as art and music, that had once been attainable only by the wealthy. More books were published for learning about music. Musical scores were also more widely available. Musicians, mainly supported by the wealthy and aristocratic, now wrote music that was accessible to the general public.

The two main composers associated with this period are Franz Joseph Haydn (1732–1809) and Wolfgang Amadeus Mozart (1756–1791). The large quantity and variety of their work and their faithfulness to the Classical style overshadowed many other composers of the time. Ludwig van Beethoven was born in 1770 and began composing in this period, but his work bridges the gap between the Classical and Romantic periods, the latter of which will be discussed later.

The idea of improvisation and exaggerated use of embellishments of the Baroque were abandoned for a more precise and balanced style in the Classical period. A balance between content of the music and the form in which it was expressed became an essential characteristic of the period.

Symphonies, sonatas, concertos, and chamber works became important vehicles in instrumental works. During this time, the **sonata-allegro form,** *a movement written in* A B A *form*, was born. In this form, there is a section, the *Exposition*, which represents the theme (A). The theme is then repeated with elaboration (A'). Many times this elaboration was improvised by the performer on the spot, and was a sign of his or her musical skills. The next section of the piece, the *Development*, was a contrasting section (B). Finally, there was a return to the original theme (A) in a section called *Recapitulation*.

Opera experienced a great reformation in the eighteenth century. Composers felt a need to remove its excess vocal acrobatics and to emphasize its drama.

Classical Music Today

You can hear Classical music performed in many places today. A Mozart Festival is held every summer in many cities in the United States. Classical music is performed in concert halls by choirs, instrumental groups, and soloists the world over. You may even hear Classical music used in television or radio commercials. Advertisers use the music to create a certain mood.

American Revolutionary War fought
1775–1783

Federal Government established in America
1789

1775
James Watt invents the steam engine

1789
French Revolution begins

1808
Roman excavations begin at Pompeii, Italy

1776
American Declaration of Independence signed

Check Your Understanding

Recall

1. What is the main difference between the Baroque and Classical styles?

2. What are the main characteristics of Classical music?

3. Name two composers who wrote during the Classical period.

4. What form was very important in instrumental compositions of the Classical period? Describe the form.

5. How did opera change during the Classical period?

Thinking It Through

1. How did the Greek and Roman cultures influence the Classical period?

2. Was the music of the Classical period enjoyed by all people, or by just the wealthy? Explain your answer.

3. If you wanted to hear examples of Classical music today, where could you find them?

4. Are there any similarities between characteristics of the Classical period and those of the society you live in today?

Classical Period **161**

Assessment

Informal Assessment
During this lesson, students showed the ability to:
- Identify characteristics of the Classical period and Classical music.
- Describe the impact of events of the Classical period.
- Compare the Classical period to today's world.
- Define *sonata–allegro form*.

Student Self-Assessment
Have students:
- Return to page 161 and answer the Check Your Understanding questions.
- Write a paragraph describing how much they understand about the development of music during the Classical period.

Individual Performance Assessment
To further demonstrate accomplishment, have students:
- Learn more about one aspect of music during the Classical period.
- Share their findings with the class in a creative way, such as a poster, demonstration, design for the cover of a CD or video, and so on.

ANSWERS TO RECALL QUESTIONS
1. Baroque is highly ornamental; Classical emphasizes clarity, repose, and balance.
2. Precision and balance.
3. Mozart and Haydn.
4. Sonata–allegro form—a movement written in AA'BA form.
5. Vocal acrobatics were diminished and drama was emphasized.

CLASSICAL CONNECTIONS

Listening to . . .
Classical Music

This feature is designed to expand students' appreciation of choral and instrumental music of the Classical period.

Choral Selection: "Non so piu" from The Marriage of Figaro by Mozart
Have students:
- Read the information on this page to learn more about "Non so piu."
- Study the Blackline Master, Listening Map 5.

Using the Listening Map
Follow the Italian text.
Have students:
- Read or echo you with the Italian text of section A on the listening map. Practice reading the words faster and faster while keeping correct pronunciation and making the words understandable.
- Read the Italian text of the coda as slowly as they can, working to make the words understandable.
- Listen to "Non so piu" as they follow the listening map.

Listening to . . .
Classical Music

CHORAL SELECTION

Mozart—The Marriage of Figaro, Act I, (Scene 6) "Non so piu"

"Non so piu" from *The Marriage of Figaro* is an aria performed by Cherubino, a young page who is in love with love itself. *The Marriage of Figaro* (written in 1786), is a comic opera or "opera buffa" and revolves around the marriage of a valet, Figaro, and maid, Susanna. The plot has many comical confusions, jealousies and deceptions, The part of Cherubino is played by a soprano in a trouser role.

INSTRUMENTAL SELECTION

Mozart— *Eine kleine Nachtmusik,* First Movement

Translated, *Eine kleine Nachtmusik* means "A Little Night Music." Originally, it was written for a string quartet, but is now performed by major string orchestras. It was written to be played at a garden party or other social event where "small talk" needed to be filtered out.

TEACHER'S RESOURCE BINDER
Blackline Master, Listening Map 5
Blackline Master, Listening Map 6
Optional Listening Selections:
The Norton Recordings, 7th edition
The Marriage of Figaro: Vol. I, CD 3, Track 27
Eine kleine Nachtmusik: Vol. I, CD 3, Track 31

National Standards
This lesson addresses the following National Standard:
7. Evaluating music and music performances. **(a)**

Introducing...

"Dies Irae"

Wolfgang Amadeus Mozart

Setting the Stage

Composed in 1791 when Mozart was 35, "Dies Irae" is from the well-known *Requiem*. Mozart did not finish this multi-movement work before he died. He left sketches of some movements which were completed by one of his pupils, Sussmayr. Maintaining the refined quality found in music from the Classical period, Mozart uses the emotion of the rhythm and notes to create a fiery picture of the Day of Judgment. The accompaniment, originally for orchestra, is constantly moving—representing the flames of hell. The notes also help depict the exit ("Quantus tremor est futurs," the trembling figure in the bass part in measure 41 and in measures 49–51). The emotion of the scene is carried from the beginning to the end with a driving rhythm from both the chorus and the orchestra. This piece should be challenging and fulfilling for you to sing.

Meeting the Composer

Wolfgang Amadeus Mozart (1756–1791)

Born in Salzburg, Austria, Wolfgang Amadeus Mozart, whose full name is Johann Chrysostom Wolfgang Theophilus, began his musical career at an extremely early age. By the time he was four years old, Mozart had already mastered the keyboard and had written his first musical piece by age five. He became a master of the violin quickly thereafter. Mozart's father, Leopald Mozart, realized Amadeus' talent and began a tour through Europe, exhibiting his young son's extraordinary talents. By age 16, Mozart had already written about 25 symphonies. While writing the *Requiem*, Mozart was stricken with an illness that left him bedridden for the final three weeks of his life.

Classical Connections **163**

Instrumental Selection:
Eine kleine Nachtmusik
Have students:
- Read the information on page 162 to learn more about *Eine kleine Nachtmusik.*
- Study the Blackline Master, Listening Map 6.

Using the Listening Map
Start at letter A and follow the numbered sections, repeating A and B as shown on the listening map. The form is ABABA with a coda.
Have students:
- Discuss the type of clothing worn by the people on the listening map. (formal evening wear from the late 1700s, circa George Washington)
- Predict how the music for such an event would sound. In pairs or small groups, brainstorm a word list to describe such an event.
- Listen to *Eine kleine Nachtmusik* and follow the listening map.

INTRODUCING . . .
"Dies Irae"
This feature is designed to introduce students to the Classical Lesson on the following pages.
Have students:
- Read Setting the Stage on this page to learn more about "Dies Irae."
- Read Meeting the Composer to learn more about Wolfgang Amadeus Mozart.
- Turn the page and begin the Classical Lesson.

Dies Irae

From *Requiem*
COMPOSER: Wolfgang Amadeus Mozart (1756-1791)
ARRANGER: Patrick Liebergen

Focus

OVERVIEW
Singing in Latin; blended choral sound.

OBJECTIVES
After completion of this lesson, students will be able to:
- Sing in Latin with correct pronunciation.
- Identify and demonstrate characteristics of choral blend.

CHORAL MUSIC TERMS
Define the Choral Music Terms for students, providing correct pronunciation, and answering any questions that may arise.

Warming Up

Vocal Warm-Up
This Vocal Warm-Up is designed to prepare students to:
- Find chords when singing solfège.
- Sing chords with good blend by keeping parts balanced.

Have students:
- Read through the Vocal Warm-Up directions.
- Sing, following your demonstration.

CLASSICAL LESSON

Dies Irae

From *Requiem*
COMPOSER: *Wolfgang Amadeus Mozart (1756–1791)*
ARRANGER: *Patrick Liebergen*

CHORAL MUSIC TERMS
allegro assai
choral blend
Classical period
unified vowels
Wolfgang Amadeus Mozart

VOICING
SAB

PERFORMANCE STYLE
Allegro assai
Accompanied by keyboard

FOCUS
- Use correct Latin pronunciation for the song text.
- Sing with a blended choral sound.

Warming Up

Vocal Warm-Up
Sing on solfège syllables, then on *low*. Listen carefully for all parts on the last chords. Hold each chord until it is tuned securely and there is balance between the parts. This exercise contains stepwise melody, a melody based on chord tones, and chords. Can you identify each of these parts? How can you tell when a chord has a good blend?

TEACHER'S RESOURCE BINDER
Blackline Master 16 *"Dies Irae" Pronunciation Guide,* page 92
Blackline Master 17, *Characteristics of Choral Blend Checklist,* page 93

National Standards
1. Singing, alone and with others, a varied repertoire of music. **(d, e)**
5. Reading and notating music. **(e)**
7. Evaluating music and music performances. **(a)**
8. Understanding relationships between music, the other arts, and disciplines outside the arts. **(b)**
9. Understanding music in relation to history and culture. **(a)**

Sight-Singing

Sight-sing these parts using solfège syllables or numbers, then repeat on *low*. Try to keep the vowel unified among voices and the notes smoothly connected as you sing. Singing in tune and unified vowels are characteristics of a good blended sound.

Singing: "Dies Irae"

Identify ingredients for making cookies. When you prepare cookies, these ingredients must be blended together. After they are mixed, most ingredients are no longer identifiable as they were in their original state. A choral blend has similar characteristics. All parts are equally mixed, and none is more identifiable than the others.

Now turn to the music for "Dies Irae" on page 166.

HOW DID YOU DO?

Think about your performance of the Vocal Warm-Up, Sight-Singing, and "Dies Irae."
1. Could you sing your part independently?
2. Describe the characteristics of a blended sound.
3. Did your sound blend with the rest of the group? How do you know?

4. How was your Latin pronunciation?
5. What characteristics of Classical music did you experience in this piece?
6. Did you find "Dies Irae" challenging? Why? Why not? Use specific musical terms and examples to explain.

Sight-Singing

This Sight-Singing exercise is designed to prepare students to:
- Sing in three parts.
- Practice good blend while singing by unifying vowel sounds.

Have students:
- Read through the Sight-Singing exercise directions.
- Read each voice part rhythmically, using rhythm syllables.
- Sight-sing through each part separately.
- Sing all parts together.
- Identify the characteristics of a good blended sound.

Singing: "Dies Irae"

Identify the concept of blending.
Have students:
- Read the text in the Singing section on this page, creating the list of ingredients.
- Relate the consistency of cookie dough to a blended choral sound.
- Hypothesize about what actions might contribute to a blended choral sound.

Suggested Teaching Sequence

1. Review Vocal Warm-Up.

Identify balance as a characteristic of blended choral sound. Have students:

- Read the Vocal Warm-Up on page 164 and identify the stepwise melody (notes 1–5), chord tone melody (notes 5–9), and chords (last three notes).
- Identify one way of blending by keeping balance between the parts—no one part "sticking out," or louder than the others.
- Repeat the exercise, blending the chords by keeping balance between the parts.

2. Review Sight-Singing.

Identify diction as a characteristic of blended choral sound. Have students:

- Review the Sight-Singing exercise on page 165, reading through each part with solfège and hand signs or numbers.
- Sing all three parts together.
- Practice singing the exercise, tuning carefully and blending vowels.

3. Learn the Latin pronunciation.

Have students:

- Look at the pronunciation guide, Blackline Master 16, *"Dies Irae" Pronunciation Guide,* for the correct Latin pronunciation.
- Speak the Latin slowly.
- Speak the Latin in rhythm from the song text.

Dies Irae

from "Requiem"

Music by Wolfgang Amadeus Mozart (1756–1791)
Edited and arranged by Patrick M. Liebergen
English setting by Patrick M. Liebergen

SAB Voices and Keyboard

† Text translation is paraphrased to accommodate the English language.

il - la,   Sol - vet sae - clum   in fa - vil - la: Te - ste
a - tor,   Hear the sing - ing,   hear the plead - ing, We a -

il - la,   Sol - vet sae - clum   in fa - vil - la: Te - ste
a - tor,   Hear the sing - ing,   hear the plead - ing,   We a -

il - la,   Sol - vet sae - clum   in fa - vil - la: Te - ste
a - tor,   Hear the sing - ing,   hear the plead - ing: We a -

Da - vid cum Sy - bil - la.
wait your fi - nal com - ing.

Da - vid cum Sy - bil - la.
wait your fi - nal com - ing.

Da - vid cum Sy - bil - la.
wait your fi - nal com - ing.

4. Sight-sing "Dies Irae" using solfège and hand signs or numbers.

Have students:

- Divide into voice sections (SAB) and read each part rhythmically, using rhythm syllables, patting the steady beat as they read.
- Read the rhythms as a full ensemble.
- Again in sections, sing their part using solfège and hand signs or numbers.
- Sing the piece through as a full ensemble using solfège and hand signs or numbers.
- Discuss problem areas, working on accurate, secure pitches, correct breathing, phrasing, and dynamics.

5. Review and refine the concept of blended sound.

Have students:

- Review the characteristics of blended sound that they already know.
- Look at Blackline Master 17 *Characteristics of Choral Blend Checklist*, identifying any new ideas.
- Discuss how they can use each term in measures 1–19 of "Dies Irae."
- Sing each phrase of this section practicing tone quality, diction, and intonation.
- Discuss places that are difficult.
- Sing the piece through as a full ensemble, paying attention to blended sound.

 MUSIC LITERACY

To help students expand their music literacy, have them:

- Conduct and speak rhythms. Conduct and speak the lyrics in rhythm.
- Use solfège syllables with the minor mode to tune the altered pitches.
- Listen for the chords vertically and horizontally. Listen to the chord

progressions and the pivoting chord tones to connect the progressions.

- Analyze how the composer "illustrates" the lyrics with his writing, such as the "tremor" section at measure 41.

Quan - tus tre - mor est fu - tu - rus, Quan - do
We shall trem - ble in your glo - ry on that

ju - dex est ven - tu - rus, Cun - cta
fi - nal day of judge - ment, Lord have

stri - cte dis - cus - su - rus!
mer - cy when you judge us!

stri - cte dis - cus - su - rus!
mer - cy when you judge us!

stri - cte dis - cus - su - rus!
mer - cy when you judge us!

Di - es i - rae, di - es
Lord al - might - y, God cre -

Di - es i - rae, di - es
Lord al - might - y, God cre -

Di - es i - rae, di - es
Lord al - might - y, God cre -

Dies Irae **169**

Informal Assessment
In this lesson, students showed the ability to:
- Demonstrate blended chords through balancing parts in the Vocal Warm-Up.
- Demonstrate blended sound through careful tuning and blending vowels in the Sight-Singing exercise.
- Sing in Latin, using correct pronunciation in "Dies Irae."
- Sing, demonstrating elements of a blended sound in "Dies Irae."

Student Self-Assessment
Have students:
- Read the How Did You Do? section on page 167.
- Answer the questions individually. Discuss them in pairs or small groups, and/or write their responses on a sheet of paper.

Individual Performance Assessment
To further demonstrate accomplishment, have students:
- Orally check a partner's knowledge of the characteristics of blended sound using Blackline Master 17.
- Perform, into a tape recorder in an isolated space, measures 10–19, demonstrating correct Latin pronunciation.

CULTURAL CONNECTIONS
Music and the Funeral

Mozart is said to have written *Requiem* for his own funeral. Music is an integral part of many social and religious functions, one of which is a funeral. Ask students:
- To share any experiences of music they have heard at funerals, and the reasons they think music is played or sung at a funeral.
- Discuss what type of music would be appropriate at a funeral, and give reasons for their answers. Be open to different opinions. Some may feel that somber music would reflect the mood, while others might suggest something lighter to lift the spirits of those in attendance, or to celebrate the life of a loved one.

Extension

The Full *Requiem*

If students are interested, have them listen to the original movement from *Requiem*. Have them identify instruments or voices that help depict the scene of the final judgment. They may also be interested in hearing other movements of the piece.

Visual Art Connection: The Day of Wrath

"Dies Irae" means "the day of wrath," a day of judgment where all must atone for their sins. Have students:

- Create a mural depicting their impression of the final judgment using colors, shapes, and textures representative of the music.
- First analyze the piece, "Dies Irae," writing down the different sections:

A=measures 1–9

B=measures 10–21

A'=measures 22–30 same text and rhythm, different melody

B'=measures 31–40 same text and rhythm, different melody

A"=measures 41–end; elaborated text, rhythm, and melody

National Standards

The following National Standards are addressed through the Extension and bottom-page activities:

6. Listening to, analyzing, and describing music. **(a)**
7. Evaluating music and music performances. **(a)**
8. Understanding relationships between music, the other arts, and disciplines outside the arts. **(a)**
9. Understanding music in relation to history and culture. **(a, b, c)**

- Divide a large paper into these sections. Then, listening to a tape recording of their performance, imagine what visual representation could occur on each section.
- Discuss the work enough so there will be some connections between similar sections, and the visual will have characteristics of the melody, rhythm, and mood of the piece.
- In groups, each group work on one of the sections of the mural. After it is completed, listen to the piece, following their visual representation, and assess how it is successful and what might be even better.

Dies Irae **171**

VOCAL DEVELOPMENT

To encourage vocal development, have students:

- Listen for the chords and chord progressions. Listen for the balance of the sound. Each note of the chord should blend together so that one voice does not overpower another.
- Use strong breath support for the dramatic energy of the movement. Forte, or full singing, must originate in firm posture and diaphragmatic breathing. Use a heavy panting, "belly laugh" feeling to support the sound.
- Sing with tall, open resonance, adding *oo* to the *ee* sounds, as in *Dies Irae*.
- Articulate the slurred notes by leaning into the first note, with a slight break after the second note.
- Follow the pronunciation guide for the Latin text. Words must be pronounced identically by all singers to create an effective blend.

Romantic Period

Focus

OVERVIEW
Understanding the development of choral music during the Romantic period.

OBJECTIVES
After completing this lesson, students will be able to:
- Compare qualities of music written in the Romantic and Classical styles.
- Identify several major composers and compositional forms from the Romantic period.
- Define *art songs, nationalism,* and *symphony.*

CHORAL MUSIC TERMS
Define the Choral Music Terms for students, providing correct pronunciations, and answering any questions that may arise.

Introducing the Lesson

Introduce the Romantic period through visual art.
Point out the artwork on this page and have students:
- Look at the picture, pointing out ways in which this painter used the elements and principles of art differently than artists of other periods studied. Ask: Is there a story in the picture?

 Emotional response is the significant feature in *Wounded Feelings* by English artist Alice Walker. Interest in exploring feelings and reactions, rather than formal structure, is typical of visual arts and music during the Romantic period.

1862. Alice Walker. *Wounded Feelings.* Oil on canvas. 101.6 x 76.2 cm (40 x 30"). The Forbes Magazine Collection, New York, New York.

176 *Choral Connections   Level 1 Mixed Voices*

TEACHER'S RESOURCE BINDER
Fine Art Transparency 4,
    Wounded Feelings, by Alice Walker

National Standards
4. Composing and arranging music within specified guidelines. **(b, c)**
6. Listening to, analyzing, and describing music. **(a)**
8. Understanding relationships between music, the other arts, and disciplines outside the arts. **(a, b)**
9. Understanding music in relation to history and culture. **(a, b, c)**

Romantic Period

After completing this lesson, you will be able to:

- *Compare* qualities of music written in the Romantic and Classical styles.
- *Identify* two major composers from the Romantic period.
- *Define* nationalism, art songs, *and the* Romantic period.

Whenever there are rules, they are challenged by some people. The **Romantic period** (1820–1900) was *a time in which artists and composers attempted to make a break from classical music ideas.* The eighteenth century came to a close, leaving behind a restrained and controlled era, and the nineteenth century brought a newly acquired political and artistic freedom. There was a revolutionary spirit in society, with ideals of liberty and individualism, dramatic action, and indepentent thought. The musical restraints and order of the Classical period soon gave way to experimentation, as composers became impatient with the older rules and traditions.

The Romantic Period—a Time of Drama

Most composers of the Romantic period kept many of the classical forms alive. However, it is their treatment of these forms that made new statements about music. **Symphonies**—*large orchestral pieces for many instruments, usually of three or four parts or movements*—began to become popular. In some symphonies, a chorus was added (e.g., Beethoven's N*inth Symphony*).

Many composers based their works on legends, dramas, or novels. In doing so, they explored through their music the heights and depths of human emotion. This innovation contrasted with previous vocal and instrumental works, many of which required musical simplicity. In general, vocal melodies became longer and more expressive, harmonies became more colorful, and instrumentation was expanded to enhance the overall possibilities of tone color in the music. Freedom and flexibility of rhythm and form brought new hues to the palette of sound composed by Romantic period composers.

Music of the Period

During the Romantic period, a new class of people—landowners, merchants, businesspeople who were not nobles—gained a powerful place in society. We refer to them as the middle class. With the help of the Industrial Revolution, which created many jobs, more and more people entered this class and took an active part in their culture and their nation. A growing pride in patriotism brought a spirit of nationalism to music. **Nationalism** in music

COMPOSERS

Ludwig van Beethoven (1770–1827)
Franz Schubert (1797–1828)
Hector Berlioz (1803–1869)
Felix Mendelssohn (1809–1847)
Frédéric Chopin (1810–1849)
Robert Schumann (1810–1856)
Franz Liszt (1811–1886)
Richard Wagner (1813–1883)
Giuseppe Verdi (1813–1901)
Clara Schumann (1819–1896)
Johannes Brahms (1833–1897)
Georges Bizet (1838–1875)
Modest Mussorgsky (1839–1881)
Peter Ilyich Tchaikovsky (1840–1893)
Giacomo Puccini (1858–1924)

ARTISTS

Élisabeth Vigée-Lebrun (1755–1842)
Rosa Bonheur (1822–1899)
Edouard Manet (1832–1883)
Edgar Degas (1834–1917)
Paul Cezanne (1839–1906)
Claude Monet (1840–1926)
Berthe Morisot (1841–1895)
Pierre Auguste Renoir (1841–1919)
Mary Cassatt (1845–1926)
Vincent van Gogh (1853–1890)
Georges Seurat (1859–1891)
Alice Walker (1944–)

AUTHORS

Noah Webster (1758–1843)
Mary Wollstonecraft Shelley (1797–1851)
Ralph Waldo Emerson (1803–1882)
Elizabeth Barrett Browning (1806–1861)
Henry Wadsworth Longfellow (1807–1882)
Edgar Allan Poe (1809–1849)
Harriet Beecher Stowe (1811–1896)
Theodore Dostoyevsky (1821–1881)
Leo Tolstoy (1828–1910)

CHORAL MUSIC TERMS

art songs
nationalism
Romantic period
symphonies

Romantic Period **177**

Suggested Teaching Sequence

1. Examine the Romantic period.

Have students:

- Read the text on student pages 177–179.
- Discuss their answers to the review questions to check their comprehension with other students, clarifying misunderstandings.

2. Examine the Romantic period in historical perspective.

Have students:

- Turn to the time line and read the citations.
- Discuss why these are considered important dates and personalities during the Romantic period.
- Compare these events to what occurred before and after the Romantic period.
- Devise a one- or two-sentence statement that describes the Romantic period based on one of the events in the time line.
- Devise one additional sentence that tells how this Romantic event is related to the student's world.

Louisiana Purchase
established
1803

Abraham Lincoln
1809–1865

Frederick Douglass
c. 1817–1895

Mary Baker Eddy
1821–1910

Monroe Doctrine created
1823

1804
Napoleon crowned Emperor

1812–1814
U.S. declares war on Britain

1821
Jean Champollion deciphers Egyptian
hieroglyphics using the Rosetta Stone

3. Define the musical aspects of the Romantic period.

Have students:

- Review the changes in music during the Romantic period.
- Define *art songs, nationalism,* and *symphony.*

Extension

Arrange a Song in Nationalistic Style

Have students:

- Choose a folk song or patriotic song that they feel expresses pride in their country, and arrange a setting of it that provides emotional impact and expresses their sense of pride. They may use traditional or non-traditional instruments, and create spoken or sung renditions of the piece.

Can a Composer Make a Living?

The Romantic period marked the beginning of the artist as a self-sustaining professional. Before this time, although some artists were not supported financially, most artists and composers were part of a "court," or on the payroll of a wealthy family. They received commissions from the church or their patron family to create compositions for certain events, or even as study pieces for lessons. As the individual emerged in society, this type of patronage dwindled during the Romantic period. Since this time, composers have had to find ways to make a living either by commissions, printing and marketing their pieces, getting a well-known performer to present the piece, or performing it themselves.

Have students:

- Research some of their favorite music to find out who the composer is and how the composer gets paid for writing the piece.

The glass-and-iron Crystal Palace was erected for the 1851 Great Exhibition in Hyde Park, London. Its naves and transepts housed the Handel Orchestra and Choir, concert halls, and exhibits of paintings and sculptures.

1851. Vincent Brooks. Crystal Palace. Lithograph. Victoria and Albert Museum, London, Great Britain.

means that composers created works that evoked *pride in a country's historical and legendary past.* Richard Wagner wanted to preserve German music and legends in his operas. Giuseppe Verdi, great Italian composer of opera, felt he should guide the younger generation to adhere to the Italian historical and cultural tradition. This nationalism spawned interest in folk music of particular nations and regions. Robert Schumann used or imitated German folk songs. The American composer Stephen Foster composed songs on themes of life in the southern United States.

The art song became the most important vocal form during the Romantic period. **Art songs** were *expressive songs about life, love, and human relationships for solo voice and piano.* The most prolific composer of art songs, known in German as *lieder,* was Franz Schubert. Others were Robert Schumann and Johannes Brahms.

Modern Innovations

The idea of "selling" music to an audience through the musicians who composed it was developed during this time. In an effort to capture the general public's interest, a colorful and controversial personal life became an important factor in the visibility of many composers. Some of these composers were Franz Liszt, Hector Berlioz, and Richard Wagner.

Another figure to emerge in the performance setting was the music critic. His or her job was not only to explain the composer and the composer's music to the public, but also to set standards in musical taste.

178 *Choral Connections Level 1 Mixed Voices*

1835–1910
Mark Twain

1844–1900
Friedrich Nietzsche

1895
Wireless telegraph developed by Marconi

The Romantic Period in Retrospect

The Romantic period was a time of exploration, imagination, and diversity. This period was diverse and complex, and it would be hard to describe with one definition all the new styles that emerged during it. The Romantic movement, however, was international in scope and influenced all the arts. The excitement of the Romantic period came from the rejection and challenge of old ways and a search for new, unique, and meaningful possibilities.

Check Your Understanding

Recall

1. Write one sentence which characterizes the mood of the Romantic period.

2. How did vocal melodies change during the Romantic period?

3. How did instrumental music change during the Romantic period?

4. Describe nationalism.

5. Define art song.

6. Name a Romantic composer of each: opera, art song.

Thinking It Through

1. Compare musical characteristics of the Classical and Romantic periods.

2. What was the role of the individual in music of the Romantic period?

3. Why was a music critic more likely to emerge during the Romantic period than before?

Assessment

Informal Assessment
During this lesson, students showed the ability to:

- Identify characteristics of the Romantic period and Romantic music.
- Describe the impact of events of the Romantic period.
- Compare the Romantic period to today's world.
- Define *art songs, nationalism,* and *symphony.*

Student Self-Assessment
Have students:

- Review the questions in Checking Your Understanding.
- Write a paragraph describing how much they understand about the Romantic period.

Individual Performance Assessment
To further demonstrate accomplishment, have students:

- Learn more about one aspect of music during the Romantic period.
- Share their findings with the class in a creative way, such as a poster, demonstration, design for the cover of a CD or video, and so on.

ANSWERS TO RECALL QUESTIONS

1. Sentences will vary.
2. Melodies were larger and more expressive, and harmonies were more colorful.
3. The music included tone color.
4. Pride in a country's historical and legendary past.
5. Expressive songs about life, love, and human relationships for solo voice and piano.
6. Opera—Wagner and Verdi. Art song—Schubert, Schumann, and Brahms.

♪♪ **ROMANTIC CONNECTIONS**

Listening to . . .

Romantic Music

Listening to . . .
Romantic Music

This feature is designed to expand students' appreciation of choral and instrumental music of the Romantic period.

Choral Selection:
"Habanera" from *Carmen*
by Bizet
Have students:
- Read the information on this page to learn more about "Habanera."
- Study the Blackline Master, Listening Map 7.

Using the Listening Map
Follow the English translation as the aria is performed in Italian. Have students:
- Look at the listening map and discuss the English translation, with emphasis on the emotions depicted in the lyrics.
- Listen as you describe the form of the piece. (verse/refrain)
- Indicate where a solo is heard and where the full group sings ensemble.
- Listen to "Habanera" while following the listening map.

| CHORAL SELECTION |

Bizet — *Carmen*, Act I, "Habanera"

Georges Bizet (1838–1875) composed the music for the opera *Carmen*, based on a novel written by Prosper Mérimée.

The story takes place in Seville, Spain, around 1820. Carmen is a gypsy girl who works in the tobacco factory. She is arrested for fighting, but Don José, a soldier, becomes infatuated with her and allows her to escape. Months later, they are reunited, but soon argue because Carmen insists he must leave the army to be with her. At first he refuses, but after a fight with an officer he decides he has no choice except to join her.

After he is with the gypsies for some time, however, Carmen tires of him and insists he return to town to care for his mother. Carmen then takes a new lover, Escamillo. Don José is devastated by her rejection and, jealous of Escamillo, ends up stabbing Carmen. If he can't have her, no one will!

| INSTRUMENTAL SELECTION |

Mussorgsky — *Pictures at an Exhibition*, "The Hut on Fowl's Legs"/"The Great Gate of Kiev"

Modest Mussorgsky (1839–1881) was a very good friend of Victor Hartmann, an architect, watercolorist, and designer. The year after Hartmann died, a grief-stricken Mussorgsky visited an exhibition of his works and then wrote ten musical sketches inspired by pictures he had seen in the Hartmann memorial show. "The Hut on Fowl's Legs" is a picture of a Russian folklore witch, Baba Yaga, and her enchanted house. "The Great Gate of Kiev" is a sketch of a gate to be built in honor of fallen Russian soldiers.

180 *Choral Connections   Level 1 Mixed Voices*

TEACHER'S RESOURCE BINDER
Blackline Master, Listening Map 7
Blackline Master, Listening Map 8

Optional Listening Selections:
The Norton Recordings, 7th edition
Carmen: Vol. II, CD 6, Track 22
Pictures at an Exhibition: Vol. II, CD 6, Tracks 24 and 27

National Standards
This lesson addresses the following National Standard:
8. Understanding relationships between music, the other arts, and disciplines outside the arts. **(a)**

Introducing...

"In Stiller Nacht"

Johannes Brahms

Setting the Stage

"In Stiller Nacht" is an example of a folk song composed during the nationalist movement during the Romantic period. Within the confines of classical forms Brahms created new expressions in the warmth of the Romantic movement. Harmonies were expanded to add more color, making the phrases more expressive (measures 1–8). The addition of harmonic tension (measures 9–12) brings the emotion of the text to a new height of expression. The warmth of harmony and text will make this piece a pleasure to perform.

Meeting the Composer

Johannes Brahms (1833–1897)

Johannes Brahms is considered one of the leading composers of the Romantic period. His virtuosity in playing the piano stems from his early years when he helped support his family by performing in taverns and theaters. He also arranged popular waltzes for a local publisher. Brahms composed symphonies and overtures for orchestras as well as a wealth of choral pieces with piano and orchestral accompaniment. One of his finest works is *A German Requiem* which was written following the death of his mother. Brahms songs for voices(s) and piano are among the most delightful and accessible to all. Based on folk melodies or themselves folk songs, these compositions are full of emotion and delight.

Romantic Connections **181**

ASSESSMENT

Individual Performance Assessment

To further demonstrate understanding of Romantic music, have students:

- Work in pairs or small groups to brainstorm words that describe Carmen's emotions in "Habanera." (shy, bold, teasing, light-hearted)
- List the elements of "Habanera" that illustrate the emotions in their lists. (The music is loud when the chorus sings "You play with fire.")
- Brainstorm musical qualities in "The Great Gate of Kiev" that show Mussorgsky's affection for Victor Hartmann.
- Describe the connection between the art of Victor Hartmann and "The Hut on Fowl's Legs."

Instrumental Selection: "The Hut on Fowl's Legs"/"The Great Gate of Kiev" from *Pictures at an Exhibition* by Mussorgsky

Have students:

- Read page 180 to learn more about "The Hut on Fowl's Legs"/"The Great Gate of Kiev."
- Study the Blackline Master, Listening Map 8.

Using the Listening Map

Follow the map for "Hut on Fowl's Legs" first. Listen for rhythm patterns notated. Notice how section 2 leads directly into "The Great Gate of Kiev." Then follow the map for "The Great Gate of Kiev." Listen for the main theme at each gate and the quieter theme at each house.

Have students:

- Speculate about the connection between the emotional power felt in "The Great Gate of Kiev" and Mussorgsky's grief at the death of his friend Victor Hartmann.
- Study the listening map for "The Hut on Fowl's Legs" as you describe the form of the piece. (ABA, with instruments featured in sections 4, 5, 6, 7, and 8 and the rhythm patterns notated on the map)
- Study the listening map for "The Great Gate of Kiev" while you sing the main "gate" theme and point out how many times it will be heard. (6) Also point out the quieter theme heard at each house and the instruments featured in each section.
- Listen to "The Hut on Fowl's Legs"/"The Great Gate of Kiev" while following the map.

INTRODUCING... "In Stiller Nacht"

This feature is designed to introduce students to the Romantic Lesson on the following pages.

Have students:

- Read Setting the Stage on this page to learn more about "In Stiller Nacht."
- Read Meeting the Composer to learn more about Brahms.
- Turn the page and begin the Romantic Lesson.

ROMANTIC LESSON

In Stiller Nacht

COMPOSER: Johannes Brahms
(1833-1897)
ARRANGER: David L. Weck

Focus

OVERVIEW
Detached and connected articulation; singing in German; sustained crescendo/decrescendo.

OBJECTIVES
Upon completion of this lesson, students will be able to:
- Articulate detached and connected pitches.
- Sing in German with correct pronunciation.
- Demonstrate sustained crescendo and decrescendo through a phrase.

CHORAL MUSIC TERMS
Define the Choral Music Terms for students, providing correct pronunciation, and answering any questions that may arise.

Warming Up

Vocal Warm-Up 1
Vocal Warm-Up 1 is designed to prepare students to:
- Feel the pull of the phrase as the students sing crescendo and decrescendo.

Have students:
- Read through Vocal Warm-Up 1 directions.
- Sing, following your demonstration.

In Stiller Nacht

COMPOSER: *Johannes Brahms (1833–1897)*
ARRANGER: *David L. Weck*

CHORAL MUSIC TERMS
articulation
crescendo
decrescendo

VOICING
SAT

PERFORMANCE STYLE
Somewhat slowly
Accompanied by piano

FOCUS
- Detached and connected articulation.
- Use correct German pronunciation for the song text.
- Sustained crescendo and decrescendo.

Warming Up

Vocal Warm-Up 1
Sing on *loo*. Notice the dynamic markings. Working with a partner, face one another, and stand with one foot in front of the other, clasping hands. As you begin to sing the crescendo, pull outward with even tension between you and your partner. Feel the "pull" of the phrase as you connect the notes together. What will the appropriate movement be during the decrescendo?

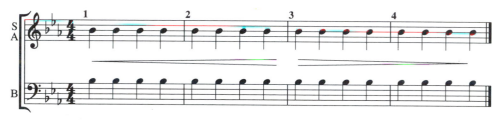

Vocal Warm-Up 2
Sing on solfège syllables, then on *hoh*. Notice the articulation markings. Sing the first four notes detached, and the second four on one connected sound. Whether you sing detached or connected pitches, maintain your breath support.

TEACHER'S RESOURCE BINDER
Blackline Master 18, *"In Stiller Nacht" Pronunciation Guide,* page 94

National Standards
1. Singing, alone and with others, a varied repertoire of music. (**c, d, e**)
5. Reading and notating music. (**b, e**)
7. Evaluating music and music performances. (**a, b**)
8. Understanding relationships between music, the other arts, and disciplines outside the arts. (**a, b**)
9. Understanding music in relation to history and culture. (**a, b, c**)

Sight-Singing

Everyone sight-sings the tenor part first, using solfège syllables and hand signs or numbers. Then sing all the parts. First sing with separated notes, then connect the notes carefully together.

Singing: "In Stiller Nacht"

If you were living with a family who did not speak your language, how would you communicate something that made you very sad?

If you could speak a little of their language, what would you do to make sure you were clearly understood?

Now turn to the music for "In Stiller Nacht" on page 184.

HOW DID YOU DO?

Think about your performance on the Vocal Warm-Ups, Sight-Singing, and "In Stiller Nacht."

1. Could you sing your part independently?
2. Describe how you used dynamics to shape the phrase.
3. Describe how you used articulation to interpret the piece.

4. How was your German pronunciation?
5. What characteristics of Romantic music did you experience in this piece?
6. Do you think the music fits the text of "In Stiller Nacht"? Why? Why not? Use specific musical terms and language to support your opinion.

Vocal Warm-Up 2

Vocal Warm-Up 2 is designed to prepare students to:
- Connect the breath support while singing detached and connected pitches.

Have students:
- Read through the Vocal Warm-Up 2 directions.
- Sing, following your demonstration.

Sight-Singing

This Sight-Singing exercise is designed to prepare students to:
- Hear and sight-sing new harmonies containing altered tones.
- Practice connecting notes together.

Have students:
- Read through the Sight-Singing exercise directions.
- Sing the tenor part first, using solfège and hand signs or numbers.
- Sing all parts together.
- Sing with separated notes.
- Sing all parts with notes connected together.

Singing: "In Stiller Nacht"

Identify the concept of blending.
Have students:
- Read the text in the Singing section on this page.
- Respond to the questions posed.
- Consider how body language, facial expressions, and voice inflections help people communicate.

TEACHING STRATEGY

Learning Foreign Text

It is very important to learn the notes of the piece first without the German. Then learn the pronunciation of the German followed by saying the text in rhythm. Finally, add the words to the notes.

Suggested Teaching Sequence

1. Review Vocal Warm-Up.

Identify and practice crescendo and decrescendo.

Have students:

- Review the Vocal Warm-Up 1 exercise on page 182.

2. Review Vocal Warm-Up.

Practice detached and connected articulation.

Have students:

- Review the Vocal Warm-Up 2 exercise on page 182.

3. Review Sight-Singing.

Read altered tones.

Have students:

- Review the Sight-Singing exercise on page 183, reading through the tenor part with solfège and hand signs or numbers, then reading all parts.
- Sight-sing all three parts together.

4. Sight-sing "In Stiller Nacht" using solfège and hand signs or numbers.

Have students:

- Divide into voice sections (SAT) and read each part rhythmically, using rhythm syllables or a neutral syllable.
- Read the piece with solfège and hand signs or English text.
- Discuss problem areas.
- Sing the piece through as a full ensemble.

5. Review and refine concepts of articulation and dynamics.

Have students:

- Sing measures 1–9 on *loo*.
- Decide how many phrases are included and where voices should crescendo and decrescendo. (Even though there is a breath mark half way through, this is one phrase. They should crescendo on the first half, and decrescendo after the breath.)

In Stiller Nacht

Johannes Brahms
Arranged by David L. Weck
English words by H.T. Duffield, alt.

SAT Voices and Accompaniment

184 *Choral Connections   Level 1 Mixed Voices*

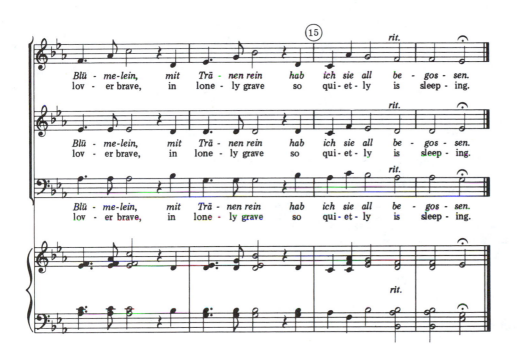

tra - gen; von her-bem Leid und Trau - rig-keit ist mir das Herz zer-flos - sen, die
bring-ing. There's no re-lief from bit - ter grief, A - las! My heart is break-ing; My

Blü - me-lein, mit Trä - nen rein hab ich sie all be-gos - sen.
lov - er brave, in lone - ly grave so qui - et - ly is sleep - ing.

In Stiller Nacht **185**

National Standards

The following National Standards are addressed through the Extension.
1. Singing, alone or with others, a varied repertoire of music. **(a)**
4. Composing and arranging music within specified guidelines. **(a)**

- From a sitting position, stand as they crescendo and sit as they decrescendo without making any sudden moves. They should be fully standing when they reach the peak of the phrase and fully sitting when they finish the phrase.
- Sing the whole piece on *loo*, standing and sitting on each phrase, with smooth articulation.
- Discuss any problems.

Assessment

Informal Assessment
In this lesson, students showed the ability to:
- Sing crescendo/decrescendo, connected articulation, and German pronunciation in "In Stiller Nacht."

Student Self-Assessment
Have students:
- Answer the How Did You Do? questions at the bottom of page 183.

Individual Performance Assessment
Have students:
- Each demonstrate correct German pronunciation by performing measures 9–16 into a tape recorder.
- Sing measures 9–16 in a trio, standing and sitting when appropriate, demonstrating a sustained, connected phrase.

Extension

Playing with Crescendo and Decrescendo
Have students:
- Choose a favorite song, and make a plan for when to crescendo and decrescendo.
- Perform their plan.

Contemporary Period

Focus

OVERVIEW
Understanding the development of choral music during the Contemporary period.

OBJECTIVES
After completing this lesson, students will be able to:
- Compare qualities of music written in the Contemporary and Romantic styles.
- Identify several characteristics and styles of twentieth-century music.
- Define *abstract, aleatoric music, dissonance, fusion,* and *twelve-tone music.*

CHORAL MUSIC TERMS
Define the Choral Music Terms for students, providing pronunciation, and answering any questions that may arise.

Three Musicians, a Cubist work by Pablo Picasso (1881–1973), demonstrates visual art based on geometric elements. In art and music, contemporary artists employ a variety of new techniques in the creation of their works.

1921. Pablo Picasso. *Three Musicians.* (Detail.) Oil on canvas. 200.7 x 222.9 cm (6'7" x 7'3¼"). Museum of Modern Art, New York, New York. Mrs. Simon Guggenheim Fund.

TEACHER'S RESOURCE BINDER
Fine Art Transparency 5, *Three Musicians,* by Pablo Picasso

National Standards
2. Performing on instruments a varied repertoire of music. **(c)**
4. Composing and arranging music within specified guidelines. **(b, c)**
6. Listening to, analyzing, and describing music. **(a, c)**
8. Understanding relationships between music and other disciplines. **(a, b)**
9. Understanding music in relation to history and culture. **(a, b)**

Contemporary Period

After completing this lesson, you will be able to:

- Compare qualities of music written in the Romantic and Contemporary styles.
- Identify several characteristics and styles of twentieth-century music.
- Define dissonance, twelve-tone music, and aleatoric, or chance music.
- Define fusion.

You live in the **Contemporary period,** the time from 1900 to right now, so you know something about contemporary music. More likely, however, there are some kinds of contemporary music that are still awaiting your discovery. One of the most important characteristics of the twentieth century has been rapid change. In this century, humans have lived through two world wars, the Chinese and Russian revolutions, the Great Depression, the Cold War, the rise and fall of Communism in many countries of the world, and many other events. Society is moving fast, and changes are constant.

A Time of Variety

Technology has had a large influence in the twentieth century, and it affects the preferences and demands of people. First, phonographs made music easily accessible to anyone who wanted to hear it. The invention of the radio brought live performances right into people's homes. Then, television captivated the world. Now tape recorder/players, CDs, and computers with interactive programs are popular, bringing us higher quality sounds and images and more possibilities. In many locations, synthesizers are taking the place of acoustic instruments, making it less expensive and easier for everyone to be involved in music-making and listening.

Looking Back

In the Romantic period, composers searched for new means of musical expression through the use of changed musical elements and larger orchestras. Many times, they were painting a story or mood in sound. As we have seen in the past, the artistic cycle tends to go from emotional to rational and back. During the twentieth century, composers and artists looked toward the abstract as a reaction to the overly emotional Romantic arts. They felt music was its own justification—it did not exist to paint some picture or evoke some emotion. Consequently, great changes occurred.

COMPOSERS

Richard Strauss (1864–1949)
Ralph Vaughan Williams (1872–1958)
Charles Ives (1874–1954)
Béla Bartók (1881–1945)
Igor Stravinsky (1882–1971)
Sergei Prokofiev (1891–1953)
George Gershwin (1898–1937)
Aaron Copland (1900–1990)
Benjamin Britten (1913–1976)
Leonard Bernstein (1918–1990)
David N. Davenport
Eugene Butler
Bob Dylan (1941–)

ARTISTS

Henri Rousseau (1844–1910)
Wassily Kandinsky (1866–1944)
Henri Matisse (1869–1954)
Pablo Picasso (1881–1973)
Georgia O'Keeffe (1887–1986)
Jackson Pollock (1912–1956)
Andrew Wyeth (1917–)
Andy Warhol (1930–1987)

AUTHORS

George Bernard Shaw (1856–1950)
Sir Arthur Conan Doyle (1859–1930)
Edith Wharton (1862–1937)
Gertrude Stein (1874–1946)
Robert Frost (1874–1963)
James Joyce (1882–1941)
Virginia Woolf (1882–1941)
T. S. Eliot (1888–1965)
William Faulkner (1897–1962)
Ernest Hemingway (1899–1961)
John Steinbeck (1902–1968)
Maya Angelou (1928–)

CHORAL MUSIC TERMS

abstract
aleatoric music
chance music
Contemporary period
dissonance
fusion
twelve-tone music

Contemporary Period **187**

Introducing the Lesson

Introduce the Contemporary period through visual art.

Point out the fine art, *Three Musicians,* on page 186, and the architecture illustration on page 188.

Have students:

- Look at the painting, pointing out ways in which this painter created art differently than the artists of other periods studied. Ask: Is there a story in the picture?

Wright Brothers' flight

1903

Model-T Ford introduced
1908

1905
First motion picture
theater opens

1914–1918
World War I

Suggested Teaching Sequence

1. Examine the Contemporary period.

Have students:

- Read the text on pages 187–191.
- Read, discuss, and answer the review questions individually, in pairs, or in small groups.
- Discuss their answers with the whole group, clarifying misunderstandings.

2. Examine the Contemporary period in historical perspective.

Have students:

- Turn to the time line on pages 188–191 and read the citations.
- Discuss why these are considered important dates and personalities during the Contemporary period.
- Compare each of these events to what occurred before the Contemporary period.
- Devise a one- or two-sentence statement that describes the Contemporary period based on one of the events in the time line. (For example: The Contemporary period is a time of great change. The first airplane was flown sometime around 1903. By 1927 Lindbergh flew across the Atlantic. By 1945 planes were being used to drop atomic bombs, and soon after that there were men on the moon.)
- Devise one additional sentence which tells how this Contemporary event is related to the student's world. (For example: Although we have technology to travel around the world, through outer space, and under the ocean, most people have not experienced these adventures.)

▲ **Just as contemporary music explores new avenues of expression, the Chapel of Notre Dame du Haut is a unique style of architecture. The massive walls and the rounded roof reflect abstract sculpture of contemporary artists. At the same time, the design is suggestive of the strength and solidity of a medieval fortress.**

1955. Le Corbusier. Frontal view of Chapelle de Notre Dame du Haut. Chapelle de Notre Dame du Haut, Ronchamp, France.

During the Romantic period, there was a change from church- and patron-sponsored composition to commissions and the sale of compositions. As the emerging middle class became the main consumer of music, the aristocracy played a less important role. Musicians' income was now provided by the sale of concert tickets and published music. In the twentieth century, serious music is supported by large and small performing groups in most cities and large towns. There is also support from nonprofit organizations, colleges, and universities.

As the twentieth century draws to a close, we can look back and see the changes from Impressionism (music that creates a musical picture with a

188 *Choral Connections   Level 1 Mixed Voices*

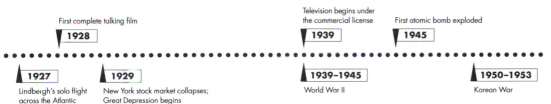

First complete talking film
1928

Television begins under
the commercial license
1939

First atomic bomb exploded
1945

1927
Lindbergh's solo flight
across the Atlantic

1929
New York stock market collapses;
Great Depression begins

1939–1945
World War II

1950–1953
Korean War

dreamy quality through chromaticism) to Expressionism (bold and dynamic expression of mood with great dissonance). Composers still use some forms from the Romantic period, such as opera, the symphony, and song form. Yet, they also continue to experiment with new ways to express themselves through music.

Music of the Period

Much of the music written before World War I was a continuation of Romanticism. After that war, composers were striving for a more objective style, a style stressing music for its own sake. There was a swing toward the **abstract,** *focusing on lines, rows, angles, clusters, textures, and form.*

Prior to the twentieth century, chords were built in intervals of a third. In the twentieth century, composers moved away from a tonal center and scalewise organization of pitch, and built *chords using seconds, fourths, fifths, and sevenths.* This resulted in a **dissonance** that sounded very harsh to those accustomed to tonal music.

Twelve-tone music was a new organization for composition. In twelve-tone music, *the twelve tones of the chromatic scale are arranged in a tone row, then the piece is composed by arranging and rearranging the "row" in different ways—backward, forward, in clusters of three or four pitches, and so on.* The mathematical possibilities are almost endless, especially when layered, instrument over instrument. Many people feel that music composed this way is more of an exercise for the composer than a source of pleasure for the listener.

Another interesting experimental type of music is **aleatoric,** or **chance music.** In aleatoric music, *the piece has a beginning and an end, and the rest is left to chance.* There is usually a score of some kind, but great freedom is allowed each performer (for example, how long to hold each pitch, which pitch to begin on, how fast to go, and when to stop).

Other compositional elements of the twentieth century include more angular contour of the melody and different concepts of harmony, which may emphasize dissonance, complex rhythms, and specific performance markings.

World Music and Fusion

During the twentieth century, folk music from around the world traveled to greater distances as people became more mobile. Immigrants and travelers shared songs from diverse cultures, and the musical styles have influenced one another. Popular music styles emerged and continue to be created, based on characteristics of different folk groups and the intermingling of ideas. Serious

Contemporary Period **189**

3. Define the musical aspects of the Contemporary period.

Have students:
- Review the changes in music during the Contemporary period.
- Define *abstract, aleatoric music, dissonance, fusion,* and *twelve-tone music.*

Extension

Creating Twelve-Tone Music

It's easy to create a tone row. Have students:

- Take a chromatic set of resonator bells and arrange them in any order, rearranging them until the sound is interesting.
- Write down the pitches on a staff.
- Brainstorm how many ways this tone row can be played. (for example: backward, from the middle—one way and then the other, in clusters of three or four sounds, and so on.)
- Perform the pieces, and evaluate what they did and did not like.

The rule is that no pitch can be repeated until all twelve are heard. It is a challenge to the imagination and intellect to construct an interesting piece using this twelve-tone style.

Creating Aleatoric Music

There are many ways to create aleatoric music. Have students:

- Use a mobile (hanging sculpture) as a score.
- Choose a sound source for each object hanging from the mobile.
- Then play the mobile starting with any one object, and continuing as the eye travels from object to object, or as a conductor points to the objects randomly.

More than one group can play the mobile at a time, starting in different places, and at different speeds. The piece begins when the first sound is played, and ends when everyone finishes.

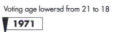

U.S. satellite put into orbit **1958**

U.S. astronaut John Glenn orbits the earth **1962**

Voting age lowered from 21 to 18 **1971**

1957 First Earth satellite put into orbit by USSR

1961 First manned satellite by USSR

1969 U.S. astronauts land on the moon

music composers also used the characteristics, melodies, and texts of folk music for their compositions. *Musical styles began to blend* in a phenomenon called **fusion.** For example, African-American, Cajun, and French Canadian musics have blended to create the fusion style called zydeco. This kind of fusion is continuing today around the world.

There is also fusion of popular and art music styles. Many folk songs are being arranged and played by symphony orchestras. For example, vocalist Bobby McFerrin collaborated with classical cellist Yo-Yo Ma in recordings and performances with symphony orchestras. Popular singers such as Linda Ronstadt and Sting perform with professional choirs and orchestras. Instruments from many cultures find their way into classical performing groups, and music from all periods is being rearranged for electronic media.

Contemporary Pop Styles

Listed below are some American styles that have emerged during the twentieth century. Some of them are still thriving, and new ones are being created every day.

- *Ragtime*—an early style of jazz, very rhythmic and syncopated.
- *Musical Stage Music*—centered around Broadway and Hollywood musicals.
- *Blues*—simple, harmonious melodies with two phrases the same, then one different.
- *Spiritual*—songs originating in the slave culture, usually religious in theme.
- *Jazz*—strong but rhythmic understructure supporting solo and ensemble improvisation.
- *Rock*—strong, steady beat.
- *Country*—based on the folk style of the southern rural United States or on the music of the cowboy.
- *Folk*—folk songs and composed songs that tell a story or sometimes have a social message.
- *Reggae*—a fusion of rock and Jamaican rhythms, instruments, and language.
- *Calypso*—an island style with strong chords and syncopation.
- *Tejano*—a fusion of Mexican and country music.
- *Zydeco*—a fusion of African-American, Cajun, and French Canadian rhythms, instruments, and lyrics.

Music's Future and You

It is important that the consumer—that's you—has a sense of quality, in both popular and classical music. That way, quality music will survive into the future.

190 *Choral Connections   Level 1 Mixed Voices*

Little League accepts girls
▼ **1975**

Fall of the Berlin Wall
▼ **1989**

▲ **1972**
Robert Moog patents the
Moog synthesizer

▲ **1975**
U.S. withdraws from Vietnam

▲ **1976**
U.S. celebrates its 200th birthday

Check Your Understanding

Recall

1. What technological inventions made music more accessible during the twentieth century?

2. Why did music change during the Contemporary period?

3. Are any forms from past periods still being composed? How are they different?

4. Describe dissonance.

5. Describe twelve-tone and aleatoric music.

6. Why is folk music still sung in the twentieth century? Name a folk song you have heard that is a twentieth-century piece.

7. Describe the result of fusion.

Thinking It Through

1. Some people say that records, tapes, and CDs are bad for society, because people never get together to sing or go out to concerts anymore. Do you think this is true? Why or why not? How do they affect the way we appreciate music?

2. If you wanted to see and hear examples of Contemporary art and popular music today, where could you find them?

Contemporary Period **191**

Assessment

Informal Assessment
During this lesson, students showed ability to:
- Identify characteristics of the Contemporary period and Contemporary music.
- Describe the impact of events on the Contemporary period.
- Define *abstract, aleatoric music, dissonance, fusion,* and *twelve-tone music.*

Student Self-Assessment
Have students:
- Review the questions in Check Your Understanding.
- Write a paragraph describing how much they understand about the Contemporary period.

Individual Performance Assessment
To further demonstrate accomplishment, have students:
- Learn more about one aspect of music during the Contemporary period.
- Share their findings with the class in a creative way, such as a poster, demonstration, design for the cover of a CD or video, and so on.

ANSWERS TO RECALL QUESTIONS

1. Phonographs, radio, television, electronic devices, and computers.
2. Composers were searching for a more objective style.
3. Yes—opera, symphony, and song; composers experiment with new forms.
4. Chords using seconds, fourths, fifths, and sevenths.
5. Twelve-tone music uses the twelve tones of the chromatic scale arranged in different ways. Aleatoric music has a beginning and an end, and the rest is left to chance.
6. There remains an interest in the music of various cultures. Responses will vary.
7. A blending of musical styles.

Listening to . . .
Contemporary Music

Listening to . . .
Contemporary Music

This feature is designed to expand students' appreciation of choral and instrumental music of the Contemporary period.

**Choral Selection:
"Mister Tambourine Man"
by Dylan**
Have students:
• Read the information on this page to learn more about "Mister Tambourine Man."
• Study the Blackline Master, Listening Map 9.

Using the Listening Map
Move from top to bottom and left to right. The form is as follows: Introduction; Chorus; Verse 1; Verse 2; Chorus; Coda.
Have students:
• Compare what they know about life in the 1960s and life as they know it today. Include discussion about fashion, music groups, fads, popular events, and so on.
• Discuss how music can convey a person's feelings.
• Listen to "Mister Tambourine Man" as they follow the listening map.

| CHORAL SELECTION |
Bob Dylan — "Mister Tambourine Man"

Bob Dylan was a prolific protest songwriter of the 1960s and 1970s. He wrote and performed music in a folk style. The Byrds, who performed "Mister Tambourine Man" on the recording you will hear, was a rock group from California. Dylan's folk style, combined with the Byrds' rock style, produced a new strand of music called "Folk Rock." "Mister Tambourine Man" was the Byrds' biggest hit and released a new wave of folk rock music that influenced songwriters in the following decades.

| INSTRUMENTAL SELECTION |
Britten — *The Young Person's Guide to the Orchestra*
(Variations and Fugue on a Theme of Purcell)

Benjamin Britten (1913–1976) was an English composer whose abilities and precociousness led him to be compared to Mozart's genius. He was commissioned by the English Ministry of Education to write a unique work for children to teach them the instruments of the orchestra. He took a theme from Henry Purcell's incidental music to *Abdelazar* and created *The Young Person's Guide to the Orchestra* that included a theme, variations and fugue.

TEACHER'S RESOURCE BINDER
Blackline Master, Listening Map 9
Blackline Master, Listening Map 10
Optional Listening Selections:
The Norton Recordings, 7th edition
"Mister Tambourine Man": Vol. II, CD 8, Track 43
The Young Person's Guide to the Orchestra: Vol. I, CD 1, Track 1

National Standards
This lesson addresses the following National Standard:
9. Understanding music in relation to history and culture. **(b)**

Introducing...

"River, Sing Your Song"

David N. Davenport

Setting the Stage

"River, Sing Your Song" by David N. Davenport is an example of twentieth century choral music that is written in the style of folk music. What might have been a solo or pop song has been harmonized and turned into wonderful choral literature. The public schools, colleges, and universities have had a tremendous influence and demand for this type of music.

Meeting the Composer

David N. Davenport and Eugene Butler

A graduate of Indiana University, Davenport has directed junior high, high school, and church choirs for many years. The thrill of hearing his first composition sung by a 300-person choir encouraged Davenport to continue writing songs. Many of his choral music songs are "mood pieces" that deal with subject matter taken from the natural elements. For example, "Sea Scenes," published some years ago, paints a musical picture of the ocean and how it moves. Another song, "Willow, Willow," deals with willow trees, whose branches are flowing gracefully in the wind. He wrote the text for "River, Sing Your Song," and then asked Eugene Butler to put music to his words.

Contemporary Connections **193**

Instrumental Selection:
The Young Person's Guide to the Orchestra by Britten
Have students:
- Read the information on page 192 to learn more about instruments in an orchestra.
- Study the Blackline Master, Listening Map 10.

Using the Listening Map
Begin at theme 1 on page 1, marked "full orchestra." Numbers 1–6 are the instrument families introducing the themes that are notated at the bottom of the map. Continue by following the numbers of the variations in the outline of the orchestra. The variations are played by each instrument of each family: #1 (flutes) through #24 (all percussion). Finish page 1 at the conductor, #25 (full orchestra). Follow page 2 of the map from instrument to instrument, starting with the piccolo and ending with full orchestra.
Have students:
- Discuss how music can be used by institutions or corporations to promote a sense of loyalty and pride, to stir emotions, to sell a product, or to educate.
- Listen to *The Young Person's Guide to the Orchestra* and follow the listening map.

INTRODUCING . . .
"River, Sing Your Song"
This feature is designed to introduce students to the Contemporary Lesson on the following pages.
Have students:
- Read Setting the Stage on this page to learn more about "River, Sing Your Song."
- Read Meeting the Composer to learn more about David N. Davenport and Eugene Butler.
- Turn the page and begin the Contemporary Lesson.

ASSESSMENT

Individual Performance Assessment
To further demonstrate understanding of Contemporary music, have students:
- Work in pairs or small groups to choose a familiar song and describe the message, if any, that the lyrics convey.
- Identify music that is used to convey the following ideas: patriotism, individualism, facts, feelings of anger or love, and trust in a person or product.

River, Sing Your Song

COMPOSER: Eugene Butler
TEXT: David Davenport

Focus

OVERVIEW
Phrasing, dynamics.

OBJECTIVES
Upon completion of this lesson, students will be able to:
- Demonstrate correct dynamics.
- Determine and perform correct phrasing.

CHORAL MUSIC TERMS
Define the Choral Music Terms for students, providing correct pronunciation, and answering any questions that may arise.

Warming Up

Vocal Warm-Up
This Vocal Warm-Up is designed to prepare students to:
- Sing short slurs.
- Sing in various keys.
- Sing, forming the correct vowel sounds.
Have students:
- Read through the Vocal Warm-Up directions.
- Sing, following your demonstration.

River, Sing Your Song

COMPOSER: *Eugene Butler*
TEXT: *David N. Davenport*

CHORAL MUSIC TERMS
dynamics
forte
mezzo forte (*mf*)

VOICING
Three-part mixed

PERFORMANCE STYLE
Flowing
Accompanied by piano

FOCUS
- Demonstrate correct dynamics.
- Determine and perform correct phrasing.

Warming Up

 Vocal Warm-Up
Sing on solfège syllables, then on the neutral syllables under the notes. Notice the slurs. Usually a phrase is marked by a long arc. In this exercise there are short arcs that tell you to slur two pitches. But where would you mark the phrase? Sing through each phrase with strong breath support.

Continue up to next key.

loo___ ee___ loo___ ee___ lah___

TEACHER'S RESOURCE BINDER

 National Standards
This lesson addresses:
1. Singing, alone and with others, a varied repertoire of music. **(a, c, e)**
3. Improvising melodies, variations, and accompaniments. **(c)**
5. Reading and notating music. **(a, b, c, d)**
7. Evaluating music. **(a)**
8. Understanding music and arts. **(a)**
9. Understanding music in relation to history and culture. **(b)**

Sight-Singing

Sight-sing the parts below separately, then in any combination. How many phrases are in this exercise? Sing each phrase with a crescendo to the "peak," and then decrescendo to the end. What do the I, IV, V markings denote?

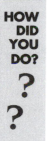

Singing: "River, Sing Your Song"

Can you improvise a melody that "describes" a river?

Listen to several classmates improvise a melody that "describes" a river. Choose one melody to sing all together.

With a partner, make up a simple movement that matches the melody.

Now turn to the music for "River, Sing Your Song" on page 196.

HOW DID YOU DO?

Think about your performance on the Vocal Warm-Up, Sight-Singing, and "River, Sing Your Song."

1. Could you describe your part independently?

2. Describe how you decided where each phrase begins and ends.

3. Describe how you used dynamics to enhance the phrases.

4. What characteristics of Contemporary music did you experience in this piece?

5. Do you think the music fits the text of "River, Sing Your Song"? Why? Why not? Use specific musical terms and language to support your opinion.

Sight-Singing

This Sight-Singing exercise is designed to prepare students to:

- Sight-sing, using solfège and hand signs or numbers.
- Combine independent lines of rhythms and perform them in an ensemble.
- Sing complete phrases.

Have students:

- Read through the Sight-Singing exercise directions.
- Read each voice part rhythmically, using rhythm syllables.
- Sight-sing through each part separately.
- Sing parts in any combination.
- Determine the number of phrases in the exercise.
- Sing all parts together.

Singing: "River, Sing Your Song"

Identify the concept of being a composer.

Have students:

- Read the text in the Singing section on this page.
- Volunteer to improvise a melody that "describes" a river.
- Choose one melody and sing it on solfège syllables.
- Write the melody on the board (with your help, if necessary).
- Choose a partner and create a simple movement to match the created melody.
- Use the new melody as a warm-up exercise, moving up or down by half steps.

Suggested Teaching Sequence

1. Review Vocal Warm-Up.
Identify phrases.
Have students:
- Review the Vocal Warm-Up.
- Repeat the exercise until the class agrees that it is well done.
- Divide into voice part sections (SAB) and find the phrases in "River, Sing Your Song" by reading through the text in rhythm.
- Still in sections, speak the phrases in rhythm, putting stress on the "peak" words and swinging an arm in an arc to simulate the rising and falling of the phrase.

2. Review Sight-Singing.
Use crescendo and decrescendo to sing phrases.
Have students:
- Review the Sight-Singing exercise, reading each part separately, then in different combinations.
- Sight-sing all four parts together.
- Practice singing the exercise using crescendo and decrescendo.

River, Sing Your Song

Eugene Butler
David N. Davenport

Three-part Mixed Voices, Accompanied

TEACHING STRATEGY
Understanding and Singing Dissonant Harmonies

If thirds are considered consonant, then seconds and sevenths create dissonance to the harmonically trained ear. Have students:
- Sing a chord on *do, mi,* and *so.*
- Then sing a chord consisting of *do, re,* and *mi.*
- Return to the *do-mi-so* chord, each section of the choir singing and holding out one of the pitches.
- As you point to one person in each section, that person should change the pitch to any other pitch. The whole section changes to the new pitch.
- Then choose someone from another section. Wait each time until the whole section tunes to the new pitch before pointing again.

Students will become familiar with the feeling of singing dissonant intervals.

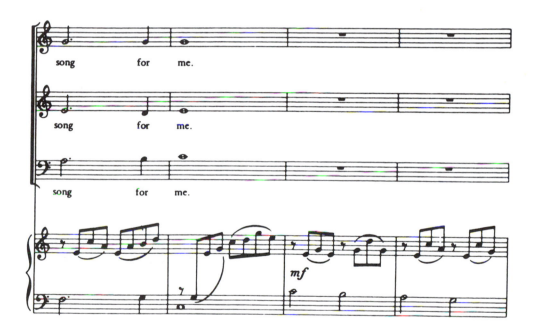

Wind - ing to the deep blue sea, O, riv - er, sing your _

Wind - ing to the deep blue _ sea, O, riv - er, sing your _

Wind - ing to the deep blue sea, O, riv - er, sing your

song for me.

song for me.

song for me.

mf

3. Sight-sing "River, Sing Your Song" using solfège and hand signs or numbers.

Have students:

- Divide into voice sections (SAB) and sing the piece with solfège and hand signs or numbers.
- Discuss and work on problem areas.
- Divide into sections and re-cite the text rhythmically for each voice part.
- Sing the piece through with text as a full ensemble.

4. Add dynamics to the piece.

Have students:

- Sing measures 5–13 three times, first piano, next mezzo forte, and finally forte.
- Find all the dynamic markings in the piece and relate them to the three levels above.
- Sing the song, performing dynamics on each phrase.

 **VOCAL DEVELOPMENT**

To encourage vocal development, have students:

- Sing the important word *river* with a stressed and unstressed *r* in the second syllable after the vowel. Modify the *er* to an *ah* for singing purposes.
- Decide whether to flip the *r* on *rippling river*.
- Tune the thirds carefully.
- Use long phrases and staggered breathing for legato singing.

 Fusion Styles

Fusion styles are emerging around the world. Some people are concerned that there will be no pure folk music anymore. Others say that folk music is always changing, and this is a natural occurrence for live art. An example in the United States is tejano style, which is a fusion of Mexican and Texas country music, incorporating elements of the mariachi tradition (trumpet, violin, and bass) and accordion. Explore performing groups in your community to see if there is any fusion music being created.

 MUSIC LITERACY

Have students:
- Read the rhythms, using rhythm syllables while conducting.
- Conduct and speak the words in rhythm.
- Identify scalewise and choral passages in the three voice parts.
- Sing the altered notes and decide whether the altered notes decorate the main melody or whether they are used to change the mode of the melody.
- Analyze the form of the song using small letters, a, b, and c for the phrase structure and capital letters for the sections, i.e., AB, ABA, and so on.
- Experiment conducting in 4 and 2. Ask: Which meter fits the character of the song?

mel - o - dy, O, riv - er, sing your_ song for me.

mel - o - dy, O, riv - er, sing your_ song for me.

mel - o - dy, O, riv - er, sing your song for me.

mf

Life like a song mov - in' a - long

Assessment

Informal Assessment

During this lesson, students showed the ability to:

- Identify and sing phrases in the Vocal Warm-Up.
- Demonstrate crescendo/decrescendo in the Sight-Singing exercise.
- Sing, demonstrating correct dynamics on each phrase in "River, Sing Your Song."

Student Self-Assessment

Have students:

- Read the How Did You Do? section on page 195.
- Answer the questions individually. Discuss their answers in pairs or small groups, and/or write their responses on a sheet of paper.

Individual Performance Assessment

To further demonstrate accomplishment, have the students:

- In trios, perform a section of the piece, demonstrating correct musical phrases.
- In double trios, perform from measure 36 to the end, showing correct dynamics.

Extension

Movement to Show Phrases

Have students:

- Use the movements created during the Singing section to create a simple choreography matching the phrases of the song.
- Find a way to write the choreography down, phrase by phrase, or videotape it for future reference. Choreography is very difficult to write down and reinterpret, which allows for lots of discussion and clarification.

A Composer's Decisions

The composer of this piece made choices from all the musical possibilities available from every period of history up to, and including, the present. Have students:

- Read the text of the piece, and decide whether they think the composer made good choices.
- Then discuss alternative treatments for this text that might be appropriate.
- Create a new setting for the poem using speech, found sounds, instruments, melody, or whatever they can imagine and justify with good musical reasons.
- Practice and perform their arrangement, revising it until it is ready for performance. It could be on a concert program along with the original piece.

National Standards

The following National Standards are addressed through the Extension and bottom-page activities:

4. Composing and arranging music within specified guidelines. **(a, b)**
7. Evaluating music and music performances. **(a, b)**
8. Understanding relationships between music, the other arts, and disciplines outside the arts. **(a)**
9. Understanding music in relation to history and culture. **(a, b, c)**

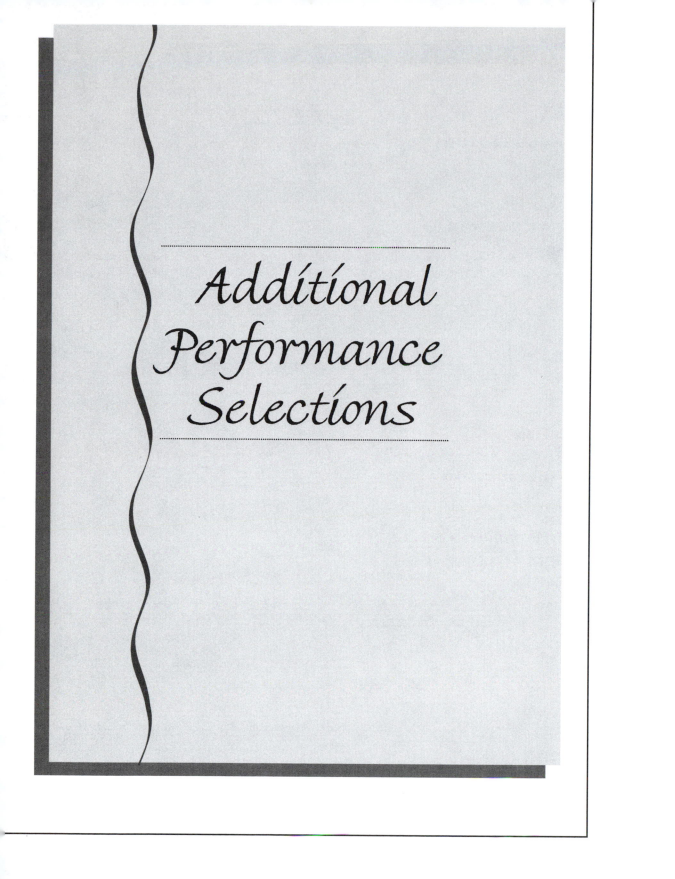

Additional Performance Selections

WARM-UPS FOR PERFORMANCE SELECTIONS

I Hear Liberty Singing

COMPOSER: Greg Gilpin

Warming Up

Vocal Warm-Up

Have students:

- Sing first on solfège and hand signs or numbers to learn the pattern.
- Then switch to singing on the syllable *loo.*
- Hold the last chord and move to the next key one-half step up.
- After the choir has moved up, sing the exercise again.

Now turn to page 207.

It's Time to Fly Away

COMPOSER: Joyce Elaine Eilers

Warming Up

Vocal Warm-Up

Have students:

- Sing the pattern using solfège and hand signs or numbers to become familiar with the key of C major.

Now turn to page 216.

VOICING

SATB

PERFORMANCE STYLE

Purposeful
Accompanied by piano

I Hear Liberty Singing

Warming Up

 Vocal Warm-Up

Sing the pattern using solfège syllables or numbers. Then switch to singing on *loo.* Hold the last chord and move one half-step up to a new key. Continue the exercise, moving one half-step up on each repeat.

Continue up by half steps.

Now turn to page 207.

VOICING

SAB

PERFORMANCE STYLE

Pensive
Accompanied by piano

It's Time to Fly Away

Warming Up

Vocal Warm-Up

Sing the following patterns using solfège or numbers.

Now turn to page 216.

204   *Choral Connections   Level 1 Mixed Voices*

VOICING
SAB

PERFORMANCE STYLE
Flowing
Accompanied by piano

Shenandoah

Warming Up

Vocal Warm-Up

Practice these intervals up and down by half steps. Sing using solfège or numbers. Do each key section all on one breath.

*Now turn to page **223**.*

VOICING
SAB

PERFORMANCE STYLE
Andante processional
Accompanied by percussion

Three Yoruba Native Songs of Nigeria

Warming Up

Vocal Warm-Up

Sing using solfège or numbers. Continue to move up stepwise.

Shenandoah

American Folk Song

ARRANGER: Brad Printz

Warming Up

Vocal Warm-Up
Have students:
- Sing these intervals using solfège and hand signs or numbers. Continue the exercise up and down by half steps. Use one breath for each three-measure phrase.

*Now turn to page **223**.*

Three Yoruba Native Songs of Nigeria

ARRANGERS: Henry H. Leck and Prince Julius Adeniyi

Warming Up

Vocal Warm-Up
- Sing these intervals using solfège and hand signs or numbers. Continue the exercise by half steps. Use one breath for each three measure phrase. Use heavier registration to prepare singing in Yoruban style.

*Now turn to page **231**.*

The Tree of Peace

COMPOSER: Fred Bock

TEXT: John Greenleaf Whittier

Warming Up

Vocal Warm-Up

Have students:

- Sing the following parts in G minor using solfège and hand signs.
- Notice where the parts are in unison, and where there are two and three parts.

Remind students that the chord tones are sometimes close together, so they will have to listen very carefully.

Now turn to page **234.**

Now turn to page **231.**

VOICING

SAB

PERFORMANCE STYLE

Moderato
Accompanied by piano

The Tree of Peace

Warming Up

Vocal Warm-Up

Sing the parts below in G minor using solfège. Notice where the parts are in unison, and where there are two and three parts. The chord tones are sometimes close together, so listen carefully.

Now turn to page **234.**

I Hear Liberty Singing

Words and Music by
GREG GILPIN

SATB, Accompanied

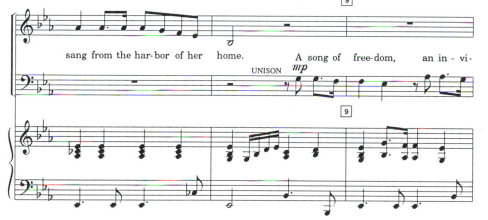

I Hear Liberty Singing

Performance Tips

- This selection is an excellent "closer" for a concert. Also, it would be a nice piece for several combined choirs to sing.
- Signing would also be an added touch to enhance understanding and meaning.

Rhythmic Focus

Have students:
Read through the piece in the following order.

- Read the rhythm with rhythm syllables or text. The rhythm of this piece fits the natural rhythm of the text. Work to keep the rhythm from becoming too metrical. Keep the rhythm of the text in mind as you learn the rhythm of the notes.

Melodic Focus

Have students:

- In voice sections (SATB), sight-sing the melody with solfège syllables or text.
- Sing the piece through as a full ensemble.

The melody of this piece flows nicely and has few surprises. Make sure students connect each note to prevent any choppy phrases. The harmony is logical and easy.

Hot Spots

- Listen for careful tuning in octave singing in measures 11, 19–20, 38, 44, and 50. Some of these measures are good recovery spots after more difficult harmony sections.
- Measure 55, one measure before the key change, needs to be secure.
- In measure 25, keep the solo as the most important part by pulling back the *oo* parts.
- When the parts split into five- and six–part harmonies, make sure they are assigned and clearly sung.

Program Ideas:

"Shalom, My Friends"—Wagner
"The Tiger"—Porterfield
"Dare to Dream!"—Lorenz
"Bound for Jubilee"—Eilers
"I Hear Liberty Singing"—Gilpin

VOCAL DEVELOPMENT

To encourage vocal development, have students:

- Identify the imitation of different voices and places where unison and part singing occurs.
- Modify vowel sounds on words such as *invitation* and *one*.
- Follow guidelines for singing *r* after a vowel, as in *years, her,* and *world*.
- Follow guidelines for singing diphthongs on words such as *night, light,* and *tired*.
- Sing balanced chords by listening carefully to the weight of each chord tone.

MORE ABOUT... Composer Greg Gilpin

Born and raised in Waverly, Missouri, composer Greg Gilpin has lived in Alexandria, Indiana since 1986. He is a graduate of Northwest Missouri State University with a degree in Vocal Music Education, K-12. Gilpin travels the United States and the world, conducting choral festivals and working as a clinician and choreographer with students of all ages and with music teachers.

This work has taken him to Japan, New Guinea, the Philippines, Germany, France, and Switzerland. To raise funds and awareness of homeless children, he worked with the organization called America Sings!

Gilpin has been published by Alfred, The Lorenz Corporation, Praise Gathering Music Group, Gilpin–McPheeters, and Warner/CPP Belwin.

Have students:
- Read rhythms using rhythm syllables while conducting.
- Conduct and speak the words in rhythm.
- Identify the new triplet rhythm at measure 21. Practice dividing two beats into three equal pieces.
- Distinguish chords in chordal passages.

turned so they could not see her flame. But I hear li-ber-ty sing-ing. Her song of free-dom is ring - ing a - round the world, strong-er than— be - fore. From shore to shore, I hear li - ber-ty

Oo I hear li - ber - ty

"I Hear Liberty Singing"

Greg Gilpin, the composer of "I Hear Liberty Singing," says, "I've always enjoyed patriotic songs and have felt they are important for our young people to learn and perform. Personally, I was tired of hearing the same message over and over again and tried to create a new lyric with a different point of view. I believe I've achieved this with 'I Hear Liberty Singing.' I approached the Statue of Liberty as an analogy of a lady singing her song or message, but everyone hated it and refused to listen. She continued to sing in spite of this, and today, all the world longs for her song of liberty and freedom. I think it is a strong message of doing what you believe in no matter what people might say or do to fight against it."

The Statue of Liberty

During the centennial celebration of the Declaration of Independence in the United States, French author Edouard de Laboulaye proposed the erection of a memorial to commemorate the alliance of 1778 between France and the United States. Auguste Bartholdi, assigned to execute the memor- ial, proposed that the French people erect a mammoth statue upon one of the islands in New York Harbor. The statue was completed for presentation to the United States in Paris on July 4, 1884. After being dismantled, it was shipped to New York and reassembled at its present location. President Grover

song._____ Like a bea- con shin-ing in___ the night,

those who

hear her   turn to see her   light.

slight rit.   **a tempo**

those who hear,   see her   light._____

Give   me   your

slight rit.   **a tempo**

Give   me   your

slight rit.   **a tempo**

cresc.

tired,   your___ poor your hud- dled   mas - ses   yearn-ing to breathe

cresc.

tired, give me   your poor_____   your hud- dled   mas - ses   yearn-ing to breathe

cresc.

Cleveland dedicated the statue on October 28, 1886. Bartholdi's statue portrays Liberty in the figure of a woman who has just won her freedom.

In her right hand she holds a burning torch and in her left hand a book of law inscribed "July 4, 1776." Broken shackles lie at her feet as she steps forward to enlighten the world.

The statue itself stands 151 feet high, although the tip of the torch is 305 feet above sea level. The width of the face is 10 feet and that of the eyes, 2 feet 6 inches. The law book in the left hand is 23 feet long, 13 feet wide, and 2 feet thick. The right arm is 42 feet long and diameter of the waist is 35 feet.

Made of hammered copper about one-eighth of an inch in thickness, the hollow,

225-ton statue is supported upon a steel frame anchored in the pedestal. The green color of the statue is the result of verdigris, or green rust of copper. The star-shaped wall around the base of the statue is part of the former U.S. Fort Wood, which was garrisoned as a part of the defenses of New York City from 1841 to 1877.

The Statue of Liberty was proclaimed a national monument by President Coolidge on October 15, 1924, and was transferred to the National Park Service in 1933. There is regular ferry service to the island from Battery Park, Manhattan.

The statue is officially entitled *Liberty Enlightening the World*. Inscribed in bronze on the pedestal is the poem "The New Colossus," written by Emma Lazarus:

Not like the brazen giant of Greek fame,
With conquering limbs astride from land to
    land;
Here at our sea-washed, sunset gates shall
    stand
A mighty woman with a torch, whose flame
Is the imprisoned lightning, and her name
Mother of Exiles. From her beacon-hand
Glows world-wide welcome; her mild eyes
    command

The air-bridged harbor that twin cities frame.
"Keep ancient lands, your storied pomp!"
    cries she
With silent lips. "Give me your tired, your
    poor,
Your huddled masses yearning to breathe
    free,
The wretched refuse of your teeming shore.
Send these, the homeless, tempest-tost to me,
I lift my lamp beside the golden door!"

free - dom ring - ing. Ah_____

ring - ing_____

ring - ing a - round the__ world, strong - er than__ be -

END DESCANT

fore. From shore to shore, I hear

strong - er than__ be - fore. From shore to shore,

li - ber - ty,   Ah

li - ber - ty   sings!

It's Time to
Fly Away

Performance Tips

Rhythmic Focus

Have students:

- Read the rhythm with rhythm syllables. The rhythm fits the natural rhythm of the text. The 4/4 meter lends itself to a smooth and pensive style. Notice the tempo changes at measures 12, 22, and 31, following the verse/refrain form of the piece.

Melodic Focus

Have students:

- In voice sections (SAB), read the melody with solfège and hand signs or numbers. The folk-like, flowing melody is carried mainly by the sopranos. From measures 22–25 the altos sing the melody. Parts should be easily sight-read.
- Read the piece through as an ensemble.

It's Time to Fly Away

Words and Music by
JOYCE ELAINE EILERS

Hot Spots

- Phrasing is very important in this piece.
- Baritones may be divided into two sections at measures 16–21 and measures 31–42.
- In measures 40–42, take the liberty of assigning a small group or solo to sing *away*. Possibly drop from full choir to small group, then quartets at the beginning of each measure or on your signal.

Program Ideas:

"It's Time to Fly Away"—Eilers
"The Tiger"—Porterfield
"In Stiller Nacht"—Brahms
"Down by the Riverside"—Printz
"Praise Ye the Lord, All Nations"—Bach/Sherman

all who would lis-ten, he sends his song, and then he flies a-

all who would lis-ten, he sends his song, and then he flies a-

all who would lis-ten, he sends his song, and then he flies a-

way. Song - bird, the

way. Song - bird, the

way. Song - bird, the

V 7909

V 7909

way.

way.

A

way.

Ab   Bb   C   C

22 **Tempo I** (♩ = 84)

Oo

chill   in the wind brings a warn-ing   of win-ter,   tell - ing the song - bird he

Oo

22 **Tempo I** (♩ = 84)

C   F   G   C   C   Em

p

V 7909

So life is a les-son in mov-in' on. It's

can-not stay. So life is a les-son in mov-in' on. It's

So life is a les-son in mov-in' on. It's

time to fly a-way.

time to fly a-way.

time to fly a-way.

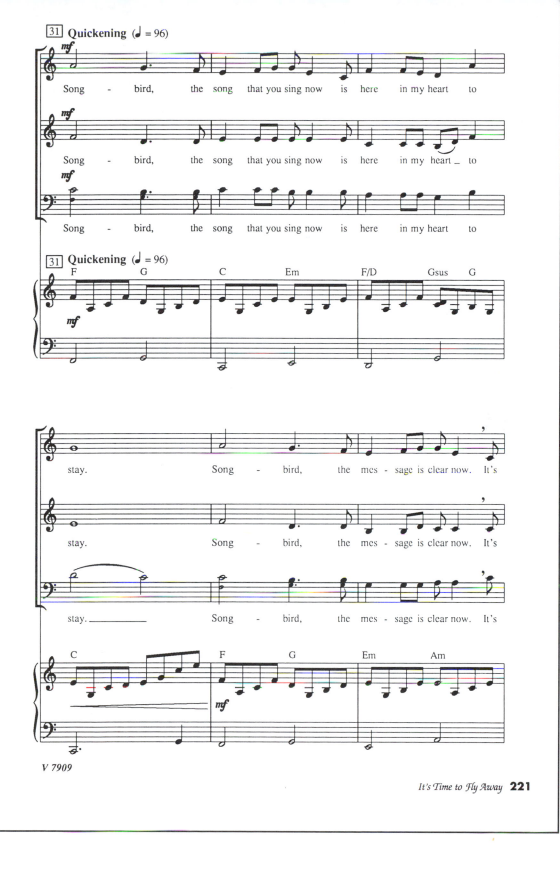

time to fly a - way.

time to fly a - way.

time to fly a - way.

(A - way.)

V 7909

*Optional - Solo or small group, Tenor or Alto.

222 *Choral Connections   Level 1 Mixed Voices*

Shenandoah

Traditional
American Folk Song
Arranged by Brad Printz

Three-part Mixed Chorus and Piano

Shenandoah **223**

MUSIC LITERACY

To help students expand their music literacy, have them:

- Read the rhythms using rhythm syllables while conducting.
- Conduct and speak the words in rhythm.
- Identify the chord changes. Ask students: Which chords are dissonant and how do they resolve?

Shenandoah

Performance Tips

"Shenandoah" is a wonderful piece for an American theme concert. The dynamics and tempo fluctuations are vital to this expressive piece of music. Do not hesitate to be creative and use some rubato techniques on the last page.

Rhythmic Focus

Have students:

- Read the rhythm with rhythm syllables. The secret to a great performance of "Shenandoah" lies in the interpretation of the long, flowing phrases. Emphasize the anacrusis at the beginning of many phrases. Watch for tied notes and rests, and watch the conductor during the multiple ritardandos.

Melodic Focus

Have students:

- In voice sections (SAB), sight-sing the melody with solfège and hand signs or numbers. This beautiful melody, and the accompanying harmony parts, have wide intervals that need careful attention. The independent voice parts require careful counting and watching for conductor's cues. There is almost an echoing effect throughout the piece.
- Sing the piece through as a full ensemble.

Hot Spots

- Rehearse the key change in measure 48 so it is smooth.
- Plan the breath mark and fermatas in measure 64 so they are executed carefully.
- Rehearse the dynamics and ritards so they are performed to give dramatic impact.
- Point out the long, smooth phrases, and teach students to stagger their breathing.

VOCAL DEVELOPMENT

To encourage vocal development, have students:

- Sing two-syllable words carefully, without creating a stress on the second syllable if one doesn't belong. For example, on the word *river* in measures 11, 33, and 55.
- Sing the diphthongs correctly on *away, wide,* and *bound*.
- Sing with expressive dynamics to create the mood of the folk song. Fragments and cadence ending repetitions should be sung softly.
- Sing each phrase with an idea of the beginning, climax point, and ending of the phrase. The dynamics often follow this arched form.

 Arranger Brad Printz

The hauntingly lyrical melody, "Shenandoah," beautiful in its simplicity, has made it a favorite folk song for many years. Believed to be a sea chantey from the early 1800s, it was originally performed by a chanteyman singing the verses and workmen echoing the refrains, "Away, you rolling river" and "Away, we're bound away, 'cross the wide Missouri." Original verses included the legend of a trader who fell in love with an Indian chief's daughter, and the word *Shenandoah* refers to the trader's homeland. The last syllable of Missouri was initially pronounced *rye,* but this has evolved with the passing of time to the present *ree.*

PROGRAM IDEAS

"Riu, Riu, Chiu"—Spevacek
"Over There"—Ray
"Bound for Jubilee"—Eilers
"Down by the Riverside"—
  Printz
"Shenandoah"—Printz

Shenandoah **225**

riv - er. _____ O ___ Shen - an-doah, _____

_____ I won't de - ceive you, _____ a -

a - way, a - way, _____ I'm bound a - way, _____ I'm bound a -

way, _____ I'm bound a - way, _____

a way, a - way, _____ I'm bound a -

Three Yoruba Native Songs of Nigeria

Arranged by
Henry H. Leck and Prince Julius Adeniyi

Unison Voiced and Percussion

1. E ORU O
"Greeting"

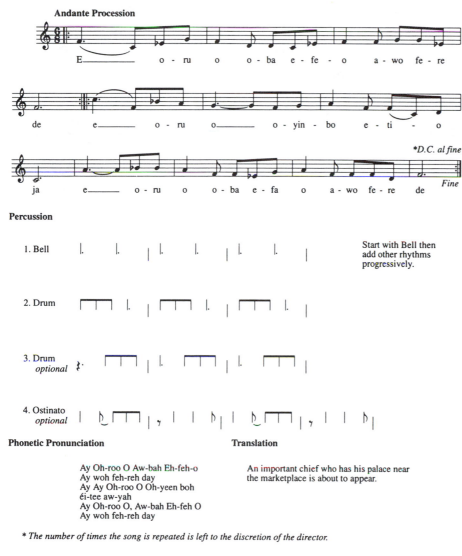

Phonetic Pronunciation

Ay Oh-roo O Aw-bah Eh-feh-o
Ay woh feh-reh day
Ay Ay Oh-roo O Oh-yeen boh
éi-tee aw-yah
Ay Oh-roo O, Aw-bah Eh-feh O
Ay woh feh-reh day

Translation

An important chief who has his palace near the marketplace is about to appear.

* The number of times the song is repeated is left to the discretion of the director.

Three Yoruba Native Songs of Nigeria **231**

MUSIC LITERACY

To help students expand their music literacy, have them:

- Conduct and speak the rhythm syllables in each song.
- Conduct and speak the text in rhythm. Ask: Does it fit the pattern of Western music scales? Why or why not?

- Analyze the intervals of the songs. Ask: Which intervals predominate?
- Practice the percussion ostinati parts and experiment with different African instruments or homemade instruments.

Three Yoruba Native Songs of Nigeria

Performance Tips

- If you do not have the instruments that are called for in the piece, create your own. Determine the number of repetitions for each section of each piece.
- The first piece is a procession, and can be used at the beginning of a program to enter, or during the program to change the staging formation of the choir. A slight swaying is acceptable performance style, and may be added to any or all of the pieces.
- Costuming might include narrow draped scarves of an African woven fabric.
- Instrumentalists should be seated or standing where they have a clear visual line of direction to the conductor.

Learn "Three Yoruba Native Songs of Nigeria"
These pieces are taught through the oral tradition in Nigeria, and so might be introduced orally through echo and repetition during the first several rehearsals. Then read through each piece in the following order:

- Read the text to discover the context of each of the "Three Yoruba Native Songs of Nigeria."
- Read the rhythm with rhythm syllables.
- In voice sections (SAB), read the melody with solfège and hand signs or numbers.

(continued on page 232)

- Learn the text pronunciation using the Phonetic Pronunciation guide on each literature page. Remember that these pieces are taught by ear, and the notation is an approximation of the rhythm. The first two pieces are in 6/8 meter with simple rhythms. The third piece is in 4/4 meter, and includes sixteenth notes. The rhythmic fun and challenge comes when you include the instrumental parts.
- Read the piece through as a full ensemble.
- Optional: Learn and include the instrumental parts.

Hot Spots
- The first rehearsals should be through oral repetition.
- Work on the vocal tone color so it is heavier (more chest voice), louder, more nasal, and has wider sounds. Listen to some Nigerian performances if possible.
- Practice the sixteenth notes in the third piece.

Program Ideas
"Down by the Riverside"—Printz
"A Red, Red Rose"—Burton
"Nightfall"—Williams-Wimberly
"Three Yoruba Native Songs of Nigeria"—Leck/Adeniyi
"Praise Ye the Lord, All Nations"—Bach/Sherman

2. ODUN DE
"New Year is Here"

Same Percussion Rhythm Patterns As "E Oru O"

Phonetic Pronunciation

Aw-doon day aw-doon day
Aw-doon day ahn-your
Ay doo-mah ray ja-war wah (g) baw peh
Wah o
Eer-ay eer-ay ay ay ay ay ay ay
Aw-doon day ay aw-doon day ay
Aw-doon day

Translation

New Year is here, New Year is here
We are happy. Almighty God.
Please accept our thanks. Blessing, blessing
New Year is here, New Year is here

 CULTURAL CONNECTIONS

If you went to Nigeria, you would hear vocal performing groups in the villages. They are not select choirs, however,—everyone sings. Each song has a special function. The singing style is different from your typical choral sound—the singing is heavier, louder, and has wider sounds. Many times there is a dance or slight movement with the songs. Instruments accompany the singing, creating exciting syncopation. Three Yoruban songs of Nigeria have been collected and arranged for you. When your students sing them, they should try to understand where they come from, what their purpose is, and try to honor the music and its original people.

3. KABO KABO
"Song of Praise in honor of a Prince or King"

Ka bo___ ka-bo ka-bo ka-bo o mo-a ba-le so-ro o mo-a ba-le so-ro ki-le la nu ka-bo. Ka-bo. A ko bi a la ke lon jo ba la ke a ko bi ku___ ku lon jo bi ni je bu-o de ka - bo___ ka - bo ka - bo___ ka - bo o mo-a ba - le so - ro o mo-a ba - le so - ro ki-le la nu ka - bo

Percussion

1. Djembe
2. Claves
3. Conga R L R R L R
4. Bells

Translation

Welcome! Welcome! The son (prince) who speaks
to the ground and makes the ground open

Verse: The first son of Alake (king) becomes the king
of Ake (a city in Nigeria)

Now the first son of Ku Ku (another king) becomes
the king of Ijebuode (a city in Nigeria)

Refrain: Kabo...

Phonetic Pronunciation

Kah-boh-o kah-boh o *(sing 2 times)*
aw-maw ah-bah leh saw raw *(sing 2 times)*
Kee-leh lah noo kah-boh

Ah-kaw bee ah lah kay lown jaw bah lah kay,
Ah-kaw bee koo koo lown jaw bah
nee-jeh-boo oh-day

Three Yoruba Native Songs of Nigeria **233**

VOCAL DEVELOPMENT

To encourage vocal development, have students:

- Distinguish the chant
  nature of native African
  songs. The songs do
  not require the Western
  music tone quality of
  the voice that is used
  by trained singers.
- Experiment with different
  "colors" of tone quality,
  such as nasal, harsh, gut-
  teral, airy, etc. Decide on
  the sound that best fits the
  African characteristics.
- The style of "E Oru O"
  is a stately processional.
  Sing legato while feeling
  the walking pulse.
- Identify the rhythmic
  variety in the third song,
  "Kabo, Kabo." Ask: How
  will this change the character of this song in comparison to the stately
  legato processional of the
  first song, "E Oru O"?

The Tree of Peace

Adapted by Fred Bock
(A.S.C.A.P.)
John Greenleaf Whittier

SAB, Accompanied

234 *Choral Connections   Level 1 Mixed Voices*

The Tree of Peace

Performance Tips

Rhythmic Focus
Explain to students:
- The piece is in 4/4 meter, at a moderate tempo.
- The rhythm is easy, but must be completely accurate and powerful.
- In measure 15, and again at 32, the tempo slows a little.

Melodic Focus
Tell students:
- The melody is often sung in unison by two or three parts.
- The soprano section carries the melody throughout.
- The melody must be accurate, but the harmonies are where the power of this piece lies.

MUSIC LITERACY

To help students expand their music literacy, have them:
- Conduct and speak the rhythm syllables.
- Conduct and speak the text in rhythm.
- Analyze the chords in the three-part section.

234

The Tree of Peace **235**

More Ideas

- Pay great attention to dynamics, and don't sing too slowly.
- This piece is very powerful and extremely moving. If performed with much emotion, the audience will sit in awe!
- As an introduction, you might have the choir do a dramatic choral speaking of the text before singing the piece. With some solos and some choral speech, it can be a powerful speech piece as well.

Hot Spots

- The piece is in a minor key. Address this immediately.
- There is a lot of unison singing—tune carefully.
- Practice the rhythms of measures 27 and 28 until they are crisp and secure.
- The dynamics are an essential part of this piece.

Program Ideas

"The Tree of Peace"—Bock
"Dare to Dream!"—Lorenz
"The Tiger"—Porterfield
"Praise Ye the Lord, All Nations"—Bach/Sherman
"Bound for Jubilee"—Eilers

Poet John Greenleaf Whittier

Because he was a devout Quaker who wrote essays and poems that expressed his strong moral values, John Greenleaf Whittier (1807-1882) is often called the "Quaker Poet." Much of Whittier's prose and poetry described the hardships of New England farm life before and after the American Civil War. The 1866 narrative poem, "Snow-Bound," is considered his masterpiece. His written works focused on two separate topics—the pastoral life in New England and his devotion to the abolition of slavery in America.

*Girls 2nd time only - Boys both times

236 *Choral Connections   Level 1 Mixed Voices*

wars' wild mus-ic o'er the earth shall cease!

earth shall cease!

Love shall put

out   the   burn - ing   fires   of   an   ger

The Tree of Peace **237**

Glossary

Choral Music Terms

A

a cappella (ah-kah-PEH-lah) [It.] Unaccompanied vocal music.

accelerando (*accel.*) (ah-chel-leh-RAHN-doh) [It.] Gradually increasing the tempo.

accent Indicates the note is to be sung with extra force or stress. (ᵃ)

accidentals Signs used to indicate the raising or lowering of a pitch. A sharp (♯) alters a pitch by raising it one-half step; a flat (♭) alters a pitch by lowering it one-half step; a natural (♮) cancels a sharp or a flat.

accompaniment Musical material that supports another; for example, a piano or orchestra accompanying a choir or soloist.

adagio (ah-DAH-jee-oh) [It.] Slow tempo, but not as slow as largo.

al fine (ahl FEE-neh) [It.] To the end.

alla breve Indicates cut time; duple meter in which there are two beats per measure, the half note getting one beat.

allargando (*allarg.*) (ahl-ahr-GAHN-doh) [It.] To broaden, become slower.

aleatoric or chance music Music in which chance is deliberately used as a compositional component.

allegro (ah-LEH-groh) [It.] Brisk tempo; faster than moderato, slower than *vivace*.

allegro assai (ah-LEH-groh ah-SAH-ee) [It.] Very fast; in seventeenth-century music, the term can also mean "sufficiently fast."

altered pitch A note that does not belong to the scale of the work being performed.

alto The lower female voice; sometimes called contralto or mezzo-soprano.

anacrusis (a-nuh-KROO-suhs) [Gk.] *See* upbeat.

andante (ahn-DAHN-teh) [It.] Moderately slow; a walking tempo.

andante con moto (ahn-DAHN-teh kohn MOH-toh) [It.] A slightly faster tempo, "with motion."

animato Quick, lively; "animated."

aria (AHR-ee-uh) [It.] A song for a solo singer and orchestra, usually in an opera, oratorio, or cantata.

arpeggio (ahr-PEH-jee-oh) [It.] A chord in which the pitches are sounded successively, usually from lowest to highest; in broken style.

art song Expressive songs about life, love, and human relationships for solo voice and piano.

articulation Clarity in performance of notes and diction.

B

a tempo (ah TEM-poh) [It.] Return to the established tempo after a change.

balance and symmetry Even and equal.

baritone The male voice between tenor and bass.

bar line (measure bar) A vertical line drawn through the staff to show the end of a measure. Double bar lines show the end of a section or a piece of music.

Baroque period (buh-ROHK) [Fr.] Historic period between c. 1600 and c. 1750 that reflected highly embellished styles in art, architecture, fashion, manners, and music. The period of elaboration.

bass The lowest male voice, below tenor and baritone.

bass clef Symbol at the beginning of the staff for lower voices and instruments, or the piano left hand; usually referring to pitches lower than middle C. The two dots lie on either side of the fourth-line F, thus the term, F clef.

beat A steady pulse.

bel canto (bell KAHN-toh) [It.] Italian vocal technique of the eighteenth century with emphasis on beauty of sound and brilliance of performance.

binary form Defines a form having two sections (A and B), each of which may be repeated.

breath mark A mark placed within a phrase or melody showing where the singer or musician should breathe. (❜)

C

cadence Punctuation or termination of a musical phrase; a breathing break.

caesura (si-ZHUR-uh) [Lt.] A break or pause between two musical phrases. (//)

call and response A song style that follows a simple question-and-answer pattern in which a soloist leads and a group responds.

calypso style Folk-style music from the Caribbean Islands with bright, syncopated rhythm.

cambiata The young male voice that is still developing.

canon   A compositional form in which the subject is begun in one group and then is continually and exactly repeated by other groups. Unlike the round, the canon closes with all voices ending together on a common chord.

cantata   (kan-TAH-tuh) [It.] A collection of vocal compositions with instrumental accompaniment consisting of several movements based on related secular or sacred text segments.

cantabile   In a lyrical, singing style.

chantey   (SHAN-tee) [Fr.] A song sung by sailors in rhythm with their work.

chant, plainsong   Music from the liturgy of the early church, characterized by free rhythms, monophonic texture, and sung *a cappella*.

chorale   (kuh-RAL) [Gr.] Congregational song or hymn of the German Protestant (Evangelical) Church.

chord   Three or more pitches sounded simultaneously.

chord, block   Three or more pitches sounded simultaneously.

chord, broken   Three or more pitches sounded in succession; *see also* arpeggio.

chromatic   (kroh-MAT-ik) [Gr.] Moving up or down by half steps. Also the name of a scale composed entirely of half steps.

Classical period   The period in Western history beginning around 1750 and lasting until around 1820 that reflected a time when society began looking to the ancient Greeks and Romans for examples of order and ways of looking at life.

clef   The symbol at the beginning of the staff that identifies a set of pitches; *see also* bass clef and treble clef.

coda   Ending section; a concluding portion of a composition. (⊕)

common time   Another name for 4/4 meter; *see also* cut time. (**c**)

composer   The creator of musical works.

compound meter   Meter whose beat can be subdivided into threes and/or sixes.

con   (kohn) [It.] With.

concerto   Composition for solo instrument and an orchestra, usually with three movements.

consonance   A musical interval or chord that sounds pleasing; opposite of dissonance.

Contemporary period   The time from 1900 to right now.

continuo   A Baroque tradition in which the bass line is played "continuously," by a cello, double bass, and/or bassoon while a keyboard instrument (harpsichord, organ) plays the bass line and indicated harmonies.

contrapuntal   *See* counterpoint.

counterpoint   The combination of simultaneous parts; *see* polyphony.

crescendo   (*cresc.*) (kreh-SHEN-doh) [It.] To gradually become louder. ⎯◁

cued notes   Smaller notes indicating either optional harmony or notes from another voice part. ♩

cut time   2/2 time with the half note getting the beat. (¢)

D ⎯⎯⎯⎯⎯⎯⎯⎯⎯⎯⎯⎯⎯

da capo   (*D.C.*) (dah KAH-poh) [It.] Go back to the beginning and repeat; *see also* dal segno and al fine.

dal segno   (*D.S.*) (dahl SAYN-yoh) [It.] Go back to the sign and repeat. (𝄋)

D. C. al fine   (dah KAH-poh ahl FEE-neh) [It.] Repeat back to the beginning and end at the "fine."

decrescendo   (*decresc.*) (deh-kreh-SHEN-doh) [It.] To gradually become softer. ▷⎯

delicato   Delicate; to play or sing delicately.

descant   A high, ornamental voice part often lying above the melody.

diction   Clear and correct enunciation.

diminuendo   (*dim.*) (duh-min-yoo-WEN-doh) [It.] Gradually getting softer; *see also* decrescendo.

diphthong   A combination of two vowel sounds consisting of a primary vowel sound and a secondary vowel sound. The secondary vowel sound is (usually) at the very end of the diphthong; for example, in the word *toy*, the diphthong starts with the sound of "o," then moves on to "y," in this case pronounced "ee."

dissonance   Discord in music, suggesting a state of tension or "seeking"; chords using seconds, fourths, fifths, and sevenths; the opposite of consonance.

divisi   (*div.*) (dih-VEE-see) [It.] Divide; the parts divide.

dolce   (DOHL-chay) [It.] Sweet; *dolcissimo*, very sweet; *dolcemente*, sweetly.

Dorian mode   A scale with the pattern of whole-step, half, whole, whole, whole, half, and whole. For example, D to D on the keyboard.

dotted rhythm   A note written with a dot increases its value again by half.

double bar   Two vertical lines placed on the staff indicating the end of a section or a composition; used with two dots to enclose repeated sections.

doubling   The performance of the same note by two parts, either at the same pitch or an octave apart.

downbeat   The accented first beat in a measure.

D. S. al coda   (dahl SAYN-yoh ahl KOH-dah) [It.] Repeat from the symbol (𝄋) and skip to the coda when you see the sign. (⊕)

D. S. al fine   (dahl SAYN-yoh ahl FEE-neh) [It.] Repeat from the symbol (𝄋) and sing to fine or the end.

duple   Any time signature or group of beats that is a multiple of two.

duet   Composition for two performers.

dynamics   The volume of sound, the loudness or softness of a musical passage; intensity, power.

E

enharmonic   Identical tones that are named and written differently; for example, C sharp and D flat.

ensemble   A group of musicians or singers who perform together.

enunciation   Speaking and singing words with distinct vowels and consonants.

espressivo   (espress.) (es-preh-SEE-vo) [It.] For expression; con espressione, with feeling.

ethnomusicology   The musical study of specific world cultures.

expressive singing   To sing with feeling.

exuberance   Joyously unrestrained and enthusiastic.

F

fermata   (fur-MAH-tah) [It.] A hold; to hold the note longer. (𝄐)

fine   (FEE-neh) Ending; to finish.

flat   Symbol (accidental) that lowers a pitch by one half step. (♭)

folk music   Uncomplicated music that speaks directly of everyday matters; the first popular music; usually passed down through the oral tradition.

form   The structure of a musical composition.

forte   (f) (FOR-teh) [It.] Loud.

fortissimo   (ff) (for-TEE-suh-moh) [It.] Very loud.

freely   A direction that permits liberties with tempo, dynamics, and style.

fugue   (FYOOG) [It.] A polyphonic composition consisting of a series of successive melody imitations; see also imitative style.

fusion   A combination or blending of different genres of music.

G

gapped scale   A scale resulting from leaving out certain tones (the pentatonic scale is an example).

grand staff   Two staves usually linked together by a long bar line and a bracket.

H

half step   The smallest distance (interval) between two notes on a keyboard; the chromatic scale is composed entirely of half steps, shown as (∨).

half time   See cut time.

harmonic interval   Intervals that are sung or played simultaneously; see also melodic interval.

harmony   Vertical blocks of different tones sounded simultaneously.

hemiola   (hee-mee-OH-lah) [Gk.] A metric flow of two against a metric flow of three.

homophonic   (hah-muh-FAH-nik) [Gk.] A texture where all parts sing similar rhythm in unison or harmony.

homophony   (hah-MAH-fuh-nee) [Gk.] Music that consists of two or more voice parts with similar or identical rhythms. From the Greek words meaning "same sounds," homophony could be described as "hymn-style."

hushed   A style marking indicating a soft, whispered tone.

I

imitation, imitative style   Restating identical or nearly identical musical material in two or more parts.

improvised   Invented on the spur of the moment.

improvisation   Spontaneous musical invention, commonly associated with jazz.

interval   The distance from one note to another; intervals are measured by the total steps and half steps between the two notes.

intonation   The degree to which pitch is accurately produced in tune.

introduction   An opening section at the beginning of a movement or work, preparatory to the main body of the form.

K

key The way tonality is organized around a tonal center; *see also* key signature.

key change Changing an initial key signature in the body of a composition.

key signature Designation of sharps or flats at the beginning of a composition to indicate its basic scale and tonality.

L

legato (leh-GAH-toh) [It.] Smooth, connected style.

ledger lines Short lines that appear above, between treble and bass clefs, or below the bass clef, used to expand the notation.

leggiero (leh-JEH-roh) [It.] Articulate lightly; sometimes nonlegato.

linear flow, line Singing/playing notes in a flowing (smooth) manner, as if in a horizontal line.

lullaby A cradle song; in Western music, usually sung with a gentle and regular rhythm.

M

madrigal A secular vocal form in several parts, popular in the Renaissance.

maestoso (mah-eh-STOH-soh) [It.] Perform majestically.

major (key, scale, mode) Scale built on the formula of two whole steps, one half step, three whole steps, one half step.

Letter Names:	G	A	B	C	D	E	F#	G
Movable Do:	do	re	mi	fa	so	la	ti	do
Numbers:	1	2	3	4	5	6	7	1

Major 2nd The name for an interval of one whole step or two half steps. For example, from C to D.

Major 6th The name for an interval of four whole steps and one-half step. For example, from C to A.

Major 3rd The name for an interval of two whole steps or four half steps. For example, from C to E.

major triad Three tones that form a major third *do* to *mi* and a minor third *mi* to *so* as in C E G.

marcato (mahr-KAH-toh) [It.] Long but separated pitches; translated as marked.

mass The main religious service of the Roman Catholic Church. There are two divisions of mass: the Proper of the Mass in which the text changes for each day, and the Ordinary of the Mass in which the text remains the same for every mass. Music for the mass includes the Kyrie, Gloria, Credo, Sanctus, and Agnus Dei as well as other chants, hymns, and psalms. For special mass occasions composers through the centuries have created large musical works for choruses, soloists, instrumentalists, and orchestras.

measure The space from one bar line to the next; also called bars.

medieval Historical period prior to the Renaissance, c. 500-1450.

medley A group of tunes, linked together and sung consecutively.

melisma (n.) or melismatic (adj.) (muh-LIZ-mah or muh-liz-MAT-ik) [Gk.] A term describing the setting of one syllable of text to several pitches.

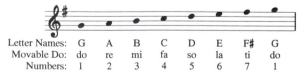

melodic interval Intervals that are performed in succession; *see also* harmonic interval.

melody A logical succession of musical tones; also called tune.

meter The pattern into which a steady succession of rhythmic pulses (beats) is organized.

meter signature The divided number at the beginning of a clef; 4/4, 3/4, and so forth; *see also* time signature.

metronome marking A sign that appears over the top line of the treble clef staff at the beginning of a piece indicating the tempo. It shows the kind of note that will get the beat and the numbers of beats per minute as measured by a metronome; for example, ♪ = 100.

mezzo forte (*mf*) (MEHT-soh FOR-teh) [It.] Medium loud.

mezzo piano (*mp*) (MEHT-soh pee-AH-noh) [It.] Medium soft.

middle C   The note that is located nearest the center of the piano keyboard; middle C can be written in either the treble or bass clef.

minor (key, scale)   Scale built on the formula of one whole step, one half step, two whole steps, one half step, two whole steps.

Letter Names:	D	E	F	G	A	B♭	C	D
Movable Do:	la	ti	do	re	mi	fa	so	la
Numbers:	6	7	1	2	3	4	5	6

minor mode   One of two modes upon which the basic scales of Western music are based, the other being major; using W for a whole step and H for a half step, a minor scale has the pattern W H W W H W W.

minor triad   Three tones that form a minor third (bottom) and a major third (top), such as A C E.

minor third   The name for an interval of three half steps. For example, from A to C.

mixed meter   Frequently changing time signatures or meters.

moderato   Moderate.

modulation   Adjusting to a change of keys within a song.

molto   Very or much; for example, *molto rit.* means "much slower."

monophonic   (mah-nuh-FAH-nik) [Gk.] A musical texture having a single melodic line with no accompaniment; monophony.

monophony   (muh-NAH-fuh-nee) [Gk.] One sound; music that has a single melody. Gregorian chants or plainsongs exhibit monophony.

motive   A shortened expression, sometimes contained within a phrase.

musical variations   Changes in rhythm, pitch, dynamics, style, and tempo to create new statements of the established theme.

mysterioso   Perform in a mysterious or haunting way; to create a haunting mood.

N

nationalism   Patriotism; pride of country. This feeling influenced many Romantic composers such as Wagner, Tchaikovsky, Dvořák, Chopin, and Brahms.

natural   (♮) Cancels a previous sharp (♯) lowering the pitch a half step, or a previous flat (♭), raising the pitch a half step.

no breath mark   A direction not to take a breath at a specific place in the composition. (or N.B.)

notation   Written notes, symbols, and directions used to represent music within a composition.

O

octave   An interval of twelve half steps; 8 or 8va = an octave above; 8vb = an octave below.

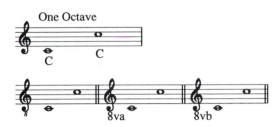

opera   A combination of singing, instrumental music, dancing, and drama that tells a story.

optional divisi   (*opt. div.*) Indicating a split in the music into optional harmony, shown by the smaller cued note.

oratorio   A piece for solo voices, chorus, and orchestra, that is an expanded dramatic work on a literary or religious theme presented without theatrical action.

ostinato   (ahs-tuh-NAH-toh) [It.] A rhythmic or melodic passage that is repeated continuously.

P

palate   The roof of the mouth; the hard palate is forward, the soft palate (velum) is at the back.

parallel major and minor keys   Major and minor keys having the same tonic, such as A major and A minor (A major being the parallel major of A minor and A minor the parallel minor of A major).

peak   The high point in the course of a development; for example, the high point of a musical phrase or the high point in a movement of instrumental music.

pentatonic scale   A five-tone scale constructed of *do, re, mi, so, la* (degrees 1, 2, 3, 5, 6) of a corresponding major scale.

Perfect 5th   The name for an interval of three whole steps and one half step. For example, C to G.

Perfect 4th   The name for an interval of two whole steps and one half step. For example, C to F.

phrase   A musical sentence containing a beginning, middle, and end.

phrase mark   In music, an indicator of the length of a phrase in a melody; this mark may also mean that the singer or musician should not take a breath for the duration of the phrase. (‾‾‾‾‾)

phrasing The realization of the phrase structure of a work; largely a function of a performer's articulation and breathing.

pianissimo (*pp*) (pee-uh-NEE-suh-moh) [It.] Very soft.

piano (*p*) (pee-ANN-noh) [It.] Soft.

Picardy third An interval of a major third used in the final, tonic chord of a piece written in a minor key.

pick-up *See* upbeat.

pitch Sound, the result of vibration; the highness or lowness of a tone, determined by the number of vibrations per second.

piu (pew) [It.] More; for example, *piu forte* means "more loudly."

poco (POH-koh) [It.] Little; for example, *poco dim.* means "a little softer."

poco a poco (POH-koh ah POH-koh) [It.] Little by little; for example, *poco a poco cresc.* means "little by little increase in volume."

polyphony (n.) or polyphonic (adj.) (pah-LIH-fuh-nee or pah-lee-FAH-nik) [Gk.] The term that means that each voice part begins at a different place, is independent and important, and that sections often repeat in contrasting dynamic levels. Poly = many, phony = sounds.

polyrhythmic The simultaneous use of contrasting rhythmic figures.

presto (PREH-stoh) [It.] Very fast.

program music A descriptive style of music composed to relate or illustrate a specific incident, situation, or drama; the form of the piece is often dictated or influenced by the nonmusical program. This style commonly occurs in music composed during the Romantic period. For example, "The Moldau" from *Má Vlast*, by Bedřich Smetana.

progression A succession of two or more pitches or chords; also melodic or harmonic progression.

R

rallentando (*rall.*) (rahl-en-TAHN-doh) [It.] Meaning to "perform more and more slowly." *See also* ritardando.

recitative (res-uh-TAY-teev) [It.] A speechlike style of singing used in opera, oratorio, and cantata.

register, vocal A term used for different parts of a singer's range, such as head register (high notes) and chest register (low notes).

relative major and minor keys The relative minor of any major key or scale, while sharing its key signature and pitches, takes for its tonic the sixth scale degree of that major key or scale. For example, in D major the sixth scale degree is B (or *la* in solfège), *la* then becomes the tonic for A minor.

D major   B minor

Renaissance period The historic period in Western Europe from c. 1430 to 1600; the term means "rebirth" or "renewal"; it indicates a period of rapid development in exploration, science, art, and music.

repeat sign A direction to repeat the section of music (‖: :‖); if the first half of this sign is omitted, it means to "go back to the beginning" (:‖).

repetition The restatement of a musical idea; repeated pitches; repeated "A" section in ABA form.

resolution (*res.*) A progression from a dissonant tone or harmony to a consonant harmony; a sense of completion.

resonance Reinforcement and intensification of sound by vibrations.

rest Symbols used to indicated silence.

rhythm The pattern of sounds and silences.

rhythmic motif A rhythmic pattern that is repeated throughout a movement or composition.

ritardando (*rit.*) The gradual slowing of tempo; also called "ritard."

Rococo Music of the Baroque period so elaborate it was named after a certain type of fancy rock work.

Romantic period A historic period starting c. 1820 and ending c. 1900 in which artists and composers attempted to break with classical music ideas.

rondo form An instrumental form based on an alternation between a repeated (or recurring) section and contrasting episodes (ABACADA).

root The bottom note of a triad in its original position; the note on which the chord is built.

round A composition in which the perpetual theme (sometimes with harmonic parts) begins in one group and is strictly imitated in other groups in an overlapping fashion. Usually the last voice to enter becomes the final voice to complete the song.

rubato (roo-BAH-toh) [It.] Freely; allows the conductor or the performer to vary the tempo.

S

sacred music Of or dealing with religious music; hymns, chorales, early masses; *see* secular music.

scale A pattern of pitches arranged by whole steps and half steps.

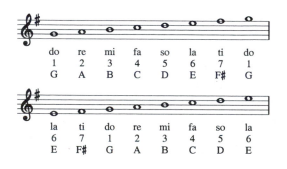

do	re	mi	fa	so	la	ti	do
1	2	3	4	5	6	7	1
G	A	B	C	D	E	F♯	G

la	ti	do	re	mi	fa	so	la
6	7	1	2	3	4	5	6
E	F♯	G	A	B	C	D	E

score   The arrangement of instrumental and vocal staffs that all sound at the same time.

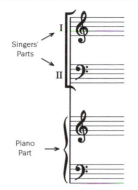

secular music   Music without religious content; *see* sacred music.

sempre   (SEHM-preh) [It.] Always, continually.

sequence   Repetition of a pattern of notes on a higher or lower pitch level.

sharp   A symbol (accidental) that raises a pitch by one half step. (♯)

sight-sing   Reading and singing of music at first sight.

simile   (*sim.*) (SIM-ee-leh) [It.] To continue in the same way.

simple meter   Meter in which each beat is divisible by 2.

skip   Melodic movement in intervals larger than a whole step.

slur   Curved line placed over or under a group of notes to indicate that they are to be performed without a break. ( )

solfège   (SOHL-fehj) [Fr.] A method of sight-singing, using the syllables *do, re, mi, fa, so, la, ti,* etc. for pitches of the scale.

solo   Composition for one featured performer.

sonata-allegro form   (suh-NAH-tuh ah-LEH-groh) [It.] Large A B A form consisting of three sections: exposition, development, and recapitulation.

soprano   The higher female voice.

sotto voce   In a quiet, subdued manner; "under" the voice.

spirito   (SPEE-ree-toh) [It.] Spirited; for example, *con spirito*, with spirit.

spiritual   A type of song created by African Americans who combined African rhythms with melodies they created and heard in America.

staccato   (stah-KAH-toh) [It.] Performed in a short, detached manner, as opposed to legato.

staff   Series of five horizontal lines and four spaces on which music is written to show pitch.

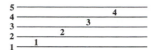

staggered entrances   Voice parts or instruments begin singing or playing at different points within the composition.

steady beat   A metrical pulse; *see also* beat, meter, rhythm.

step   Melodic movement from one note to the next adjacent note, either higher or lower.

stepwise melodic movement   Motion from one note to an adjacent one.

stress   Emphasis on certain notes or rhythmic elements.

strong beat   Naturally accented beats; beats 1 and 3 in 4/4 meter, beat 1 in 3/4 meter.

strophic   Description of a song in which all the stanzas of the text are sung to the same music; opposite of *through-composed*.

style   The particular character of a musical work; often indicated by words at the beginning of a composition, telling the performer the general manner in which the piece is to be performed.

subito   (sub.) (SOO-bee-toh) [It.] Suddenly; for example, *sub. piano* means "suddenly soft."

suspension or suspended tone   The tone or tones in a chord that are held as the remainder of the notes change to a new chord. The sustained tones often form a *dissonance* with the new chord, into which they then resolve.

sustained tone   A tone sustained in duration; sometimes implying a slowing of tempo; *sostenuto* or *sostenendo*, abbreviated *sost.*

swing   This is a performance style in which a pair of eighth notes ( ) are no longer performed evenly, but instead like a triplet ( ), yet they are still written ( ); usually indicated at the beginning of a song or a section.

symphony   An extended work in several movements, for orchestra; also an orchestra configured to perform symphonic music.

syncopation   Deliberate shifts of accent so that a rhythm goes against the steady beat; sometimes referred to as the "offbeat."

T

tempo   A pace with which music moves, based on the speed of the underlying beat.

tempo I or tempo primo   Return to the first tempo.

tenor   A high male voice, lower than the alto, but higher than bass.

tenuto   (teh-NOO-toh) [It.] Stress and extend the marked note. ($\bar{\rho}$)

text   Words, usually set in a poetic style, that express a central thought, idea, moral, or narrative.

texture   The thickness of the different layers of horizontal and vertical sounds.

theme and variation form   A musical form in which variations of the basic theme comprise the composition.

tie   A curved line connecting two successive notes of the same pitch, indicating that the second note is not to be articulated. ( )

timbre   Tone color; the unique quality produced by a voice or instrument.

time signature   The sign placed at the beginning and within a composition to indicate the meter; for example, 4/4, 3/4; *see also* cut time, meter signature.

to coda   Skip to the ⊕ or CODA.

tonality   The organized relationships of pitches with reference to a definite key center. In Western music, most tonalities are organized by the major and minor scales.

tone   A sound quality of a definite pitch.

tone color, quality, or timbre   That which distinguishes the voice or tone of one singer or instrument from another; for example, a soprano from an alto or a flute from a clarinet.

tonic chord   (TAH-nik kord) [Gk.] The name of a chord built on the tonal center of a scale; for example, C E G or *do, mi, so* for C major.

tonic or tonal center   The most important pitch in a scale; *do*; the home tone; the tonal center or root of a key or scale.

tonic triad   A three-note chord comprising root, third, and fifth; for example, C E G.

treble clef   The symbol that appears at the beginning of the staff used for higher voices, instruments, or the piano right hand; generally referring to pitches above middle C, it wraps around the line for G, therefore it is also called the G-clef. 🎼

triad   A three-note chord built in thirds above a root tone.

trill   A rapid change between the marked note and the one above it within the same key. (*tr*~)

triplet   A group of notes in which three notes of equal duration are sung in the time normally given to two notes of equal duration.

troubadour   A wandering minstrel of noble birth in southern France, Spain, and Italy during the eleventh to thirteenth centuries.

tuning   The process of adjusting the tones of voices or instruments so they will sound the proper pitches.

tutti   (TOO-tee) [It.] Meaning "all" or "together."

twelve-tone music   Twentieth-century system of writing music in which the twelve tones of the chromatic scale are arranged into a tone row (numbered 1 to 12), and then the piece is composed by arranging and rearranging the "row" in different ways; for example, backward, forward, or in clusters of three or four pitches.

U

unison   Voice parts or instruments sounding the same pitches in the same rhythm simultaneously.

upbeat   A weak beat preceding the downbeat.

V

variation   *See* theme and variation form, musical variations.

vivace   (vee-VAH-chay) [It.] Very fast; lively.

voice crossing (or voice exchange)   When one voice "crosses" above or below another voice part.

W

whole step   The combination of two successive half steps. (⌊_⌋)

whole tone scale   A scale consisting only of whole steps.